DATE DUE

D1444384

EXECUTION'S DOORSTEP

Contents

Introduction

Our lives begin to end the day we become silent about the things that matter.
—Martin Luther King, Jr.

The individuals whose stories appear in this book were sentenced to death for crimes they did not commit. They spent from two to seventeen years incarcerated in cells smaller than the standard-size dog pen at a boarding kennel.

A circuitous path led me to these men. I have always opposed capital punishment, but my reasons were vague and poorly defined until five years ago, when I authored an article investigating the movement to declare a moratorium on executions in Tennessee. Stunned by what I learned and convinced that no reasonable person could be in favor of the death penalty if they knew the facts, I soon found myself addressing civic and faith-based groups, encouraging them to support a moratorium on executions, as a stepping-stone toward abolishing capital punishment.

My "facts" were no match for questions like, *What about that monster Scott Peterson who murdered his pregnant wife, Laci? What if Laci Peterson was your daughter, how would you feel?* Statistics showing that execution did not deter crime and cost far more than confining the offender for life paled against the faces of innocent victims.* Then, in the spring of 2004, through my

---

*Even death-penalty advocates acknowledge that capital punishment does not deter crime. Homicide rates are 48 to 101 percent higher in states that practice execution. When Oklahoma and California resumed executions, after a twenty-five-year moratorium, homicide rates increased. "Fact Sheet: Deterrence," National Coalition to Abolish the Death Penalty (NCADP) website, www.ncadp.org, retrieved 26 July 2007; "Issues, Facts about Deterrence and the Death Penalty," Death Penalty Information Center (DPIC), www.deathpenaltyinfo.org, retrieved 26 July 2007. Most of the expense in capital cases is incurred during the investigation and original trial, not during the appeals process. In Florida, each execution cost the state $3.2 million compared to $600,000 for life imprisonment. "Cost," Tennessee Coalition to Abolish State Killing (TCASK), www.tcask.org, retrieved 26 July 2007.

affiliation with the Tennessee Coalition to Abolish State Killing, I arranged
for death-row exonerated Ray Krone to speak at the University of the
South, in Sewanee, Tennessee. You could feel the emotional barometer in
the room rising as Ray told his story, about how he was convicted and sentenced to death on the basis of a bite mark on the victim that allegedly
matched his teeth. The prosecution concealed evidence that hair and footprints at the crime scene were not his. The dental expert who testified to
the bite-mark match received fees in excess of $50,000. Ray's court-
appointed attorney was paid $5,000 and had a total budget of $2,500 for
expert-witness fees. Ray appealed his conviction, won a new trial, and was
found guilty a second time. Harboring doubts about his guilt, the judge reduced his sentence to life. After ten years in Arizona penitentiaries, DNA
evidence conclusively proved his innocence. The gazes that followed Ray
as he walked slowly back to his front-row seat were a mixed lot—some
members of the audience were weeping; others were wide-eyed and incredulous; still others scowled, their expressions locked in an angry,
clenched-teeth grimace, enraged by what they had just heard. I was told afterwards that several ardent supporters of capital punishment reversed
their position as a consequence of hearing Ray Krone speak.

Ray Krone's presentation compelled me to pen a collection of narratives—
adhering to the literary maxim, "Don't tell me, show me"—recounting the
experiences of men like him. These stories invite the reader to stand in the
shoes of the accused and, at the same time, to have a bird's eye view of
the legal proceedings and crime. My purpose was twofold: To give the
wrongfully accused voices and faces—to make them real for the reader—
and to school readers in the workings of the capital-conviction process so
they could better understand how and why wrongful convictions occur. A
study conducted by Professor James Liebman of the Columbia University
School of Law, at the request of the U.S. Senate Committee of the Judiciary,
reported that for capital convictions reviewed on appeal from 1973 to 1995,
the courts found "reversible error" in 68 percent of the cases—that
is, error in the trial or pre-trial procedures that sufficiently distorted information available to the jury to make the verdict and/or sentence subject to
being reversed.[1] Although the doctrine *innocent until proven guilty* is embedded firmly in the tradition of Anglo-American jurisprudence, in actuality
the investigative team and prosecution often presume guilt based on a
shred of suspicion and then set out to prove their hunch correct. The five
men whose stories appear in *Execution's Doorstep*—Michael Ray Graham, Jr.,
Ron Keine, Juan Melendez, Madison Hobley, and Randal Padgett—were
not sentenced to death by virtue of some honest mistake. In all instances,
individuals directly responsible for their conviction—police, sheriff's

officials, and/or prosecuting attorneys—concealed evidence pointing to their innocence. All five men likely would have been executed were it not for fortuitous quirks of fate: an appellate attorney's chance encounter with a former law-enforcement official who revealed previously undisclosed information about the disappearance of a rifle that was likely the murder weapon; a transcript of the real killer's tape-recorded confession discovered among files stored in a garage; the actual killer's religious conversion that compelled him to turn himself in to the police. None of the five were exonerated by DNA evidence.

Since the death penalty was reinstated after a brief hiatus in the mid-1970s, 124 individuals sentenced to death have been found innocent of the crimes for which they were convicted.* Virtually all of the exonerated men and women suffer from posttraumatic stress disorder. After long years in a cell, in isolation, where someone else scheduled every aspect of their day in a routine over which they had no control, autonomous self-directed behavior and decision-making pose Herculean challenges. Many exonerated individuals turn to alcohol and drugs. Some commit suicide. In the vast majority of cases, the exonerated prisoners are released into the free world with no money, no job, and no support system. Although innocent, they are tainted. Says Ron Keine, "One guy told me he couldn't hire me, because I would scare the women who worked there." The allure to resort to crime to survive is strong. Preliminary to writing the book, I reviewed the hundred-plus documented cases of innocence since the death penalty's reinstatement and talked with a number of the exonerated individuals or their legal representatives. In selecting subjects, I held to two criteria: that the candidate had remained crime-free since being released, and that the candidate was willing and able to participate in a series of interviews. Of the men whose stories are included here, three are Caucasian, one African American, and one Hispanic.† Prior to their sojourn on death row, three had at-

*The U.S. Supreme Court, 1972, *Furman v. Georgia* cited racial bias and other factors to conclude that the death penalty was applied in an arbitrary and unfair manner and, as such, constituted "cruel and unusual punishment" in violation of the U.S. Constitution. Beginning in 1976, cases brought before the Supreme Court indicated its approval of revised state statutes that addressed the concerns raised in *Furman v. Georgia*, bringing the death penalty back into use. "Facts, History of the Death Penalty, Constitutionality of the Death Penalty in America," DPIC.

†Of the individuals executed since the death penalty's reinstatement, 58 percent were Caucasian, 34 percent African American, 7 percent Hispanic, and 2 percent other races. Of the individuals currently on death row, 45 percent are Caucasian, 42 percent African American, 10 percent Hispanic, and 2 percent other races. Women commit 10 percent of homicides, but receive only 2 percent of death sentence. "Race of Death Row Inmates Executed Since 1976," DPIC; "Women and the Death Penalty," DPIC.

tended college and one held a bachelor's degree. Only one of the five had a previous arrest for a violent crime.

For the subjects who I selected and who agreed to work with me, the first leg of my research began with an Internet search, which invariably turned up newspaper articles and an occasional court order, leaving me with more questions than answers. I next conducted a series of in-depth personal interviews with the subjects—a rich and emotionally charged experience. Some wept, some became angry, others frustrated. Often times what I had read about their cases in the press proved misleading or inaccurate. Committed to understanding how and why justice went awry, I contacted the relevant law enforcement agencies and court authorities for police reports and trial transcripts. Some were cooperative, others not, as might be expected, since suppression of evidence contributed to the wrongful conviction of all five men.* Similarly, some defense attorneys declined to speak with me, while others agreed to lengthy interviews, granted me access to transcripts and legal documents in their possession, and directed me to source materials and other individuals knowledgeable about the case. In writing the stories, I use single quotation marks to indicate reported conversation, that is, when the speaker or person credited as the source is quoting someone else. When a person quoted has denied making a statement or remark, I indicate as much. I made best effort to verify reported conversation, as well as reported circumstance.† For each story I found a legal mentor, the subject's appellate attorney or current legal advocate, who reviewed a draft of the final manuscript, fact-checking for accuracy. The statistical information and circumstances recounted in *Execution's Doorstep* reflect the information available through my research prior to January 1, 2008.

The appeals process. Significantly, the two men defended by private attorneys, rather than relying on state-appointed legal counsel, spent the least amount of time incarcerated.[2] Incompetent defense attorneys and suppression of evidence by the state (that is, Brady violations, as defined by the U.S. Supreme Court decision in *Brady v. Maryland*, 1963) are the two most common causes of wrongful death sentences. Once convicted and condemned to death, the wrongfully accused's only recourse is to prove his or her innocence through the appeals process.

---

*The Court Recorder for the Marshall County, Alabama, Circuit Court refused to provide me with Randal Padgett's trial transcript, and the Chicago Police Department refused to release any information on Andre Council, a convicted felon whose testimony against Madison Hobley played a key role in his conviction.

†Attorneys Roger Alcott, Dwight Wells, and Mark McDaniel did not respond to my efforts to contact them by phone or e-mail. Alcott represented Juan Melendez at trial, and Wells also figured in the Melendez story. McDaniel represented Randal Padgett at his first trial.

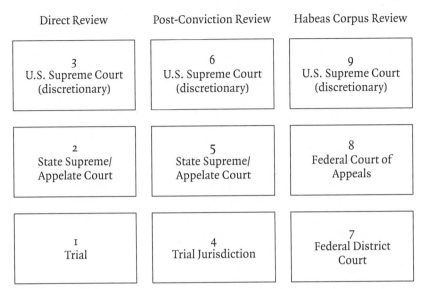

Direct Review	Post-Conviction Review	Habeas Corpus Review
3 U.S. Supreme Court (discretionary)	6 U.S. Supreme Court (discretionary)	9 U.S. Supreme Court (discretionary)
2 State Supreme/ Appelate Court	5 State Supreme/ Appelate Court	8 Federal Court of Appeals
1 Trial	4 Trial Jurisdiction	7 Federal District Court

Capital Conviction Appeals Process.

Laws vary from state to state, but in general, there are three levels of appeal: direct review, post-conviction review, and federal habeas corpus review (see diagram, Capital Conviction Appeals Process).

At the direct-appeal level, a higher state court, usually the state supreme court, reviews the trial and pre-trial proceedings for "serious error," meaning error that has undermined the reliability of the outcome or otherwise harmed the defendant. Many states do not allow new evidence to be introduced at the direct-appeal level. If the state supreme court affirms the defendant's conviction and death sentence, the defendant can ask the U.S. Supreme Court to review the trial and related proceedings, through certiorari. When a writ of certiorari is granted, the court examines the extant records in a case for error, but it does not consider new evidence. While everyone convicted of a criminal offense is automatically entitled to direct review at the state level, the U.S. Supreme Court considers only those cases that they conclude merit their attention.[3]

If a defendant's conviction and death sentence are affirmed at the direct-review level, the case enters the post-conviction phase. The defendant can introduce claims not entertained at the trial or direct-appeal level, most often, new evidence (either suppressed or previously unavailable) or ineffective assistance of counsel at the trial or direct appeal level. Frequently, the trial attorney handles the direct appeal, as well. The closer an individual gets to death, the more skilled his or her legal representation. A post-conviction attorney may discover errors overlooked by trial and/or direct-appeal attorneys. The defendant's motion for post-conviction review goes first to the trial court jurisdiction, often the same judge who presided at trial. If the trial court jurisdiction refuses the motion, the defendant can appeal to the state supreme court. If refused by the state supreme court, the defendant can request certiorari by the U.S. Supreme Court; but again, review by the U.S. Supreme Court is highly discretionary.

The third level of appeal, federal habeas corpus review, derives from the constitutionally guaranteed right to a "writ of habeas corpus," which orders that an imprisoned person be brought before the court to determine if the petitioner is being detained lawfully and if his or her right to a fair trial as provided for by the U.S. Constitution was violated. Habeas corpus review occurs, first, in the relevant federal district court. If the federal district court concludes the individual is being detained lawfully, the petitioner can request habeas corpus review by the federal court of appeals. If denied relief by both lower courts, a defendant can request certiorari by the U.S. Supreme Court.

The 1996 Antiterrorism and Effective Death Penalty Act discourages and limits second and successive federal habeas petitions. The U.S. Supreme Court decision in Herrera v. Collins (1993) reasoned that the due process clause of the U.S. Constitution required only that a person receive a "fair trial," and, by inference, actual innocence was not a constitutional bar to execution.

At any level of review, the presiding judge or judges can grant a hearing to allow for more thorough and in-depth presentation of the evidence by the defendant's attorneys, or variously, the court can deny a hearing and render a decision based on a cursory review of the claims raised in the defendant's motion.

At any level of review, the presiding judge or judges can order the defendant's conviction overturned, and as a consequence, order that the defendant be granted a new trial, or variously, order the lower court to conduct a hearing to determine if the defendant is entitled to a new trial.

In the event that a defendant is granted a new trial, the jury invariably knows that he or she previously was found guilty. Capital defense attorney Richard Jaffe, who represented Randal Padgett, put it quite bluntly: "In a death penalty case at retrial, the client is already considered guilty, and you're considered to be a sleaze ball for defending him. The attitude of everyone in the courtroom is let's get this disposed of so we can go home."[4]

A wrongfully accused individual who fails to secure relief via the appeals process can petition the governor for a pardon. Seven of the 126 individuals exonerated since the death penalty's reinstatement were excused of all blame through gubernatorial pardons. Pardons are exceedingly rare.[5]

. . .

Many of the terms associated with the capital conviction process have circumstance-specific connotations or are unfamiliar to those outside legal circles. To that end, a short glossary follows.

Writing *Execution's Doorstep* took me into a world that I did not know existed. My guides on the journey were the exonerated individuals and the dedicated attorneys who fought to prove their innocence—often pro bono. My worldview has changed forever. Says Juan Melendez of the prosecutor who condemned him to death, knowing that the actual killer had confessed, "I forgive Prosecutor Hardy Pickard, but I do not respect him. For me to respect him, he would need to admit his mistake. The thing about forgiving is that, after forgiving, only then can you start to heal." While working with the five men whose stories appear here, although at moments I saw anger, I never saw hate, bitterness, or vengefulness. I strongly sensed that their willingness to help me was an effort on their part to give back, generosity of spirit born of their gratitude for their freedom. Ironically, they have received little or no compensation for the lost years of their lives. Only 14 states pay restitution for wrongful capital convictions, and the laws are such that qualifying for monetary recompense often requires conviction of the actual killer or DNA proof of innocence (see appendix).

Some of the exonerated individuals have filed civil suits against the officials responsible for their wrongful convictions, but the 1976 U.S. Supreme Court decision *Imbler v. Pachtman* set forth the precedent that an official who "acted within the scope of his duties . . . is absolutely immune from a civil suit for damages" brought by wrongfully accused individuals deprived of their constitutional right to liberty. The burden of proof rests with the accused, who must show that officials intentionally acted in bad faith; neglect and ignorance qualify for "scope of duties" immunity. The occasional substantial settlement granted to a wrongfully accused individual rates grandiose media coverage and distorts the picture. Jury awards are extremely uncommon.[6]

On a personal level, I feel I owe these men a debt I can never repay. I remain eternally grateful.

Glossary of Context-Specific Death-Penalty Terms

Aggravating—circumstances increasing the defendant's culpability and potential for posing a future danger, such as a prior criminal record and facts of the crime that were particularly cruel, heinous, or atrocious.

Arraignment—the formal declaration of charges before the court in response to which the defendant enters a plea of guilty or not guilty.

Bifurcated trial—a trial consisting of two stages, a guilt or innocence phase and a penalty phase. (All capital trials are bifurcated.)

Capital—punishable by death.

Death-qualified jury—a jury composed of individuals who have no ideological objection to the death penalty and to recommending a death sentence if the accused is found guilty.

Defense—the attorneys representing the accused; the evidence offered by the accused's attorneys as proof of innocence.

Exculpatory—tending to clear from guilt, blame, or fault.

Grand jury—a body of citizens who decides whether or not there is sufficient evidence to try the accused.

Impeach—to call into question or cast doubt on.

Indictment—formal written accusation by the grand jury authorizing the commencement of criminal proceedings against the accused.

Mitigating—circumstance reducing a defendant's moral culpability and so recommending a less severe penalty, such as lack of a prior criminal record, remorse, or mental illness.

Plea bargain—when the defendant agrees to plead guilty in exchange for reduced charges, dismissal of some charges, or a less severe penalty.

Pro bono—when an attorney represents a client without recompense, from the Latin *pro bono publico*, for the public good.

Prosecutor/prosecution—the attorneys for the State and the agents and officers who assist them; the evidence offered by the State as proof of guilt.

State—the government and its agents, who represent the victim and people under the government's jurisdiction in bringing charges against the accused.

RON KEINE

Condemned by the False Testimony of a Motel Maid Who Was Thrown in Jail When She Tried to Tell the Truth

When a guy goes to prison for a crime he commits—robbery, drugs, whatever—when he gets out, there are support programs, counseling services. Parole officers will try to get guys in school or vocational training if they don't have any skills, to get them off the dope-dealing streets and make them productive members of society. But an innocent man coming off death row, he's got no parole officer. He's got nothing. He's been stuck in a six-by-nine cell, for no telling how many years. His three meals have been shoved through a gate like he was an animal. If he's lucky, he might have gotten out for a shower and exercise once a week. He didn't work. Someone else scheduled every aspect of his day in a routine that he had no control over—including the day they'll end his life for a crime he didn't commit. Then by some miracle they discover he didn't do it, and he gets out. He doesn't know how to make decisions for himself. He's got no money. There are no government agencies or services to help him readjust to life on the outside. Friends turn the other way when they see him coming, afraid he'll ask them for a job. No one will hire him. If he's got a wife and kids, she's supporting them. If he doesn't have a girl, he can't get one. No one wants to go out with him—what's he got to offer? He feels like a piece of shit. I know what these guys are going through just off death row—I was there.

—Ron Keine, who was nine days away from the New Mexico gas chamber when an appeal stayed his execution and that of the three men convicted along with him. All four eventually were proved innocent, but within five years of their release, the other three were dead.[1]

The Crime: 6 February 1974, Albuquerque, New Mexico

Kerry Rodney Lee had been in Albuquerque only a few weeks. Lee, age twenty-three, made his way in the world by selling illegal drugs and by serving as a police informer. His charming, charismatic personality quickly won over nearly everyone he met, a trait enhanced by his dark curly hair, hazel eyes, and fetching smile. Women found him irresistible. He once boasted he could seduce any woman or man he set his sights on.

His new girlfriend, Jan McCord, was a student at the University of New Mexico. Her friends Steve Lent and Pat Spahn had introduced Jan McCord to Kerry Lee. They met him at Okie's Bar, a popular hangout across the street from the University of New Mexico campus. Although Jan McCord had known Kerry Lee only a very short time, she clearly was infatuated. She had persuaded Steve Lent to let Kerry Lee room with him, although the arrangement did not last long. On the fourth day of his stay, Lent discovered Kerry Lee engaged in a sexual act with a 15-year-old Chicano boy and told him to move out.[2]

On the evening of February 5, Kerry Lee had use of the Thunderbird that Jan McCord's father, William McCord, had given Jan to drive. In the glove compartment was an Ivor Johnson .22 pistol, which Lee had taken from William McCord's gun collection. When Kerry Lee stopped by Steve Lent's apartment, Lent was not particularly happy to see him, given the past circumstances. And Lee was seriously drunk, probably stoned on downers, too, Steve Lent guessed.[3]

Sensing the extent of his unwelcome, Kerry Lee cut his visit short, mentioning on his way out that he had some important business to take care of, although the business was likely nothing more urgent than more drinking. Lee made his way to Okie's, where he struck up a conversation with William Velten, age twenty-six, who worked at a nearby Chinese restaurant. The two men had never met before and became acquainted over multiple rounds of tequila, along with an added boost from some Seconals, a strong pharmaceutical analgesic. Feeling no pain, they left the bar.[4]

After stopping briefly at Pat Spahn's, where Lee and Velten never even got around to taking off their jackets, the pair drove out of town to a deserted arroyo. Lee bottomed out the T-bird on a sandy rise in the creek bed.

For reasons that have never been entirely understood, Kerry Lee and William Velten ended up in a death match outside the car. During a struggle over possession of the Ivor Johnson .22, stray bullets struck the T-bird, and Velten pulled a buck-hunting knife. Lee gained control of the pistol and fired. Velten went down. Drunk and enraged, Lee emptied the pistol in

Velten's head, and with Velten's buck knife, slashed the man's chest, castrated him, and stuffed his severed penis in his mouth.[5]

Lee heaved the pistol into the shadows and dragged the body beneath the cover of a nearby bush. After scouring the area for spent cartridges, he walked back to the main road, to the Western Skies Motel. At the coffee shop, he met a police officer, who had received a call to investigate a report of gunfire. Lee and the officer had coffee. He told the officer about getting stuck in the sand and said he had been hassled by rowdy kids who threw firecrackers at his car—a tidy explanation accounting for both the gunshots and his unkempt appearance.[6]

The police officer bought his story and phoned for a wrecker.[7]

Lee was soiled and dusty from the struggle with Velten. There was no blood on his clothes or person, though. He had done his work with the knife after Velten was dead, and the corpse bled very little.[8]

But the gunshot wounds to Velten's head were another matter. Had he kicked sand over the bloodstain where Velten went down?

The alcohol and downers had taken their toll on Kerry Lee. He rode with the tow-truck driver back to the arroyo, and the driver pulled the T-bird out, no questions asked. Afterwards, Lee decided to spend the night at the motel, registering under the name David Morningstar. In his pocket, he discovered the spent cartridges that he had retrieved from the scene, and he hid them under the carpet in the motel room.[9]

During the course of the day that followed, February 6, Lee and Jan McCord drove into the arroyo in a borrowed Land Rover. Horrified when she realized the nature of their errand, Jan McCord watched while Kerry Lee dragged a man's body further into the brush. Lee later returned on horseback, hoping to move the corpse to a still more remote location, but he did not get far. He tied a rope to the corpse, but the horse tangled in the makeshift harness and fell. Burying the body was out of the question with the ground frozen. Exhausted, he gave up and crudely concealed the body under a sage bush.[10]

Lee rented a metal detector and returned to the scene of the crime a third time to search for the Ivor Johnson pistol, but he never found it.[11]

A few weeks later, Kerry Lee left town.[12]

Ron Keine: 8 February 1974, El Monte, California

Late on the evening of February 8, Ron Keine and four of his buddies, bikers like himself, set out from El Monte, California, in a flashy orange van with a custom paint job. They were headed back to Michigan for motorcycle parts. Michigan was Ron's home state, and the home state of all but one of the others. They were members of the Vagos, a coalition of southern California bikers who had aligned themselves against the notorious Hell's Angels.

Ron was twenty-six. He had been in California just under a year. The Vagos were his reason for being there— "The Vagos had the reputation of being the baddest bikers around, and that was what I wanted to be."

Ron was born in 1947 to a doting, loving mother and an abusive, alcoholic father. As a child, he was nervous and emaciated. A battery of tests at a local hospital revealed nothing physically wrong with him. "I wouldn't eat, because I didn't want to sit at the table with my dad. Mealtime was hell. You couldn't say anything, or you got backhanded off your chair, and wound up with a mouthful of blood and loose teeth."

The array of hospital tests also included psychological assessments, which indicated that Ron was extremely intelligent. As a consequence, things at home got even worse for Ron. His father relentlessly berated him for being an underachiever.

"My dad would come in late, drunk, yank me out bed, and smack me around. One time he swung at me, missed, and punched the thermostat through the wall. He said it was my fault, threw me out of the house, and said I couldn't come back until I gave him $87 to have it fixed—I was fifteen. My mom paid for the thermostat so I could come home."

Throughout his adolescence, Ron managed to stay in trouble of one kind or another, mostly petty neighborhood vandalism. "I was a tough guy, a punk," he concedes. He got a job at Ford Motor Company and saved up enough money to buy a motorcycle. When he was seventeen, he threw a rock through a storefront window and wound up in Youthful Offender Prison, convicted of malicious destruction of property. He finished high school there.

An instructor picked up on how bright he was, and encouraged him to further his education. After he was paroled, Ron enrolled in junior college, paying his way by working in a steel mill. To manage the grueling schedule of full-time school and ten-hour shifts, he started taking amphetamines. Before long, he realized he was an emotional wreck and developing a chemical dependency. He signed himself into a treatment program. The counseling and therapy sessions intrigued him. Fascinated by what he had learned of the behavioral sciences and psychology, he applied to study at the Gestalt Institute, in Cleveland. "They accepted me. I couldn't believe it. I was the first person they ever admitted who didn't have at least a bachelor's degree." Ron's life was finally coming together. He was upbeat and optimistic about the promise the future held in store.

One weekend, he drove home from Cleveland to visit his mom and friends. Saturday night found him cruising the strip, hanging out with the hometown crowd at a local drive in. "This guy asked me if I'd give him a lift to his house. He dealt drugs and word on the street was that he was a snitch. I didn't use drugs. I'd had my fling with that and was done with it. But I figured, what the heck, I'll give the guy a ride. We were about to take off, and he tells me he needs to make a phone call. So I wait. He comes back, and we don't get two blocks down the road before the cops pull us over. They tell us to get out, search us. I'm not worried, because I know I'm clean, but the cops find a bag of pot on the ground under my car. The snitch had dropped it. He made his points for the night. For me, it meant a parole violation. There was no hearing, no trial. To rehabilitate me, they pulled me out of college and sent me back to jail—how much sense does that make?—and not the juvenile facility this time. I served out the rest of my sentence in Jackson State Prison. After that, I had a real serious attitude problem."

Ron was twenty-four when he was released. He found a job working as a motorcycle mechanic and enrolled in classes at the Michigan Motorcycle Mechanic Institute with the intention of becoming certified. Craving the camaraderie of other motorcycle enthusiasts, he joined the Minutemen, a Detroit-based motorcycle club. Ron's habit of showing up for meetings dressed in his greasy mechanic's togs led the more urbane members of the group to nickname him Grub. "A lot of the guys were clean-cut businessmen types," Ron points out, "Family riders into weekend camping trips and Sunday afternoon picnics, that sort of thing. It was a real lightweight club."

Ron found a soulmate, though, in Richard "Doc Sly" Greer.

Ron and Doc eventually broke with the Minutemen. "Doc and I wanted to join up with a hard-riding, hard-drinking, outlaw-type club—a Hell's Angels type club. The way we saw it, being a biker was a way of life, not just something you did on the weekends. Doc took off for California, to check out the Angels firsthand. I stuck around to finish school. I could make double the money once I was certified."

In early 1973, Doc phoned Ron. "'Come on down here, man,' Doc says to me, 'I found us a club. Forget about the Hell's Angels. We were misled.' From what we had heard, the Angels were the baddest bikers around. Doc had been hanging out with the Angels, getting to know some of the guys. He was at this bar with twenty or so Angels and in come four bikers from this other club, the Vagos. They cleaned the place out, put the Angels on the street. They asked Doc, 'Are you with them?' and he said, 'No, I believe I want to be with you guys.' A lot of the Angels weren't even serious riders any more. It was nothing but an organized drug syndicate."

Ron had not finished his certification, but the prospect of reuniting with Doc and joining up with the Vagos overrode his intentions. February 14, Valentines Day, 1973, he said adios to his girlfriend and set out for California on his bike, with a break-down shotgun and a fishing pole rolled into his sleeping bag.

Ron's passion for hunting and fishing were legacies from his maternal grandfather, a bright spot in his otherwise bleak adolescence. The Vagos were a perfect fit, outlaws and serious riders, with a group ethic underscored by rugged adventurism. Once a month there were mandatory runs, long bike excursions up into the California mountains or across the border into Mexico. Ron talks about butchering a poached cow on one trip, how his expertise and skill as an outdoorsmen set him apart. He knew how to field dress a carcass, knew the best cuts of meat. "I sliced off the back strap and tenderloin for me and Doc and my other close buddies. A lot of the guys in the club were city dwellers. I had to teach them how to cook meat on a stick over an open fire." As to the outlaw image, for the Vagos, bar fights were a recreational pastime. "Bar fighting, that was one of my favorite things. I was a hell of a scrapper. I used to start fights just to prove to my club brothers how tough I was."

Ron earned his keep providing protection for several women who worked as strippers. A number of his club brothers worked as bouncers in bars. The Vagos—Spanish for vagabond—had two rules: no drugs and no homosexuals. "When you get in a bar fight you don't want some junky watching your back. As to the homosexual thing, well, you get that many drunk guys with an attitude together, you've got to have something to hate."

All five of the bikers en route to Michigan in the orange van on the evening of 8 February 1974 were in their twenties and all had had previous run-ins with the law, though only for minor offenses. None of them had ever been convicted of a crime involving aggressive violence. Clarence "Sandman" Smith had an indecent exposure conviction, stemming from when his pants ripped in a bar fight. Like Doc Greer and Ron, Sandman Smith and fellow biker Art Smith hailed from Michigan, although Ron had not known them there. The two Smiths were not related. Art Smith was Doc Greer's cousin. "Art never would have made it in the Vagos without Doc," Ron insists. "He was a baby, just a big dumb kid. Doc took Art under his wing, and looked after him." The fifth biker, Tom Gladish, was a California native.[13]

The Vagos had a strict code of bylaws. The only excuse for missing a mandatory meeting was jail. All five bikers had attended the February 8 meeting, on the afternoon of the day they left for Michigan. The next mandatory meeting was scheduled for February 15. They had exactly one week to make it to Michigan and back. They drove all night, drinking nonstop, and at daybreak, on the morning of February 9, stopped at a roadside diner in Arizona for breakfast. "We all ordered pancakes. It was the cheapest thing on the menu. We were operating on a tight budget. When it came down to choosing between beer and food, we chose beer." Crossing Arizona, they made several stops for gas. Doc Greer paid, with a stolen credit card.

The bikers breezed through Albuquerque, New Mexico, without stopping, and just outside Albuquerque, picked up a hitchhiker from a local commune, Kathy Ibrahim. "People asked what we were doing picking up hitchhikers. Hippies, low-riders, bikers—we were all part of the same subculture," says Ron, "We got along with hippies." But the drunken bikers were too rowdy for Kathy Ibrahim's tastes. Ron stripped and jumped naked into her lap. The hysterical Kathy Ibrahim began chanting Hail Marys, and they complied with her request to be let out. She was no fun at all.

At a burned-down gas station and curio shop, the bikers pulled off the road for a pee stop. Sifting through the rubble, Ron unearthed a pair of steer horns mounted on a plaque. Doc came up with the idea of attaching the horns to the handlebars of his bike, and they tossed them in the van. A little further on down the road, they picked up two more hitchers, both males. The bikers gave their two new riders a beer. Things were friendly enough until Ron caught one of them cramming beers into his knapsack. The bikers' hospitality affronted, Ron demanded that the hitchhikers pay for the beer they drank and chip in for gas. Art Smith, acting the tough guy, snatched Doc's .22 pistol out of the glove compartment and spun it on his finger cowboy fashion. The gun went off, grazing one of the hitchhikers behind the ear. 'What in the hell—you dumb ass kid!' Doc raged, grabbing the pistol from his cousin. Ron doused the wound with beer and mopped up the blood with a T-shirt. By then the other hitchhiker had offered up a dollar and some change to pay for the beer they drank. "We felt real bad about Art shooting that guy," Ron says. "We talked about if maybe we should take him to a doctor, but he appeared to be okay. It was just a flesh wound. We carried them with us for a ways further, and on a deserted stretch of highway in north Texas, we let them out. If they decided to turn us into the cops, it would be a while before they caught another ride, and we'd be long gone."

By the wee hours of February 10, the bikers had left Texas behind and cruised into Oklahoma. They did not get far before blue lights showed in their rearview mirror. They pulled over, and when ordered to come out with their hands up, they obeyed, except for Sandman Smith. Sandman, so named because he had a habit of getting drunk and passing out, was asleep. A search of the van yielded up Sandman, and numerous incidentals including a ratty green blanket belonging to Sandman's girlfriend, the steer horns, two .22 pistols, and Ron's broken-down shotgun. Each of the bikers was carrying a knife, of the pocket variety, except for Sandman Smith, who wore a large hunting knife strapped to his leg.

The hitchhikers had filed armed robbery charges against the bikers. Charges were also pending, of an unspecified nature, regarding the Kathy Ibrahim incident. The bikers spent the next five days in a jail in Weatherford, Oklahoma. For the most part they thought it was a big joke. How bad could it be? They had taken the dollar the hitchhiker offered for the beer and let him keep the change. His buddy was not seriously hurt. Ron expected an indecent exposure charge for the Kathy Ibrahim shenanigans and, at worst, a $25 fine—that was what Sandman's torn-pants episode had cost him. When Ron's turn came to make the phone call he was entitled to by law, he ordered a pizza. The officer yanked the receiver out of his hand and smacked him in the head with it. Of primary concern to the bikers at the time of their arrest was that the unexpected delay would make them late for next week's mandatory Vagos meeting.

A Castrated John Doe

Early on the morning of February 13, a crow hunter tramped the frozen earth in the Tijeras Canyon and stumbled on a castrated corpse crudely concealed beneath a sage bush. Albuquerque City Police were first to arrive on the scene, but the Bernalillo County Sheriff's Department took over the investigation when it was determined the body was on county land.[14] The victim, a young male, wore an army-green jacket with an orange lining.[15] His pants were pulled down around his knees. In addition to being emasculated, the victim had been shot in the head and slashed across the chest. There was a rope tied to his ankles, suggesting the body had been dragged to its present location.[16]

With no wallet and no identification of any kind found on the corpse, the authorities were stumped. Dr. James Weston, the state's chief medical examiner, was at a conference in Texas. Weston had assisted in the autopsy of JFK and had impressive credentials. Out of state, so unable to participate in the autopsy of the castrated John Doe, Weston provided what help he could over the phone. After consulting with a colleague at the conference, a leading authority on sex-related crimes, Weston provided the Bernalillo Sheriff's Department with a profile of the killers. He characterized the murder as a gang-style killing by individuals with a homosexual background.[17]

Chief Detective Santos Baca of the Bernalillo County Sheriff's Department remembered hearing a February 9 radio advisory to be on the lookout for five robbery suspects traveling east in an orange van with California tags. The dispatch had come in from Quay County, east of there, meaning the van likely had passed through Albuquerque. It was worth checking out. When Baca phoned the Quay County Sheriff's Department, he learned that the suspects had been apprehended.[18]

On February 15, the bikers were extradited to Tucumcari, New Mexico, and incarcerated in the Quay County jail, the county where the hitchhikers and Kathy Ibrahim had filed charges. Bernalillo County Sheriff's Department deputies Robert Tena and Gilbert Candelaria traveled to Tucumcari to interview the bikers. On February 16, Bernalillo County Sheriff Lester Hay told the press that the bikers were "good suspects" and that they initially were arrested for the armed robbery of a Tucumcari service station. The article in the *Albuquerque Tribune* went on to say that the bikers had guns and knives and had threatened the proprietor, 'We'll cut you up like we did that guy back in Albuquerque.'[19] The quote was actually a distortion of what one of the hitchhikers reported to law enforcement officials. The hitcher said the bikers ordered him to hand over his wallet, sealing the demand with the threat: 'If you get smart, we'll kill you like we did a guy a ways back.' Nothing of the kind was ever said by any of the bikers. In their report, Detectives Tena and Candelaria inflated the hitchhiker's fraudulent statement still further, to suggest it pointed to the Albuquerque murder, and attributed it to the bikers in conjunction with a service-station robbery that never happened.[20]

The bikers had readily admitted to taking the steer horns from the charred ruins of the service station and curio shop near Tucumcari. But why were the cops making such big deal about it, they wondered? Robbery? The place was burned to the ground and abandoned. What the bikers did not know was that the hitchhikers, as hitchhikers were wont to do, had hit the road. Without witnesses, the charges filed by the hitchhikers would never hold up in court. Suspicion of armed robbery related to an incident at a Tucumcari service station and curio shop was added to the bikers' list of offenses, in order to keep them under lock and key until their possible involvement in the Albuquerque murder of the castrated John Doe could be investigated. Given the sexual nature of the crime, Ron's jumping naked into Kathy Ibrahim's lap lent credibility to the sheriff's department's theory that the bikers were the killers, but Ron's drunken shenanigans did not constitute an offense serious enough to prolong their incarceration.

Ron and company had no idea that they were suspects in a homicide. "We thought they were just harassing us because we were bikers," Ron says, "and after a few days they'd get tired of the game and let us go."

But back in Albuquerque, the bikers were already making the news, portrayed in the papers and on local TV stations as the men under investigation for the murder of the castrated John Doe. The killing appeared to be either "sexual or gang-style," Chief Detective Baca told the press. It was an election year, and Sheriff Hay welcomed the media coverage of his department's round-the-clock efforts to solve the crime.[21]

On February 22, nine days after the corpse was discovered, the body was identified as that of William Velten, Jr., an Albuquerque resident and former student at the University of New Mexico.[22] Judith Weyer, a waitress at a local eating spot and maid at the Bel Air Motel in Albuquerque, had been following the story on TV. Like many Albuquerque residents, she thought the California bikers sounded like the very sort who would mutilate and murder a man. Earlier in the month, a rowdy group driving a car with California tags had stayed at the motel. They registered under the false name Mr. and Mrs. Butts.[23] One member of the Butts group had asked Judy for a rope to tie something to their car, and she had supplied one.[24] Judy Weyer told a co-worker at the motel about the suspicious Butts family, and the co-worker notified the Albuquerque police.[25] Officer James Boman talked with Judy Weyer, but she insisted she did not know anything about the murder.[26]

Judy Weyer gradually changed her story, though, after several interviews with Sheriff's Detectives Tena and Candelaria.[27] It was a difficult time in Judy Weyer's life. She was estranged from her husband and had lost custody of her children.[28] The detectives made her feel important.[29] To begin with, Judy Weyer thought the detectives were asking her about the Butts group. The detectives supplied her with details about the crime. The autopsy had shown that Velten had eaten hot dogs, the detectives told her, and Judy Weyer responded that she had seen wieners in the motel room.[30] And then there was the business about Velten's body being dragged with a rope. One of the California men who had stayed at the motel asked her for a rope, and she had given him one, Weyer acknowledged in talking with the detectives. Before long, she had talked herself into a corner. She was worried the detectives would think she was lying if she denied knowing anything about the murder.[31]

In her first official statement to Detectives Tena and Candelaria, dated

March 2, Judy Weyer hedged, saying she did not know anything about William Velten being killed, but she identified Ron and one of the other bikers from photographs as the men who had stayed at the motel for three days.[32] On March 6, she traveled to Tucumcari with the detectives to get a first-hand look at the detainees the detectives seemed certain had killed William Velten.[33]

A trustee at the jail told the bikers a woman was coming to identify them. "We were expecting the Kathy chick we picked up hitchhiking," Ron says. "We were waiting there in our cell, and when this woman peeked at us through the poop shoot, the slot where they slide in the food trays, Tom Gladish hollered out, 'There she is.' We saw her face for a second, and then she was gone. We were shaking our heads, saying 'Gee, that didn't look like the hippie chick from the commune.' We were really drunk when we stopped to give her a ride, but none of us remembered her looking anything like the woman who stuck her face in the poop shoot."[34]

The detectives took a second statement from Judy Weyer on March 7. It was not until her third statement, on March 11, that Judy Weyer finally gave the detectives what they wanted: Citing a Bel Air motel guestroom as the murder scene, she said, the bikers raped her and forced her to watch while they slashed, sodomized, castrated, and shot William Velten.[35]

On March 12, mug shots of the bikers made the front page of the *Albuquerque Tribune*. The headline of the four-page article read "Secret Witness Links Cycle Gang to Slaying."[36] Most people decided at a glance that the bearded, tattooed California bikers were guilty. They were an ill-kempt, vicious-looking lot.[37] The sheriff's department reported hiding a "pretty young woman" who saw the five members of the California motorcycle gang mutilate and kill William Velten, Jr. In a television interview, Sheriff Hay played to the hysteria and fear, claiming that the bikers had "disposed of other witnesses in other parts of the country . . . We're gonna give her all the protection we can . . . she saw the whole thing." According to the official statement from the sheriff's department, the bikers had picked up Velten hitchhiking. Bond for the five men, still incarcerated in the Tucumcari jail, had been set at $100,000 each. "We've got a real good case, and it's due to the efforts of Santos Baca and Detectives Gil Candelaria and Robert Tena," the sheriff boasted.[38]

On March 13, first-degree murder charges were filed against the bikers. Ron and company were transported to the Bernalillo County Jail in Albuquerque. They had no idea they were murder suspects. "We figured any day now they were going to let us go," Ron says. "It was a whole lot of shit for that Kathy Ibrahim chick and the hitchhikers we took a dollar from. Art grazing the guy with the pistol wasn't cool, but stuff a lot worse than that happened all the time in bar fights. We didn't think we were in any kind of serious trouble. We may have talked with a public defender when we were still in Tucumcari—I'm not sure. We never asked to talk to an attorney. We expected to get slapped with a $25 or $50 fine for what I did—the indecent exposure thing—and that would be the end of it.

"In Albuquerque, they put the five of us in the bull pen with a gay guy. We could tell he was a flamer. Back then I was anti-gay. We all were. It was part of the Vagos creed. We didn't want him around us. We said, 'Look, we're not your kind of people so you stay completely the fuck away from us. If we're out here playing cards or reading, you stay in your fucking cell. You come out of your cell, we're kicking your ass.' We basically put him in isolation. Looking back at it, he was probably a snitch. They were probably trying to find out if we were homosexuals—to see if we'd say something to him or do something with him—because of the nature of the murder. But we didn't know anything about the murder. We didn't even know we were suspects in a murder, not until a few days before the indictment."

The March 13 Albuquerque Tribune reported that the sheriff's office believed the "secret witness" was in grave danger. They had placed her in police custody and were keeping her hidden. One thousand motorcycle gang members were rumored to be headed for Albuquerque on their bikes to avenge their fellow bikers' arrest.[39]

"Secret witness" Weyer was staying with sheriff's deputy Ida Maynard.[40] Ida Maynard noticed marks under Judy Weyer's breasts and on the backs of her legs. The marks were caused by her overly tight bra and jeans, but Judy had become skilled at embellishing her story. She said the marks were scars from knife wounds inflicted by the bikers. The doctor who examined her concurred.[41]

When the bikers found out what they were up against, they contacted their club brothers. The Vagos sent club attorney Allan Well of Relondo Beach, California. Because Well was not licensed to practice law in New Mexico, he hired Albuquerque attorney Ron Ginsburg to serve as cocounsel. Judy Weyer's deposition testimony was replete with contradictions, Ron recalls. "'Is this story true or is the story you told before true?' our attorneys would ask her. 'Were you lying in this story or telling the truth in this story?' And she would look at them all confused and say, 'What story?'" But Judy Weyer succeeded in convincing the grand jury. On March 20, a week after arriving in Albuquerque, and only days after learning they were murder suspects, the bikers were indicted. District Judge William Riordan set the trial date for 6 May 1974.[42]

The bikers were immediately hustled off to the New Mexico State Penitentiary. "They are dangerous and we don't want to take a chance," Sheriff

Hay explained in a public statement, seizing the opportunity to flaunt the sheriff's department's commitment to protect the community.[43]

Death Row from Day 1

In the multi-tiered cellblock at the New Mexico State Penitentiary, the basement level was designated as death row. The only glimpse of daylight came from high windows on the ground floor. The bikers were incarcerated on death row from the very first day of their arrival.

"They were trying to intimidate us," Ron speculates, "to break us down, hoping maybe one of us would confess. We were completely incommunicado. For an attorney to come see us, they had to drive all the way to Santa Fe and then wait for the prison to clear them—it took half a day, so our attorneys didn't visit us much. We'd get a note from them every so often, but every letter we got from the attorneys had been opened. It was a violation of attorney-client privilege for the prison to open our mail, but they did it anyway. We told our attorneys what was going on, and after that, they didn't write much either. My mom got me a subscription to the *Albuquerque Journal*, and I kept up with our case by reading the paper. Sometimes they'd hold my papers for five or six days, and give me all of them at once, but I got them eventually. It really pissed me off what was being printed. They wouldn't let our attorneys tell their side."

Several important developments in the case didn't make the news. In mid-April, a thirteen-year-old boy out riding his bike with three friends found a .22 Ivor Johnson pistol in the arroyo not far from where Velten's body had been discovered. Ballistic tests by the State Police Crime Laboratory were inconclusive.[44] The report the bikers' attorneys received from the prosecution indicated that the four bullets taken from Velten's body could not be matched to the Ivor Johnson. This did not rule out the possibility that the pistol might be the murder weapon, but it was a big *if*, one that did nothing to prove the bikers' innocence.[45]

Meanwhile, Assistant District Attorney Brian Gross and a team of sheriff's officers were busy rehearsing Judy Weyer for the trial, in grueling sessions sometimes lasting as much as eight and nine hours.[46] Judy Weyer began to crack under the pressure. "I didn't see the killing," she confided to her guardian, policewoman Ida Maynard. But Maynard simply shrugged it off, and said 'Come on, let's have lunch.'[47] When Weyer told Sheriff's detectives Tena and Candelaria she had not witnessed the murder, they laughed at her.[48] In a chance encounter at the District Attorney's Office with the Albuquerque police officer who first questioned her, James Boman,

Judy Weyer broke down and started crying. She was being forced to fabricate testimony against the bikers, she confided to Boman; she hadn't seen any of it, she wasn't there when the murder happened. This was exactly what Judy Weyer had told Boman when he first talked with her. When Boman informed the sheriff's officers working the case that Judy Weyer had just divulged to him that she did not know anything about the Velten murder, the officers dismissed the information with the remark 'she's done this before.'[49]

But the prosecution clearly had a problem on its hands. Their entire case against the bikers rested on Judy Weyer's eyewitness account.

Assistant D.A. Gross and six sheriff's officers proceeded to subject Judy Weyer to a brutal nine-hour interrogation session.[50] When she insisted that she had not seen the bikers kill Velten and that she knew absolutely nothing about the murder, the interrogation team threatened to put her in jail for perjury. Judy Weyer failed to understand that lying to police did not constitute perjury, that perjury meant lying in court.[51] Sheriff's Sgt. Donald Heavner made a show of looking up the penalty for perjury in a criminal codebook, implying that she would spend five years in prison for lying to the detectives if she did not testify.[52]

When Judy Weyer held firm and refused to implicate the bikers, the interrogators changed their tact. They said they had information that her boyfriend Jose Rivera was involved. Rivera was staying at the Bel Air Motel during the month of February 1974, which was how Judy Weyer came to meet him. Judy Weyer's earlier statements, which pointed to the Bel Air Motel as the crime scene, had thrown suspicion on Jose Rivera, who had been in trouble before. Lacking evidence linking Rivera to the murder, authorities had picked him up and incarcerated him on the grounds that he was a dangerous habitual felon.[53]

Hammering Judy Weyer with questions and prompting her with innuendo, the interrogation team tried to persuade her to include Jose Rivera in her testimony. In room 45—the room determined to be the crime scene from Judy Weyer's earlier confused and conflicting statements—investigators had discovered a desert landscape painting disfigured by a bullet hole and a crude sketch of a hangman stick figure, with the caption, "Say Please." The interrogation team pressured her to say that Rivera had disfigured the painting and made her move it from his room into room 45, to throw suspicion on the bikers.[54] For Judy Weyer, it was a lose-lose situation: frame the bikers or frame her boyfriend.

Weyer refused to do either. Assistant D.A. Brian Gross ordered her booked on the charge of accessory to murder. She was jailed, and placed in a cell next to Jose Rivera, where the two could talk.[55]

Chief Detective Baca and Detective Candelaria visited Judy Weyer at the jail. The detectives promised her that both she and Jose would go free, if she testified against the bikers, and went on to sweeten the pot, plying her with bribes: They would help her get her kids back and they would provide her with room, board, and tuition to secretarial school, with the official assistance to begin immediately and to continue until she got a job.[56]

For two weeks, Judy Weyer denied having any knowledge of the murder.[57] But finally she came around to the detectives' way of thinking. She refused to say that Jose Rivera had anything to do with killing Velten, but she agreed to testify against the bikers.[58]

The sheriff's department made good on one point in the bargain: Judy Weyer was provided with room and board. She was kept in protective custody up until and throughout the trial, lodging either with Assistant D.A. Brian Gross and his family or in a motel, guarded by Sgt. Donald Heavner.[59] Both the press and defense attorneys were denied access to her.[60]

As to the promise that in return for agreeing to testify both she and Jose Rivera would be set free, Rivera was packed off to the New Mexico State Penitentiary in Santa Fe, where the bikers were incarcerated on death row.[61]

In prison, Rivera was assigned the duty of picking up trash in the yard. A sock, with a rock inside for weight, hit the bars of Ron's cell late one afternoon. "I was sitting there reading a magazine. If it hadn't been for the bars, the thing probably would have hit me in the head. I grabbed it real quick and pulled it in. I figured someone must have thrown it through one of the ground-level windows. There was a note inside. After I read it, I passed it down to the other guys. The note said Judy Weyer was lying. She hadn't seen the murder and didn't know anything about it. The note was signed by Jose Rivera.

"We thought for a long time that Rivera murdered Velten. We knew we didn't. Why would this girl lie? Because she was covering for the man she loved. Our attorneys thought that, too. It made sense, once they found out that Jose Rivera was Judy Weyer's boyfriend. A lot of energy got spent on trying to put these pieces together, and they were not part of the puzzle."

George Henry "Hank" Farrah from the Albuquerque public defender's office had joined the bikers' defense team.[62] Word got back to Farrah that for a period of several weeks, Judy Weyer had done a complete about-face, recanting her earlier statements identifying the bikers and insisting that she hadn't witnessed the killing. Farrah finally received permission to talk with Judy Weyer, but the interview was cut short after only two questions.[63]

Peso Chavez, investigator for the defense, traveled to the state penitentiary in Santa Fe to interview the bikers. The bad press had taken its toll on Chavez. The papers had painted the five bikers as vicious sadists, and Chavez was afraid of them. But in talking with the men one on one, Chavez quickly realized that they were just regular guys—rowdy bikers, yes, but not psychotic homicidal maniacs, not by a long shot. Chavez questioned each man separately, and each man recalled different details in recounting the drive across Arizona, New Mexico, and north Texas, into Oklahoma. It was obvious to Chavez that they hadn't gotten together and choreographed a story to tell the authorities, and equally obvious that while different incidents stuck out in each man's mind, the diverse accounts correlated to form a definitive timeline of events, beginning with their departure from El Monte, California, on February 8, and culminating with their arrest in Weatherford, Oklahoma, on February 10. They clearly were not anywhere near Albuquerque, New Mexico, on February 8, the date law enforcement officials maintained the murder occurred.[64]

Chavez requisitioned the court for travel expenses to research the case. The court was not readily forthcoming with funds to cover the expenses of the defense, but Chavez persisted and his request eventually was granted. He set out on a road trip of his own to retrace the bikers' path. One of the bikers had described a roadside diner in Arizona where they stopped for pancakes on the morning of February 9. Chavez found the diner easily enough from the description. He went in, ordered a cup of coffee, and explained to the waitress why he was there. She remembered the bikers, all right, "They were obnoxious as all get out," adding that they didn't get many drunks at sunup.[65] She searched the records in the back room and found the dated receipt. The five bikers had ordered pancakes.

The bikers' breakfast at the diner, credit card receipts for gas purchased with Doc Greer's stolen card, and an automobile accident the bikers recalled seeing all verified that they were traveling east through Arizona on February 9 and didn't get to New Mexico until later that same day, the day after Judy Weyer said the murder occurred. One of the bikers received a traffic ticket in California, on February 8. Chavez followed up on this lead as well, and verified the ticket with the officer who wrote it. The officer, however, refused to come to Albuquerque to testify when the court denied the requisition to pay his travel expenses and compensate him for time lost from his job.

Lack of funds hampered the defense from the outset. Vagos attorney Allen Well and co-counsel Ron Ginsburg withdrew from the case after the bikers were indicted, complaining of the expense involved.[66] "We had our friends on the outside selling our motorcycles, practically everything we owned, to pay attorney fees," says Ron, "and our families were chipping in.

Sandman's parents gave ten grand or so." Ginsburg and Well ultimately rejoined the defense team, and along with public defender Hank Farrah, represented the bikers at the trial. The bikers hoped to receive financial assistance from Brothers In Chains, a Vagos defense fund that Ron, as a financial officer in the club, had helped establish. "We never got a penny from the Brothers In Chains fund, not even cigarette money," Ron recalls somewhat bitterly, "but the Vagos did do one thing for us. Our club brothers went around and talked to people who saw us on February 8. They helped our attorneys locate alibi witnesses—the guy I paid my rent to on February 8, the guy who owned a motorcycle shop where one of us had done business that day, a club brother who had a clean record to testify we were all at the February 8 club meeting."

The Trial

The original trial date of May 6 had been rescheduled for May 20. Hoping to shore up their case against the bikers, sheriff's detectives contacted a young woman who had stayed at the Bel Air Motel from February 7 to March 4. Sixteen-year-old Shelley Fish had since moved to Maryland with her husband, a Marine sergeant. The court paid Shelley Fish's travel expenses and flew her back to Albuquerque just as the trial was commencing. It would be a short visit, a day at the most, the detectives had promised Shelley Fish when they spoke to her by phone. They wanted her to look at photographs of some men from California to see if she could identify them.

Shelley Fish remembered meeting five surfers from California, a group who had registered at the motel under the alias Mr. and Mrs. Butts. The surfers had stayed in room 45, the room where authorities contended William Velten was slain. Shelley Fish assumed the surfers were the men under suspicion. The detectives showed her photographs of the bikers and their orange van. She did not recognize any of the men in the photograph and had never seen the van before, she told the detectives.

The detectives accused her of lying. After several days of questioning, Shelley Fish said she wanted to go home. The officers took her airplane ticket away, insisting that they knew from Judy Weyer that she met one of the bikers, Ron Keine, on the night of the murder when he came to Judy's room to get a key—why didn't she just tell them the truth? Shelley Fish's husband had tried repeatedly to phone his wife, but officials refused to let him speak with her. Frustrated and angry, he threatened to take legal action against the Bernalillo County Sheriff's Department. His wife had been in Albuquerque almost two weeks. The detectives gave up on Shelley Fish and sent her on her way. The officer who drove her to the airport advised her to leave town immediately and not to talk with anyone about her interrogation experience.[67]

Ron and company temporarily had left death row. They were moved back to the Bernalillo County Jail in Albuquerque for the duration of the trial. At the time, one of the California surfers from the Butts group also was incarcerated in the county jail. Talk buzzed among the inmates that the bikers were saying some guys named Butts stayed at the Bel Air Motel in February, and the Butts were the ones who murdered Velten. The surfer spoke out against the accusation; he was the one who signed the guest register Mr. and Mrs. Butts, not his real name, and he and his friends had not killed anyone. Word got back to the bikers. They notified Vagos attorney Allen Well that one of the Butts was in jail with them.

Allen Well never followed up on the lead. Ron does not look favorably on Well's contribution to the defense. "Allen Well took our money, showed up in court, and that was about it. But Hank Farrah, he fought like a son of a bitch for us. He was just a green attorney then, and he did the best he could. At the trial, they had everything stacked against him."

District Attorney James Brandenburg and Assistant District Attorney Brian Gross presented the case for the prosecution. At every photo opportunity, Gross wore a hangman's noose lapel pin, reminding the public of the hangman's image disfiguring the painting found in the room where the murder allegedly took place. Adding fuel to already inflamed public opinion, Judge Riordan warned the six men and six women serving on the jury that they would see evidence of a "very brutal and very horrendous crime."[68]

Judy Weyer testified that she first met Ron at a local eatery, Der Wienerschnitzel, insinuating a link to the medical reports that Velten's last meal was hot dogs. "Grubby" and his friends needed a place to stay—Weyer referred to Ron by his biker nickname. She gave the bikers a room at the motel. Grubby later came to her room and said he had something to show her. She went with him to room 45, where she first saw Velten, his one arm tied to the bed and the other arm tied to a chair.

Grubby heated a knife in a wall heater, and slashed Velten's chest, "his legs, his arms, his hands, all over," Judy Weyer told the spellbound jurors. Next it was her turn. Grubby cut her under her breasts, then he sodomized Velten. Both Grubby and Sandman Smith raped her. After that, Grubby gave Doc Greer the knife, and Greer castrated Velten. The bikers wrapped Velten in a blanket and took him out to the van, where she was also herded, blindfolded.

Bikers en route to the courtroom, left to right: "Doc" Greer, "Sandman" Smith, Tom Gladish, Ron Keine. [*Albuquerque Journal*]

It was a graphic retelling, but with a few inconsistencies. Judy Weyer's timing varied as to when Velten was shot, and she was uncertain about whether or not Velten was dead when he was emasculated.[69]

In coaching Judy Weyer, the detectives had provided her with the information that Velten's wounds were inflicted with a hot knife and that he had been sodomized.[70] The detectives' source was Dr. James Weston, the state's chief medical examiner, whose profile of the killers had guided the investigation since the day the body was discovered.[71]

At the trial, Dr. Weston expanded on his theory that it was a gang-style killing by individuals with a homosexual background. As he had explained previously to sheriff's officials, "with this type of mutilation, almost invariably there is a female present," Weston noted, pointing out that Judy Weyer's inclusion in the ritual was consistent with research and literature documenting similar cases. In his opinion, the slashes and castration were done "with a cutting instrument which was hot, explaining to some degree, absence of any blood." Weston acknowledged that he had not been present at the autopsy, but he personally examined the lab specimens and determined "the presence of spermatozoa, that is, intact with head and tails attached."[72]

The prestigious Dr. Weston gave the stamp of authority to Judy Weyer's horrific, if somewhat confused, account of Velten's mutilation and murder.

Hitchhiker Kathy Ibrahim verified the bikers' credentials as homosexuals by testifying that when Ron jumped naked into her lap, he announced, 'Normally I prefer boys, but in your case I'll make an exception.' Kathy

Ibrahim also said she heard the bikers talking about a rape and fight during which a woman 'squealed like a stuck pig,' leading to the conclusion that the woman they were speaking about was Judy Weyer.[73] Years later, at a commune encounter session, Kathy Ibrahim admitted that none of the bikers had said any of these things. When they questioned her, sheriff's officials had portrayed the bikers as killers and rapists who preyed on hippies, and convinced her that she would be doing a justice if she helped get them off the road.

Additional hearsay testimony came from Charlie "The Rat" Duran, so named for his reputation as a jailhouse snitch. D.A. Brandenburg promised Duran a transfer out of the New Mexico State Penitentiary in return for taking the witness stand.[74] The absurdity of Duran's testimony outrages Ron: "Duran said he overheard us talking among ourselves about the murder, bragging about what we did to Velten. Duran wasn't even on death row. He was on the other side of the cellblock, a couple floors up. You couldn't hear to talk to a guy four cells down, except at night when it was real quiet. The structure was stone and steel. The din from the echo during the day was deafening. We'd never seen Duran or heard of him either one, until the trial."

Dr. Weston's hot-knife theory appeared to rectify the odd fact that no blood was found anywhere in room 45 at the Bel Air Motel or in the bikers' van. There were several small bloodstains on the green blanket confiscated from the van, the blanket belonging to Sandman Smith's girlfriend. The bloodstains matched her blood type and that of William Velten.[75] At the trial, Smith's girlfriend testified the stains were from her menstrual blood and that the blanket was hers. The prosecution contended the bikers had taken the blanket from the motel, but the motel owner could not confirm this. A few hairs were found on the blanket, which may have belonged to Velten and may not have belonged to Velten. The lab tests were inconclusive.[76]

In the bikers' favor, ballistic test showed that neither of the two .22 pistols confiscated from the van were the murder weapon and that the knives they carried showed traces of animal blood, from the cow they butchered, but no human blood.[77] The two pistols and Ron's shotgun were lawfully registered. To avoid arousing undue suspicion in the eyes of the jury, defense attorney Hank Farrah decided to admit all the knives and guns into evidence, with the exception of the large hunting knife that Sandman Smith wore strapped to his boot—it looked too threatening, even though it contained no traces of blood whatsoever.

The thrust of the prosecution's case against the bikers rested on Judy Weyer's eyewitness account. Several days into the trial, Judge Riordan dismissed charges against Art Smith. In Judy Weyer's description of the killing and torture, Art Smith only watched and was not an actual participant. Art Smith's release ultimately proved unfortunate for the other four. The bikers' attorneys had exercised their option not to have their clients testify, since in cross-examination, the prosecution could question them about past convictions, which might prejudice the jury against them. Art Smith was fair game once charges against him were dropped. The prosecution put him on the witness stand, and Assistant D.A. Gross asked Smith if the bloodstains on the blanket could have been from the incident involving the two hitchhikers they let out in north Texas. Art Smith declined to answer on the grounds that he might incriminate himself.[78] The jury was left to make of it what they would.

A long parade of alibi witnesses testified that the bikers were in El Monte, California, on February 8, the day the murder allegedly occurred. Ron's rental house super came, with the receipt dated February 8 in hand, and testified that Ron was a good tenant, always timely about paying; but the prosecution argued the Vagos had intimidated the rent collector into testifying on the bikers' behalf. The club brother who testified that all five bikers had attended the February 8 meeting had long hair and walked with a cane from a bike accident. "He looked like a biker," says Ron, "like us. The bad guys. He probably hurt us more than helped us."

The fire chief who worked the accident, which the bikers recalled seeing on February 9, testified that the mishap was not spectacular and did not make the news; the bikers would not have known about it unless they actually had seen it. Testimony of the Arizona waitress and gas station credit card receipts likewise corroborated that the murder occurred before the bikers ever got to Albuquerque. One receipt had been dated incorrectly February 8, but several attendants from the service station testified that they sometimes forgot to change the date on the machine.[79]

The oversight cost the bikers. Assistant D.A. Gross argued that they killed Velten, then backtracked into Arizona before heading east again, establishing a trail of credit card receipts dated February 9, for the specific purpose of creating an alibi.[80] Given that the credit card was stolen, and not registered in the name of any of the bikers, the credibility of the argument left something to be desired, presupposing that the bikers sought to create an alibi by using a false identity and credential.

Up to this point in the trial, the evidence—aside from Judy Weyer's testimony—supported the bikers' claim that they were nowhere near Albuquerque, New Mexico, on February 8. Then the prosecution pulled a trump card. With defense attorneys set to present their closing arguments, the prosecution introduced three additional witnesses who said they saw the bikers in Albuquerque on February 8. Judge Riordan permitted their testimony, even though the defense had not had an opportunity to investigate the witnesses' contentions and reliability. An Albuquerque resident testified that he saw Doc Greer and Tom Gladish outside Der Wienerschnitzel on the morning of February 8, and the man's son recalled seeing the orange van. A local bar owner testified that he saw Ron and Doc Greer circulating among the crowd on the evening of the murder.[81]

The jury was not sequestered. During the closing days of the trial, an alternate juror reported that she received a phone call, warning her to 'watch out,' and that she and the juror riding with her had been followed home by a bearded longhair on a chopper. Defense attorney Allen Well pointed out that her description matched that of an undercover narcotic's agent with the sheriff's department. The day before deliberation was scheduled to begin, the same juror received an obscene phone call and death threat. She said she was too upset to take part in the decision process. Judge Riordan excused her and offered the defense a mistrial. Ron and company did not want to go through another trial. They had alibi witnesses and proof of their whereabouts on both February 8 and February 9. The only evidence against them was the testimony of Judy Weyer, who could not even remember when it was they supposedly shot Velten. They all believed they would be found innocent.[82]

They were wrong. On 5 June 1974, all four men were found guilty of first-degree murder and sentenced to die in the New Mexico gas chamber.

It took the jury fifteen-and-a-half hours to reach a unanimous verdict.[83] Clearly, the decision had not been an easy one. Afterward, Hank Farrah polled the jury members. Like the bikers, Farrah believed that the dated credit card receipts and numerous alibi witnesses were sufficient proof that Judy Weyer was lying. What had swayed the jury members in their decision, Farrah wanted to know. The answer shocked and saddened him— it was Sandman Smith's knife. When she testified, Sandman's girlfriend had mentioned that Sandman wore a large, heavy-bladed knife strapped to his boot. The jury had been shown the knives the other four bikers carried. What happened to Sandman's knife, the jurors wanted to know? They decided that the bikers had used Sandman's knife to emasculate and torture Velten and then disposed of it.[84]

The day the trial ended, Judy Weyer was ousted from the motel where she had been kept in protective custody. Her official assistance officially had ended. It quickly became evident to her that the sheriff's officers had no intention of keeping their promise to send her to secretarial school. With no money and no job, Judy Weyer appealed to a local priest for help. He gave her money for plane fare, and she left town.[85]

Nine Days from the Gas Chamber

The bikers' execution was set for 1 August 1974.[86] While capital judgments now are appealed automatically, and an execution date is never set until after the appeal, in 1974 the execution date could be set immediately after sentencing.[87] No one had been executed in New Mexico since the 1972 U.S. Supreme Court ruling *Furman v. Georgia* challenged and temporarily halted executions.[88] *Furman v. Georgia* nullified all existing capital-punishment laws. The decision cited racial bias and other prejudices as operative factors in assignment of the death penalty and argued that because the death penalty was arbitrarily and capriciously applied, it constituted cruel and unusual punishment.[89] New Mexico's new capital-punishment law presumed to guarantee unbiased application of the death penalty by making execution mandatory for *all* first-degree murder convictions. The bikers' pending execution tested the constitutionality of the new law. If the bikers' execution was not challenged on constitutional grounds, the recently instated New Mexico death-penalty statute would be construed as having received the U.S. Supreme Court seal of approval.*

The main facility at the New Mexico State Penitentiary was known as the Dungeon, a reference to the Dungeon Hole, a punishment chamber at the prison where problem inmates were stripped naked and left for days in darkness, in solitary confinement, with only a hole in the floor for a toilet.[90] Ten days before he was scheduled to die, the assistant warden asked Ron about his last meal and any other final requests. Ron replied, "I want you to be holding my hand when they put me in the gas chamber and drop the pellets.

"I was being a smart ass," Ron admits. "I'd made a pledge to myself I was not going to make it easy for them. As ridiculous as it may seem, I even practiced holding my breath.

"They tried to beat us down emotionally. The whole system was geared to that. In your six-by-nine cell was a bunk, a toilet, and a little bitty sink with push buttons so you couldn't leave the water on and cause a mess. It also meant you couldn't wash properly. I figured out how to jam the knobs with toothpicks. They let us out for one shower a week if we were lucky, one man at a time. The cell doors were electric and controlled by the guards. The showers were at the end of the row of cells. All you could take with you was a towel, which you'd wear wrapped around your waist to

---

*Laws that provided a mandatory death penalty for specific crimes later were declared unconstitutional; see *Woodson v. North Carolina*, 428 U.S. 280 (1976), and *Roberts v. Louisiana*, 428 U.S. 325 (1976); "Four Members of Cycle Club Sentenced to Gas Chamber."

maintain some sense of dignity. Sometimes I would refuse to go back in my cell after a shower. I knew the prison rule was that they couldn't come onto death row without six guards, so I'd visit with my bros in the other cells until the goon squad arrived. Then I would go back in my cell like a good dog, and they would close my cell door again. The only other time we got out was when we had a visitor, and it was always in full leg shackles and handcuffs.

"We never got out for exercise, no time in the yard whatsoever. Most guys made a table from rolled-up newspapers and magazines, tied together with strips of bed sheet. Depending on the size of your table, you had roughly two feet by three feet of walking space. They'd give you all the Thorazine you wanted—it's a sedative—what they give mental patients. Thorazine is the chemical equivalent of doing a lobotomy on somebody. I always traded mine for cigarettes. Some guys liked taking it. You could pick them out by their gait—we called it the Thorazine shuffle.

"If you got sick, too bad. There was no medical attention. I had a kidney stone attack and lay on the floor of my cell for 18 hours, until I passed it. They were going to kill me anyway, so why waste time and money on keeping me alive—that's what one of the guards told me. You can become a sociopath in there. You're totally isolated. One thing we had going for us was that the four of us were on death row together. We could talk and pass notes back and forth. We learned how to communicate with guys on the floors above us, too, by what was called a 'kite.' A guy above us would wrap a note around a bar of soap, attach it to a rope made by tying together strips of bed sheet, pitch the bar of soap through his cell bars, and let it drop down to death row. We'd snare the kite with a paperclip hook tied to a bed-sheet rope.

"Nine days before our rendezvous with the cyanide gas pellets, our attorneys filed an appeal asking for a new trial, alleging, among other things, the judge's failure to sequester the jury and prejudicial pretrial publicity. That stayed our execution, temporarily. They couldn't kill us until the court ruled on the appeal. Nothing on the inside changed, though. Being in that hell pit takes its toll on you. It wasn't long before Doc and Sandman started losing it.

"Doc was in touch with this journalist on the outside. She sent him a Carlos Castaneda book and got him interested in transcendental meditation and astral projection—mind travel. He'd tell us about leaving his cell three and four times a day, and meeting with her and making love and drinking beer. He wasn't just saying this stuff. He believed it.

"Sandman cried all the time. He was an emotional wreck, whining about how much he missed his girlfriend and new baby—she was pregnant

mates staged a hunger strike to protest the unfair treatment. He managed to smuggle out a few letters to the press. Media coverage of the inmates' protest called public attention to the subhuman conditions that prevailed at the penitentiary. The inmates held their ground and had refused all food for over a week, when a guard congenially informed them, 'We're gonna let you take time in the yard. Who wants to go first?'

Ron volunteered. The guards told him to strip, shackled him, cuffed him, and shoved him out the door in below-freezing temperatures with snow on the ground. Entitled to twenty minutes in the yard, he made the best of it, jogging shackled, barefoot, and naked until he judged his allocated time had elapsed. But when he beat on the door, the guards refused to let him in. "I probably spent 30 to 40 minutes in the yard that first day," Ron recalls. "The next day, when they asked 'who wants to go,' I volunteered again. It seemed right. I was the one who started the protest. If no one went out, they would rescind our yard privileges—that's what they told us. Day two, it was the same thing—strip, shackles, handcuffs, out the door. I went to the yard that way three days in a row. By then, I had a real nasty cough. 'They're tryin' to kill you, man,' the other guys said to me, 'You're comin' down with pneumonia. It's not worth dying for.' The fourth day, I didn't go out, and neither did anyone else. That was the end of our exercise. Still, it was worth it. We made a point. We called attention to what was going on in there."

A New Trial?

Several weeks before the bikers' hearing requesting a new trial was scheduled to begin, an inmate from the New Mexico State Penitentiary, Eugene Greer (no relation to biker Doc Greer) wrote to the Detroit News claiming that another inmate, L. D. Bickford, had bragged to him about murdering William Velten. Bickford had two prior murder convictions.[105] The most recent was for a New Mexico castration-murder, in which testimony by Eugene Greer that Bickford had confessed to him was in part responsible for Bickford's conviction.[106]

The bikers' hearing for a new trial began on 31 March 1975. Teary-eyed and pregnant, Judy Weyer gave a detailed account of the coercion, bribes, and humiliation sheriff's officials had subjected her to and how they had supplied her with details about the murder. "They told me the victim had been sodomized . . . [They] told me they knew a girl was raped here in town. They kept after me, and I finally agreed it was me." She was never cut, she admitted—the marks under her breasts came from "a too tight bra." Why was she changing her testimony now? "I couldn't hold it inside anymore. I hadn't seen any of it."[107] She apologized to the bikers and asked them to forgive her.[108] She had never seen any of them until they were in custody, she told the court between sobs.[109]

Former prosecutor Brian Gross, who had resigned as assistant D.A., acknowledged that before the trial Judy Weyer had denied witnessing the murder. "I did not believe her," Gross said, "I told her I was going to charge her as an accessory to murder . . . to impress on her the seriousness of what she was doing." Gross contended that he didn't expect Sgt. Heavner to put her in jail. Gross, who had so proudly sported his hangman's noose lapel pin during the trial, acknowledged that he had requested permission to witness the biker's execution.[110]

To counter Judy Weyer's accusations, D.A. Brandenburg played a tape of his pre-trial interview with Weyer to demonstrate that she told him her story without coaching or coercion.[111]

Two prison inmates testified that Bickford had talked about murdering Velten. Eugene Greer, the inmate who contacted the *Detroit News*, also testified that he was a homosexual, that Bickford was his former lover, and that they had had a falling out when he refused Bickford's advances.[112] Bickford denied knowing anything about the Velten murder except what he heard that day in court.[113] Dr. Weston, the prosecution's star medical expert at the original trial, testified that the Velten murder and the two murders that Bickford had been convicted of were dissimilar, even though one involved emasculation. Asked to elaborate, Weston stressed that Velten was mutilated prior to his death, alluding to the hot-knife theory he advanced at the trial to explain the absence of blood.[114]

Ron testified that he had never even seen William Velten, and that it was the bikers who advised Eugene Greer to contact the *Detroit News*, when in a conversation through the prison vents, Greer told them Bickford had confessed to murdering Velten. It was the first and only time any of the bikers were put on the witness stand.[115] Why Ron and not the others? "The other guys were pretty much basket cases by then," Ron says.

The hearing lasted five days. Sheriff's Detective Ida Maynard, who served as Judy Weyer's guardian, and Albuquerque police officer James Boman both testified that Weyer told them before the trial that she never saw the murder. Corroborating the sheriff's office use of unprofessional tactics, Shelley Fish testified that detectives had also pressured her to identify the bikers and that they took her plane ticket away when she insisted she had never seen any of them before.[116]

Immediately upon presentation of closing arguments by D.A. Brandenburg and defense attorneys, Judge Riordan began reading his pre-prepared opinion. Apparently, he had arrived at a decision before the final day of courtroom testimony was heard. Judge Riordan could not accept Judy Weyer's confession that she had lied. The bikers' request for a new trial was denied.[117]

Riordan made few references to the testimony by the other witness and made no comment whatsoever regarding the testimony by the two prison inmates who named Bickford as a suspect, even though the M.O. in the Velten murder and the murders Bickford committed were stunningly similar.[118] Defense attorneys immediately filed an appeal. D.A. Brandenburg unwittingly had given them ammunition. The taped interview that Brandenburg presented as evidence that Judy Weyer was not coerced contained numerous discrepancies contradicting her trial testimony. Defense attorneys also had learned of another taped interview, conducted by a district attorney's office investigator prior to the trial, in which Judy Weyer flatly denied witnessing the murder.[119] Judge Riordan agreed to a second hearing for a new trial, and then recused himself, transferring the case to District Judge H. Verne Payne.[120]

Judge Payne denied the motion for a new trial, when the defense failed to produce the promised evidence.[121] The interview tape with Judy Weyer's statement that she never witnessed the murder, mysteriously, had disappeared.[122]

Detroit News reporters Cain and Glaizer continued with their personal probe into the case, but met with repeated frustration. A friend of William Velten's left town for an extended visit with his father when the reporters expressed an interest in interviewing him. In a prior phone conversation, he had told the reporters that sheriff's officers dramatically altered his statements to them about when he last saw Velten alive. The Albuquerque father and son who had testified that they saw the bikers' van, Doc Greer, and Tom Gladish outside Der Wienerschnitzel on February 8 had moved, forwarding address unknown. The Albuquerque bar owner who identified two of the bikers, became quarrelsome when the reporters pointed out that he testified the men were at his business at 9:00 P.M., which was when the prosecution contended they were at the motel murdering Velten.[123]

"I Started to Believe I Was Going to Die in There"

Ron and the other bikers found an unexpected ally in a guard they nicknamed Chilly Willy, a play on his surname, Freeze.

"The prison assigned Chilly night watch. He was a college student, a psychology major. After he'd been there a couple weeks, Chilly started talking to me and the other three guys and playing cards with us through the bars. And then one night, our four cell doors opened, all at the same time. We didn't come out. We thought it was a setup, that we were in for an ass-kicking, that if we came out a goon squad of guards would jump us and beat the crap out of us. We'd seen it before. We were scared shitless, when here comes Chilly strolling down the row, with a blanket and a bag of cookies his wife had baked. He spread the blanket on the floor like he was going to have a picnic and hollers, 'Come on. Let's play cards, guys.' We stepped out of our cells, real slow, still not sure. 'Aren't you afraid of us?' I asked 'According to the papers we're homicidal maniacs. We might jump you and beat you up, or worse.' 'Are you havin' a bad day?' Chilly asked back, 'Shut up and let's play cards. I've been around here long enough to know who's a murderer and who's not.' Chilly let us out for late-night blanket poker games whenever he could, when there were no other guards around. He wasn't even supposed to come onto death row by himself—six guards, that was the rule. We never gave Chilly a hard time like we did the other guards. Sometimes the guys on death row would go to beating on their cell bars and hooting, creating an uproar, just for the hell of it. If Chilly asked us to quiet down, we did. Most of the other guards treated us like animals, and that's how we acted. But Chilly was a real decent guy. We respected him, because he respected us."

Life on death row was taking its toll, though. Ron was beginning to lose hope. Sometimes, even now, thirty years later, the state of mind he calls The Syndrome still plagues him—"I'll be reading or working a crossword puzzle, and that kind of idle activity puts me back there. I forget I'm free. Except when Chilly let us out, the occasional shower or visitor, and the two court appearances, for 22 months every day and every night was the same. The same bars, the same bunk, the same sink, the same six-by-nine cell, the same concrete floor. For breakfast, lunch, and dinner, chopped potatoes with chili sauce splattered on them. It looked like something somebody already tried to eat. For a while we got a hard-boiled egg on Sunday, until somebody lobbed one through the cell bars and smacked the assistant warden in the back of the head. That made for some excitement, but it cost us our Sunday egg. I missed that egg. An egg was something to look forward to all week.

"I started to believe I was going to die in there."

William Velten's Murderer Hears the Voice of God

September of 1975 found Kerry Rodney Lee down on his luck, stranded in North Charleston, South Carolina. Lee was on his way to Florida, when he ran out of money. He sought shelter in a Baptist home for young wanderers. There, Kerry Lee found Jesus.[124]

Feeling a deep need to clear his conscience about the murder of William Velten, he spoke with a minister at the Charleston Heights Baptist Church. When Kerry Lee told the minister that he had killed a man, the minister advised him to talk with the police. Kerry Lee agreed.[125] On Friday, 19 September 1975, Kerry Lee walked into a North Charleston police station and confessed to the Albuquerque murder of a man named William Velten. North Charleston authorities notified New Mexico law enforcement official and the bikers' defense attorneys. The attorneys left immediately for South Carolina, to interview Lee. Lee's sworn statement included a map of the area where the murder occurred and an account of the events leading up to and immediately following Velten's death. Lee's story was painstakingly specific, beginning with his meeting with Velten at Okie's bar and culminating with Lee's returning to the arroyo the next day in a borrowed Land Rover, and later on horseback, to move the body.[126]

Lee gave the date of the murder as February 6.[127] He said he had lived in Albuquerque during February of 1974 and that he first met Velten on the evening of February 5; the car he was driving that night, a Thunderbird, belonged to his girlfriend Jan McCord's father, as did the gun he used to kill Velten; he and Velten had fought, and in the struggle over possession of the gun, stray fire struck the T-bird; he lost the gun in the arroyo.[128]

Based on Lee's sworn affidavits and a taped interview, defense attorneys petitioned the court for another new-trial hearing.[129] The Ivor Johnson .22 found in the arroyo by the boys riding bicycles suddenly assumed new significance. The boys happened on the pistol in mid-April 1974, two months after the crow hunter had stumbled on Velten's body. The pistol leaped to the fore, becoming the keystone of the investigation.[130] The court was scheduled to rule on the request for a hearing on October 1, but delayed its decision until October 22, to give the district attorney's office and defense attorneys additional time to clarify the mounting evidence supporting Lee's story.[131]

Jan McCord was questioned, and admitted to being with Kerry Lee when he returned to the arroyo the day after the murder to hide Velten's body.[132] She confirmed that Lee used her car in early February and that she later noticed what looked like two bullet holes in the Thunderbird. Ballistics tests showed that a spent bullet found embedded in the Thunderbird had been fired from the Ivor Johnson, and William McCord, Jan McCord's father, identified the Ivor Johnson as a gun belonging to him and taken without his knowledge from his gun cabinet.[133] The police officer, who responded to the report of gunshots in the vicinity of the Western Skies Motel in the

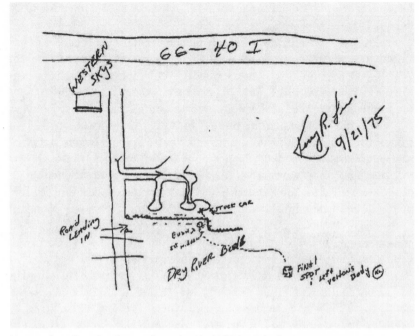

Map murderer Kerry Lee drew to show where he hid Velten's body. [*Courtesy of Hank Farrah*]

early morning hours of February 6, recalled having coffee with a young man whose car was stuck and who explained away the racket as firecrackers.[134] The motel records for February 6 listed a guest registered as David Morningstar, the alias used by Lee; and an equipment rental dealer verified that Lee had rented a metal detector, corroborating Lee's account of returning to search for the pistol.[135]

No charges had been filed against Kerry Lee. D.A. Brandenburg maintained that Lee's account of the Velten murder was unbelievable. In his sworn statement, Lee said that he and Velten drove out to the arroyo to consummate a drug deal, and that the fight erupted when Velten discovered he had a gun.[136] Since D.A. Brandenburg refused to extradite Kerry Lee or to take any legal action against him, the South Carolina law-enforcement officers set him free.[137] Lee agreed to return to New Mexico voluntarily in a plane supplied by Bernalillo County, then changed his mind, afraid the Bernalillo County officials might try to throw him from the aircraft.[138] Lee was hotly suspicious of the New Mexico authorities' motives, given their refusal to file formal charges against him.[139] For a time, Lee disappeared.[140]

When the court granted the request for a hearing, Lee returned to Albuquerque on his own, but went into hiding and negotiated with authorities via his attorney. Following his attorney's advice, Lee refused to testify at the hearing to avoid incriminating himself, but he agreed to appear in the courtroom, as necessary, for identification purposes.[141]

The new trial hearing began on 1 December 1975.[142] Witness after witness corroborated Kerry Lee's story that he had killed William Velten in the early morning hours of February 6. District attorney's office investigator Jim Plagens testified that there was no evidence Velten was alive after February 4, when a close friend had last reported seeing Velten. Investigator Plagens also testified that seven .22 caliber cartridges were found in the room at the Western Skies Motel where Lee had spent the night.[143] The wrecker driver remembered pulling the T-bird out of the arroyo and identified Kerry Lee when he appeared in the courtroom.[144] Pat Spahn recalled being visited by Lee and Velten on the night of the murder and said that both men were either drunk or on downers. Spahn only saw Velten that one time and could not identify him from a photograph, but she remembered his army-green jacket and that he was wearing something orange underneath—Velten's jacket had an orange liner.[145] Steve Lent testified to having been visited by Lee earlier that evening; that Lee was intoxicated; and that Lee mentioned having an important appointment. Lent also testified that Kerry Lee roomed with him for a time and that he had asked Lee to move out when he discovered him engaging in a sex act with a fifteen-year-old Chicano boy.[146]

The allusion to Kerry Lee's homosexual inclinations corroborated Dr. Weston's trial testimony that the murderer was a homosexual, but other conclusions that Weston had advanced at the trial did not hold up so well at the hearing. Acknowledging that Kerry Lee's confession did not include the event of a sexual encounter between him and Velten, Dr. Weston said he could not stake his reputation on finding spermatozoa on the corpse, a fact about which he had been quite certain at the trial.[147] More embarrassing still, testimony by pathologist Dr. Charles S. Petty contradicted Weston's hot-knife theory.

Dr. Petty stated that in his tests, cuts made using a hot knife and a cold knife had the same coagulation time. The victim had not bled significantly, Petty maintained, because the chest slashes and amputation of the penis occurred post-mortem. Furthermore, in his tests using a hot knife, the blade became almost useless as a cutting instrument, reducing the possibility of making multiple slashes of any length. In a total about-face, Dr. Weston said that he no longer believed Velten was cut with a hot knife and that he agreed with Dr. Petty's conclusions.[148]

According to Petty, Velten died from the four gunshot wounds.[149] A

State Police crime-lab expert and an FBI crime-lab expert both testified that, absolutely and without question, the Ivor Johnson pistol fired the bullets taken from Velten's body. Comparison of the bullet found embedded in the T-bird with two bullets taken from Velten made possible a definitive match to the pistol.[150]

On December 4, Judge Vernon Payne delivered his opinion. He stressed the new evidence of the McCord gun and the ballistics tests, information which, had it been available at the original trial, likely would have resulted in a different verdict. The request for a new trial was granted.[151]

Ron describes the moment. "We knew there was a chance, but we knew better than to be hopeful. Judy Weyer had sat there on the witness stand and said she made the whole thing up, and they sent us back to prison. 'I grant the defendants a new trial'—when the judge said that, we almost couldn't believe it. We're standing there, dumbstruck, and the next thing you know these guards come up and start snapping the handcuffs back on us.

"'Get the fuck away from me,' I say. 'You're not putting those cuffs on me.'

"'What's going on over there?' the judge asked.

"'We've got to take them back to the prison to process them and to get their belongings,' the guard says.

"And the judge came back with, 'These are free men. Let him go.'

"Hank Farrah sent somebody to the prison to get our stuff. We went upstairs to Hank's office, and he broke out a bottle of champagne. I took one sip and said, 'I want a beer, man.'

"Hank gave me some money and sent me off with one of his aides. She had a Corvette, and she let me drive. When I got behind the wheel—you can't believe how good it felt—and, yeah, I significantly broke the speed limit.

"By the time we got back to the office, another aide had gone out and bought us some clothes. I gave Hank my prison shirt for a souvenir. He still has it. One time when he was wearing it, a door-to-door salesman came to his house. When Hank opened the door wearing prison togs, the guy freaked."

The bikers were never retried. On 15 December 1975, District Judge Philip Baiamonte quashed the murder indictments against them, stating that ballistic tests conclusively linked the murder weapon to the confessed killer, Kerry Lee.[152]

D.A. James Brandenburg never produced an indictment against Kerry Lee. His successor, D.A. Ira Robinson, appointed a special prosecutor to handle the Velten murder case, and Lee finally was tried in May of 1978, two and half years after his September 1975 confession. The jury accepted

Lee's claim that he killed Velten in self-defense and found him guilty of second-degree murder, sentencing him to a prison term of fifteen to fifty-five years.[153]

Home for the Holidays

Christmas of 1975 found all of the bikers at home with their families. It was the last holiday Ron would spend with his mother. She died a few months after his release.

Freedom was bittersweet. Life on the outside took some getting used to. The first time Ron went through an airport security check station, he started to take off his belt, conditioned by prison life to expect a strip search.[154] Friends would turn the other way when they saw him coming, afraid he might ask them for a job. No one would hire him. One employer told him that having him around would be bad for employee morale and scare the women. "People read the headlines, but they didn't read the whole story," Ron says, reflecting on the early days of his freedom. "The crime is smeared all over the papers when it happens and you're accused, but when they find you innocent, all you get is a paragraph at the bottom of page 9. What people remembered was that I was involved in a murder."

Virtually everything he owned had been sold to pay attorney fees. Penniless, he and a friend from high school, likewise down on his luck, came up with a scheme for getting an occasional free meal. One of them would order dinner in a restaurant, asking for a window seat, while the other one kept track of the progress of the meal, watching from the outside. When the desert course came, the watcher would step into the restaurant and call out, 'Anybody in here drive a blue Pontiac? You left your lights on.' The eater would jump to his feet, 'That's mine,' and excuse himself to see to his car, leaving the bill unpaid. At the next restaurant, they swapped roles. "If we had any money at all, we'd leave a tip," Ron says, "I felt especially bad about ripping off the waitress, but you do what you have to do to eat."

In a New Year's Day interview with the *Detroit News*, Ron told the press, "If the four of us have a New Year's resolution in common, it must be to clean up our acts a little and try to get things right this time."[155]

Law-enforcement officials weren't making the difficult business of readjustment any easier for them. By mid-January, scarcely a month off death row, three of the four bikers had seen cell bars again. Sandman Smith was stopped for a driving violation and spent the night in jail before being fined; Tom Gladish was picked up for an old probation violation and spent five days in jail before he could scrape up the money to pay $800 in costs and restitution; and Doc Greer was arrested for possession of a stolen firearm.[156] A sheriff's motorcycle squad had pulled Greer over, claiming he had a faulty taillight. The officers ordered him to get out of his car and lie face down on the ground, refusing to let him check the light. They discovered the pistol in an illegal search of the car and didn't seem in the least surprised. But Greer was—he had no idea the pistol was hot. A friend had given it to him for a gift, at a family Christmas celebration. After two nights in jail, Greer managed to borrow the $5,000 he needed to make bail.[157]

Ron nearly landed back in jail as well. Recognizing how desperate he was for work, *Detroit News* reporter Doug Glazier hired him to do some painting. Ron accepted a pickup truck as part of his pay and used the cash he earned to buy bagged rock salt. Ever enterprising, Ron capitalized on the cold and snowy Michigan winter, peddling the bagged salt door-to-door, to grateful homeowners eager to de-ice their slippery sidewalks and driveways. While he was driving home one evening with the truck sorely overloaded with salt, a police officer who passed him going the other direction made a U-turn, and the next thing Ron knew, there were blue lights in his rearview mirror. When the officer accused him of not dimming his headlights, Ron apologized and explained that his lights were dimmed, but the front end of the truck was high from the load. The officer ho-hummed over the explanation and told Ron to wait, while he ran a check on his driver's license. Within minutes, a horde of whining sirens and flashing blue lights appeared on the scene. The six squad cars surrounded Ron's truck, forming a barricade. The license check showed that he was on death row in New Mexico State Penitentiary, convicted of first-degree murder. Fortunately, one of the officers who responded to the call knew him and corroborated Ron's story about being proved innocent. After two hours of head scratching and data checking, they let him go.

Ron contacted Hank Farrah about what had happened. The New Mexico conviction should have been expunged from his record, but it took an additional legal action to accomplish what ought to have been done as a matter of course. Attorneys Farrah and D'Angelo also had filed a ten-million-dollar damages suit on the bikers' behalf, directed against the New Mexico officials responsible for their wrongful conviction. After two years of haggling, an out-of-court settlement was reached with Sheriff Hay, Deputies Tena and Candelaria, and Dr. Weston. As prosecutors, Gross and Brandenburg were ruled immune to the civil suit's allegations.*

---

*In the aftermath of the scandal trailing upon the bikers' wrongful conviction, Detectives Robert Tena and Gilbert Candelaria and Sgt. Donald Heavner were dismissed.

Ron at the office in his "salt business" days. [*Courtesy of Ron Keine*]

The bikers received $5,000 each and reimbursement of attorney fees for the civil suit. Greer, Smith, and Gladish were satisfied with the agreement. Ron wasn't—"I wanted to see them in court, to put them on trial, like they did to us." If he had the means, Ron would have kept up the fight.[158]

Flying to New Mexico for the courtroom confrontation, which never took place, and taking time off from his salt business cost him nearly half of his settlement. Ron made what money was left work for him. He started investing in rental properties, fixer-uppers, doing the repairs himself, bit by bit piecing together a new life. Things did not go so well for the other three.

During the time of his confinement on death row, Doc Greer lost 50 pounds. In prison, he escaped by mind travel, astral projection; on the outside, he turned to alcohol. He worked sporadically driving a truck. "The last time I saw Doc," Ron says, "He got drunk and beat up a friend of mine. He was an alcoholic. I told him that if he went to AA and got straightened out, I'd give him a job." The next account Ron had of Doc, he was dead of a shotgun wound to the head, self-inflicted.

Sandman Smith and Tom Gladish had returned to California, and soon found themselves caught up in gang warfare. Eventually, both Sandman

Smith and Gladish decided they wanted to mend their ways, but by then it was too late. They had made too many enemies. Sandman and his wife were murdered on a pig farm in Arizona, where they had hoped to start a new life and escape his past. Tom Gladish moved to Oregon and was living under an assumed name. Ron received word from Gladish's girlfriend, that Gladish, too, had been murdered.

Ron never attempted to get in touch with Art Smith, who had been released mid-trial when Judy Weyer testified that he did not take part in Velten's torture and slaying. When Ron talks about Art Smith, the hurt in his voice betrays his stoic exterior. "After Judge Riordan dismissed charges against Art, Art forgot all about us. It was like we didn't exist. He didn't do a thing to help us. He never even so much as wrote us a letter or sent cigarette money. I heard through the grapevine that Art went back to the Vagos. I probably could have found him, but it wasn't at the top of my list."

"Had the State of New Mexico Gotten its Way, I'd be Dead Today"

Ron had an eye for a diamond in the rough and built several businesses from the ground up. In time, he came to be regarded as a respected member of the community and served for a number of years as local chairman of the Republican Party, at one point even considering a bid for the state senate.

He raised four daughters, weathering several stormy relationships and a broken marriage. He finally was able to let go of his tough-guy façade, finding spiritual peace through his training in the martial arts— "My sensi [teacher] refused to advance me until I mastered my ego. The Warrior Code teaches honesty and honor. It is your duty to use your skill to help others, but you never fight just to prove yourself." Ron trained for twenty years and rose to the rank of instructor. When his young charges squabbled, he punished them by making them hold hands.

Ron met the love of his life at a Parents Without Partners gathering. He had forgone his wild and reckless ways, but not his passion for motorcycles and fast cars. Pat Ameel grew up with her head under a car hood, wrenching with her dad. Being picked up for a date by a guy on a Harley was just fine with her.

In early 1998, Ron received a phone call from Rob Warden, director of the Center on Wrongful Convictions, inviting him to the National Conference on Wrongful Convictions and the Death Penalty at the Northwestern University School of Law. The Center would cover all his travel expenses and that of his spouse or companion and pay him $250 for attending.

Ron and his bike. [Photo by Pat Ameel]

Ron mulled the matter over. Twenty-two years had passed, but he still shunned discussing his death-row experience. Recalling a circumstance in which he was a powerless victim was sheer hell. He had no interest in becoming involved in the movement to abolish the death penalty.

On the other hand, it was a free trip to Chicago. "What the heck," he said to Pat, "Let's go. All I have to do is stand up and read this one sentence: *Had the state of New Mexico gotten its way, I'd be dead today.*"

Twenty-eight exonerated former death-row prisoners appeared onstage to read those same words, altered to include the name of the state where they were convicted. The effect was stunning. For the first time in history, media coverage gave a face to the people sentenced to die for crimes they did not commit.

For Ron, though, the most powerful part of the Chicago experience arose from the unsanctioned men's room sessions, where he and the others gathered to smoke and share their stories. And suddenly it dawned on him, "I could help these guys. My guys—Doc, Sandman, Gladish—they were all dead. I knew what it was like to be out there just off death row. How it was when nobody would hire you and you'd all but forgotten how to relate to people on the outside. Forgotten how to make decisions for yourself, because in there, you aren't allowed to make any decisions. Every aspect of your existence is decided by someone else in a routine you have no control over. You're sitting there waiting for them to kill you for a crime you didn't commit. The other people in your life, your wife and kids, they don't understand what you've been through. Guys are tough, they don't want to come off like a wimp, whining to their old lady about their problems. But me, these guys could relate to me, they could talk to me."

"Ron gave the other exonerated men hope," Pat says, recalling the Chicago conference. "They would say to him things like, 'We want to be like you. You're normal again.' And Ron would reassure them, 'You're where I was, but you can do it'—they were so in need of hearing that from someone who had been on death row, from someone who truly understood."[159]

Not long afterward, Ron and Pat attended training sessions at Northwestern, sponsored by the University of California, Berkeley, "Life After Exoneration Project." Again, Ron found himself playing a pivotal role in seminars and discussions. "The other exonerated guys would tune out the counselors, but me they would listen to. I was a little older, I'd been out for a while, and I'd already dealt with the things they were struggling with. I had solutions to their problems.

"I realized, then, that I could help even more by working to end the flawed system that put them on death row to begin with. Becoming involved in the movement to abolish the death penalty was the natural next step."

Returning to the Scene of the Crime

In February of 2005, Ron returned to Albuquerque to lobby members of the state legislature and to take part in a panel discussion at the University of New Mexico. Friend and fellow death-row-survivor Juan Melendez had persuaded him to make the trip—'Your case is all they ever talk about in New Mexico. You could make a difference,' Melendez insisted, 'A bill to abolish the death penalty has made it through committee and is up for a vote.'

Ron put aside his personal reservations. He had not set foot in the state in nearly 30 years. He was struck by how beautiful New Mexico was when he first arrived. His death-row experience had clouded his memory.

The face-to-face meetings with state legislators proved fruitful. One congressional representative changed his position and voted for abolition after talking with Ron, and another representative, a swing vote, was convinced to align himself with the pro-abolition cause after learning the bikers' story.

Ron Keine and Attorney Hank Farrah reunited 28
years after Ron's release. [Photo by Pat Ameel]

Hank Farrah, former defense attorney for the bikers, greeted Ron with
a warm hug when they were reunited at the University of New Mexico Student Union prior to the onset of the panel discussion. Farrah would join
Ron on the platform as a panelist, along with two other familiar faces:
Peso Chavez, investigator for the defense, and Judge Vernon Payne, who
granted the bikers a new trial.

In welcoming the crowd, the moderator extended a special greeting to
a member of the audience who had played a key role in the bikers' case, former D.A. and prosecutor James Brandenburg.

Each panelist made brief opening remarks. Farrah, Chavez, and Payne
recounted the bikers' story from a personal perspective, highlighting the
roles they played in securing the bikers' release from death row. Judge
Payne spoke about being the only district judge willing to rule on the bikers' request for a new trial and stressed that he found the case troubling
from the outset. When Ron's turn came to speak, he cited problems with
death-penalty law, pointing out that his home state, Michigan, abolished
the "archaic, barbaric" practice, after eleven people it already had executed
were later proved innocent. A member of the audience asked Ron if he
had ever received a public apology.

"No one ever apologized to us for what happened," Ron said, and then he turned to look at former D.A. Brandenburg, "I've been waiting thirty years to tell you this—I forgive you for what you did to us."

No sarcasm was intended in Ron's words. His offering of forgiveness was 100 percent sincere. In his bid for re-election following Kerry Lee's confession and the bikers' release from death row, District Attorney Brandenburg was criticized harshly for failing to produce an indictment against Kerry Lee. Brandenburg lost the election. The Velten murder case had ruined James Brandenburg's political career. Pain and tragedy had shadowed everyone touched by the murder of William Velten, and for Ron, it was time to put that all behind them. Ron did not expect a thank you or an apology from the former district attorney, just, perhaps, a nod of acknowledgement, some small sign that Brandenburg regretted the way sheriff's deputies had manipulated Judy Weyer—which had been the start of it all.[160]

James Brandenburg leaped to his feet. The panelists had "misled this audience," Brandenburg charged, "The body of evidence that convicted those gentlemen was overwhelming." The audience listened, stunned, as Brandenburg proceeded to reiterate the details of this evidence, asserting that bloodstains and hair samples matching Velten were found on a blanket confiscated from the bikers' van.

"That's an outright lie," Ron fired back, in a rare emotional outburst, breaking from the prepared agenda of death-penalty facts that he hoped to have an opportunity to present.[161]

What is true is that the jury members based their verdict on the information they had—primarily the fraudulent eyewitness testimony of Judy Weyer. The *inconclusive* incidentals—the bloodstains, the hair samples, the knife the jury was not permitted to examine—only lent fuel to the fire kindled by the inflammatory pretrial publicity and Judy Weyer's disturbing account of the murder. But, as Judge Payne emphasized when he granted the bikers' a new trial, had the jury had the evidence related to the Ivor Johnson pistol and the conclusive ballistics tests, which corroborated Kerry Lee's confession, they very likely would have reached a different verdict.

Judy Weyer had recanted her entire testimony. So what exactly was former D.A. Brandenburg's point? *Did he still believe that the bikers' murdered Velten?* the moderator asked.

Brandenburg's reply was shocking: "I still do. I believe Kerry Lee didn't do it."[162]

At his May 1978 trial for the murder of William Velten, Kerry Lee testified that Velten made homosexual advances toward him, an account of the circumstance leading up to the murder that differed somewhat from the statement Lee gave in September of 1975, when he first confessed. What actually happened that night probably will never be established definitively. William Velten is dead, and Lee had consumed vast quantities of alcohol and drugs on the evening of the murder, calling into question his memory of the events, even if his intent was to portray the episode truthfully. When Kerry Lee was paroled in 1986, he moved to Florida, and in 1987, he committed a second murder. At his trial, in 1993, Lee again argued that he killed the victim in self-defense, and again, the jury accepted his explanation of events. Lee was convicted of manslaughter and sentenced to fifteen years. Paroled in 2000, Lee went back to prison in 2002 for a parole violation, felon in possession of a firearm. Lee is incarcerated at Beaumont Federal Correctional Institution, in Beaumont, Texas. His projected release date is 2012.[163]

Given Kerry Lee's history as a repeat offender who confessed to and was convicted of a second murder, taken together with the overwhelming evidence corroborating Lee's confession to the murder of William Velten, former D.A. Brandenburg's public proclamation that he still believed the bikers were guilty and that Kerry Lee "didn't do it," verges on the incredible.

Unfortunately, it is not uncommon for prosecutors to continue to maintain that wrongfully accused individuals are guilty long after they have been proved innocent and fully exonerated. A May 2003 *Chicago Tribune* article recounts numerous cases in which law enforcement officials refused to acknowledge the innocence of defendants exculpated by the indisputable proof of DNA evidence.[164]

As district attorney, Brandenburg relied on the information supplied to him by sheriff's deputies and Assistant D.A. Brian Gross. The deputies and Gross were well aware that Judy Weyer had denied witnessing the murder prior to the trial. Did Brandenburg know? And would it have mattered if he did?

Suppression of evidence by law-enforcement officials and prosecutors is a factor in 16 to 19 percent of wrongful-death penalty convictions.[165] Is the primary role of the prosecution to serve the cause of justice? Or is the prosecution's primary role to win a conviction for the State? In a judicial system in which the U.S. Supreme Court consistently has held that prosecuting attorneys are "absolutely immune from a civil suit for damages . . . for alleged deprivations of the accused's constitutional rights," winning triumphs over justice. The Court has extended this same immunity to legislators, judges, and police officers, maintaining that these individuals acted within the scope of the duties of their office.[166] For winning a conviction, prosecutors and the law-enforcement officials who assist them are rewarded with job advancement, re-election, or election to even more prestigious public offices. For not winning a conviction, they are chastised and shamed.

As unhappy as Ron Keine was with the out-of-court settlement of the damages suit that his attorneys filed, Ron and the other bikers were fortunate to receive what they did. By settling out of court, the sheriff, sheriff's deputies, and Dr. Weston avoided further negative publicity and costly attorney fees; but had the case gone to court, they may well have prevailed. Most wrongly convicted individuals receive no restitution whatsoever.*

"Before death row, I didn't have an opinion on the death penalty," Ron Keine concedes, "My opinion was apathy. The death penalty was the law. There wasn't anything I could do to change that." These days, he is fond of quoting Irish philosopher and politician Edmund Burke, who speaks to his newfound conviction: "All that is necessary for the triumph of evil is that good men do nothing."

---

*Only fourteen of the thirty-six death-penalty states pay compensation for wrongful convictions. Adele Bernhard, "When Justice Fails: Indemnification for Unjust Convictions," table summarizing state statues on indemnification for unjust convictions (University of Chicago Law School, Roundtable 73, 5 October 2005); "State by State Information," Death Penalty Information Center.

JUAN ROBERTO MELENDEZ

Convicted by the Lies of a Heroin Addict Who Earned Five Grand for His Testimony

When I speak at conferences, and law colleges, and churches, I urge people to write to law makers and tell them to pass legislation to hold prosecutors and law investigators accountable who proceed with a death penalty case when they know they have an innocent man on their hands. The Supreme Court has ruled that prosecutors and law officers have total immunity when prosecuting a case. It gives them a license to kill without consequence.

When the prosecution and investigators were spending all this time and energy and money trying to kill me, when I did not do the crime and they knew it, how about the real killer? What do they think he was doing?

—Juan Roberto Melendez, who served seventeen years, eight months, and one day on death row before being exonerated.[1]

The Crime: 13 September 1983, Auburndale, Florida

Delbart Baker owned and managed two cosmetology schools in Polk County, Florida—one in the city of Auburndale and the other in Lakeland.[2] Located on the periphery of a predominantly African-American neighborhood, most of the employees and students at the Auburndale school were Black, as were most of the customers who availed themselves of the business's hair-styling services. Delbart Baker was Caucasian, but the neighborhood residents generally held him in high regard for bringing jobs and skills training to an economically depressed part of town. They called him "Mr. Del."

On the evening of 13 September 1983, shortly before 6:00 P.M., Terry Barber—a frequent costumer and friend of Mr. Del's—stopped by the Auburndale shop to chat. It was after hours, but Mr. Del answered when Terry Barber knocked on the door. From the front of the shop, Barber could see into the back room. Mr. Del had company. Terry Barber cut his visit short.

It was no secret to most of the neighborhood crowd that Delbart Baker was a homosexual. Baker, fifty-seven, fancied sexual encounters with young black men and had a reputation for hosting after-hours parties where the illegal drugs flowed freely.

On that evening, Baker's housemate (and business partner) Ed McDonald had expected him home by 7:00, at the latest. Baker had said he might stop by Sears to check on some draperies. By 7:30, Ed McDonald was becoming worried. He called both businesses, and getting no answer, phoned Baker's sister and brother. Both resided in Lakeland, but neither one of them had seen their brother that day. The stormy weather roused concerns that Baker may have had an accident, but nothing had been reported. At McDonald's urging, Delbart Baker's sister phoned the police and asked them to send an officer to see if her brother's car was at the Auburndale business.

Law enforcement officials arrived at the beauty school at 9:29. Inside, they found the body of Delbart Baker on the floor, awash in a sea of blood, with his throat slashed and three gunshot wounds to the head and shoulders. He wore only socks and white jockey shorts. The medical examiner estimated Baker's time of death at 7:30 P.M. A stray bullet had ricocheted off the refrigerator, and the walls and ceiling were splattered with blood, suggesting that there may have been a struggle, and that Baker had resisted his attackers. A spent .38 caliber cartridge was recovered from the scene. Baker's diamond rings, gold bracelet, watch, and the gold neck chain he always wore were missing, as well as the petty cash, which Baker kept in his desk drawer, but the day's cash receipts were still in his briefcase.

When Terry Barber heard what had happened to Mr. Del, he went to the police. Terry Barber identified the men he saw in the backroom of Mr. Del's shop earlier that evening as Vernon James and Harold "Bobo" Landrum, neighborhood residents, both in their twenties. Both men had a history of prior arrests for minor offenses, as well as felony convictions—James for burglary and Landrum for armed robbery. Landrum's rap sheet also included solicitation to prostitute and contributing to the delinquency of a minor.

On the morning of September 14, Auburndale police took James and

Landrum into custody for questioning. The tread pattern on Landrum's sneakers matched bloody footprints at the crime scene, but both James and Landrum denied having anything to do with Delbart Baker's murder. Landrum claimed he was at his job at Morrison's Cafeteria. After talking with Landrum's employer, who evidently vouched for his whereabouts (police records are vague on this point), Landrum was dropped as a suspect. As for Vernon James, word on the street was that he was a police informer who worked closely with Auburndale Police Detective John Knapp, the chief investigator assigned to the Delbart Baker murder case. Although the extent of James's relationship with Detective Knapp is not known, earlier police reports verify that Vernon James had given law-enforcement officials information in the past. Vernon James clothes initially were seized by police, but returned to him without being tested for possible blood traces or other evidence. Vernon James was dropped as a suspect as well. An official police report on the Delbart Baker murder was never filed until six months later, in March of 1984.

The Trail of Lies That Led to Juan Melendez

Juan Melendez was born in 1951, in Brooklyn, New York. His father was killed in a bar fight before Juan was born. He remembers the super of the apartment building where he lived with his mother as her boyfriend, but Juan never regarded the man as a father figure. "He would beat my mama. One time she came running into the bedroom battered and bleeding, screaming that I must come with her, we must run away. I told her to hide behind a mattress leaning against the wall. The man came charging into the room with a baseball bat. 'Where is she?' he asked me. I pointed to the door, saying she was gone. He would have killed her."

When Juan was six, he and his younger half-brother and mother left New York for Puerto Rico, the country of her birth. She had come to the United States with the help of her aunt, to find work and a better life, but it was not the dream she had hoped for. Juan flew fare-free sitting in the lap of his great aunt and godmother, while his younger half-brother rode in his mother's lap.

The family lived in the agrarian community of Maunabo. There was no lack of love in the home, but money was in short supply. Juan went to school barefoot. At the age of fourteen, at the end of the ninth grade, he left school and began working in the fields cutting sugar cane.

In April of 1970, just a month before his nineteenth birthday, Juan returned to the United States to work on a farm in Magnolia, Delaware, picking vegetables. When cold weather set in, he followed the work south and picked fruit in the Florida citrus groves. Juan liked Florida. The abundance of sun and balmy climate reminded him of home.[3] But before long, he got caught up in the Florida drug scene. In 1975, he robbed a convenience market and spent nearly six years in prison.

After his release, Juan went back to farm work. It was what he knew from his youth in Puerto Rico, and he loved the outdoors. He wanted never again to see the inside of a jail cell.

Juan Melendez has never set foot in Auburndale, Florida. In September of 1983, Juan was living in the Polk County, Florida, town of Lakeland. He was involved intimately with a married woman, Dorothy Rivera. Juan knew Dorothy Rivera's husband Philip. Like Juan, Philip Rivera was Puerto Rican and worked as a migrant. Dorothy Rivera was African American. In the Lakeland community, during the 1980s, the two ethnic groups congenially intermingled and marriages were not uncommon.

That September, Philip Rivera was in Pennsylvania for the fall orchard harvest, picking fruit.[4] Says Juan of the affair, "It was one of those things—it just happened." September 13, 1983, the day of Delbart Baker's murder, was Dorothy Rivera's first wedding anniversary. Dorothy was living with her sister and brother-in-law, Marie and Wilson Angelo Graham. On the afternoon of September 13, Juan stopped by the house. Juan had come on his bike, and when he got ready to head home, Dorothy asked Angelo to give her a ride to Juan's apartment in his car. That Dorothy intended to celebrate her first wedding anniversary with her lover did not sit well with Marie. After Juan left, Marie confronted her sister, but Dorothy wasn't swayed. Angelo obliged Dorothy and drove her to Juan's, and the couple spent the night together as planned.[5]

Dorothy Rivera and Juan Melendez broke off their relationship when Dorothy's husband Philip returned from his job in Pennsylvania. Juan and Dorothy continued to be friends, though, and to see one another on a casual basis. Dorothy Rivera's stepfather was Puerto Rican, and he and Juan frequently worked on the same crew.

The Luna family also figured among Juan's close acquaintances in the local Puerto Rican community. David Luna Carrucini and his wife were very fond of Juan and the sentiment was mutual. Juan called them "Pa and Mama." In December of 1983, Pa Luna received word that his son by his first marriage, David Luna Falcon, had gotten into some trouble in Puerto Rico.* Pa and Mama Luna decided to travel to the island to find out exactly

---

*In keeping with the Puerto Rican convention of naming, Puerto Ricans typically use two last names, the father's surname followed by the mother's maiden name, for example, David Luna Carrucini, David Luna Falcon.

what was going on and to see if they might be able help. They asked Juan if he would look after their place while they were gone. Juan was more than happy to oblige them. The Carrucinis had animals that needed cared for, and Juan also agreed to do some painting while he was staying at the house.

David Luna Falcon had been in and out of mental hospitals and diagnosed with undifferentiated schizophrenia, compounded by cocaine use and heroin addiction. He supported his habit by whatever illegal means he could and offered police the occasional tip to keep out jail. But the game had gone bad for David Falcon. He had made the wrong people mad in the world of the Puerto Rican underground, and feared for his life. Prompted by his father and stepmother's offer of assistance, David Falcon fled Puerto Rico and returned with them to Florida.

Perhaps it was Pa Luna's anxiety over his son that caused him to lash out at Juan when they got back, upbraiding him. "He did not find the house like he wanted," Juan says with a wounded shrug. He had taken on the responsibility as a favor. He was angry and hurt. He no longer felt welcome in the Carrucini home.

And as for David Falcon, Juan had no use for him. Falcon's half-sister Millie had filled Juan in on Dave's addiction and checkered past. "She told me he was bad business, that he brings trouble wherever he goes. She warned me not to hang out with him." Juan used to buddy around with David Falcon's half-brother, Gilbert. "Gilbert changed, once Dave got a hold on him," Juan recalls wistfully. Juan and David Falcon's paths crossed on one or two occasions, and that was enough. Juan chose to keep his distance. Juan and Pa Luna might have made amends eventually, but David Falcon's appearance on the scene strained Juan's relationship with the entire family.[6]

During January and February of 1984, Juan worked with his regular crew, picking oranges and grapefruit. In late February, a brutal freeze wrecked havoc in the Florida citrus groves. The trees shed their fruit, much of it still immature. "We picked up what we could salvage from the oranges and grapefruit on the ground, but that was the end of the harvest. We were out of a job." Juan traveled with the foreman and crew to a farm in Mechanicsburg, Pennsylvania, to prune apple and peach trees. The pruning job paid meager piecework wages, $2.50 per tree. The gusting wind was bone chilling for the men working on ladders in the orchards, but Juan needed the income.

Meanwhile, back in Florida, Juan was being framed for murder.

The reason behind what happened in Lakeland, Florida, in Juan's absence, is a matter of some speculation. David Falcon, a man with a drug habit to support, may have hoped to earn some easy cash. In the early days of the Delbart Baker murder investigation, police had posted a notice offering a $5,000 reward for information. No information was forthcoming. By March of 1984, the Delbart Baker murder case was cold. There were no leads. Given the crowd David Falcon ran with, he undoubtedly had heard talk about the Baker murder and reward money, and may have even seen a reward flyer. Snitching had served David Falcon well in the past, at least for a time, and giving information on the Baker case could be expected to yield both a get-out-of-jail-free card and money to feed his drug habit. Also, since the police were no longer snooping around asking questions and appeared to have lost interest in the Baker murder case, it was fair to assume that any story he concocted was not going to be shot down by a hot new lead. There was also the matter of Juan Melendez's formerly close relationship with David Falcon's parents and siblings. The family was struggling financially. David Falcon moved into the Luna home and contributed nothing, which may have led to family comparisons to Juan Melendez, the dethroned "good son." David Falcon did not have a job and did not seem interested in getting one. Making his way in the world by legitimate enterprises was not David Falcon's tack. Was David Falcon jealous of Juan Melendez? Perhaps. One thing is certain: Judging from remarks David Falcon made to people in the neighborhood, he clearly did not like Juan Melendez.[7]

'I'll either kill Melendez or have him killed,' Falcon boasted, complaining that Juan Melendez wouldn't sell drugs for him and wouldn't help him with robberies; chest thumping delivered in the context of 'he thinks he's too good for the likes of me.'

The truth of the matter was that David Falcon had never approached Juan about taking part in a robbery or drug scheme. Heeding the advice of Falcon's half-sister Millie's—*he brings trouble wherever he goes*—Juan had made it a point to cut David Falcon a wide circle. Juan was doing his best to stay out of trouble. He refused to have anything to do with David Falcon, blunt rejection that likely contributed to Falcon's hatred.

For the most part, people in the neighborhood turned a deaf ear to the slanderous accusations and threats that David Falcon began making against Juan in Juan's absence. On the evening of March 6, though, David Falcon decided to make good on his threats. 'I'm gonna get him killed, and if they don't kill him, I will,' Falcon raged, when he was visiting at the apartment of Ruby and Angelo Colon, Dorothy Rivera's mother and stepfather. The Puerto Rican families stuck together and went out of their way to extend hospitality to struggling newcomers—and David Falcon was clearly a troubled man. Ruby had heard David Falcon lash out verbally at

Juan Melendez before, unprovoked, senseless ranting. Using the phone at Ruby and Angelo's apartment, Falcon made a call—'meet me at the stadium, three blocks from here'—and left.

David Falcon rendezvoused with Florida Department of Law Enforcement (FDLE) Agent Tom Roper. Falcon said he had information about the murder of Delbart Baker. He named Juan Melendez, along with an African-American man called "John," and "another Black man." Melendez had told him all about it one evening at a nightclub when they were drinking and snorting cocaine, Falcon claimed. He proceeded to give Agent Roper an account of the role each man played: "John" was the driver, Melendez was the shooter, and "the other Black man" slashed Baker's throat. He described the car as a three-color late-model Dodge and gave the street address where police likely would find it parked.[8]

Juan Melendez had a good buddy in the neighborhood by the name of John Berrien. Juan had met John's wife when he first moved to Florida fourteen years before, and he counted the couple among his closest friends. Immediately following the interview with David Falcon, Roper and police officers checked out the lead on the three-color late-model Dodge. The car was parked on the street just as Falcon had said it would be, in front of John Berrien's home. John Berrien was an African American. From Falcon's description of the car and a Black man named "John" as the driver, police easily made the connection that the driver was John Berrien. They took Berrien into custody and subjected him to a middle-of-the-night interrogation session at the Lakeland Police Department (LPD).[9]

Agent Roper and four police detectives fired questions at a terrified John Berrien. Yes, he lived in Lakeland. Yes, he and Juan Melendez were friends, but *murder? What murder?* The murder of Auburndale beauty school owner Delbart Baker, the officers informed him. A reliable source had said his car was involved. "I don't know nothin' about no murder," Berrien insisted. The officers demanded an explanation for why his car matched the description they were given.[10] John Berrien had several prior convictions, including sale of marijuana and burglary, and was currently on probation. He did not need this kind of trouble. It would mean a parole violation. Desperate and trapped, John Berrien said he drove Juan Melendez to Mr. Del's Beauty School to have his hair done. The police persisted. They knew from their confidential source that there was a third person with them in the car that day. Who was it? Grasping for an acceptable answer, John Berrien told his interrogators that on the way to the beauty school, he and Juan Melendez picked up a man by the name of David Files, a friend of his who lived in Auburndale. Following the interview, John Berrien was released.[11]

Auburndale Police Detectives Gary Glisson and John Knapp were among the officers who questioned Berrien, and a week later, Glisson and Knapp picked up John Berrien a second time and took him to the Auburndale Police Department.[12] They set the stage with a series of threats. 'We're going to stick you with it . . . You're going down by yourself . . . You could end up like Mr. Del.'[13] Guided by a handwritten outline, the detectives coached John Berrien through a tape-recorded interview, turning the recorder off while they alternately threatened him, promised to protect him, and prompted him with the correct answers. The final, official version of the interview included a reference to a .38 caliber firearm, three rings, a bracelet, and a watch, conveniently corroborating police-investigation data from ballistic tests and an inventory cataloguing Baker's missing jewelry. David Files, who John Berrien had mentioned in the first interview, was a white man—information contradictory to David Falcon's account. Pressed to tell the truth about the third person involved, John Berrien changed his story and said it was a Jamaican named Tabu. At the conclusion of the interview, rather than helping him as they had promised, the detectives charged John Berrien with first-degree murder and armed robbery, and incarcerated him, without bail, in the Polk County Jail.[14]

David Falcon, meanwhile, had been showing up at Ruby and Andrew Colon's apartment, at what have must been pre-appointed times, to receive phone calls. Ruby eavesdropped when the phone calls came in. She had no idea who was phoning David Falcon, but she was struck by the way he talked to the people on the other end of the line, like they were partners.[15]

Two days after John Berrien's arrest, Detective Glisson and David Falcon visited John Berrien at the jail. 'Melendez already confessed to doing it,' Falcon informed him. This, of course, was a lie. Juan Melendez was in Pennsylvania pruning fruit trees and did not even know he was a suspect. At some point, a reference to John's cousin George Berrien was introduced into the conversation. Police were getting nowhere tracking leads based on the street-name Tabu. John and George Berrien had a cousin who was an instructor at the beauty school. (The business had remained open under the management of Delbart Baker's sister.) George Berrien was also a long-time friend with one of the students, and occasionally he stopped by the shop, and the two men went out for lunch. 'Go ahead, man, you'll be all right, help them out,' Falcon prompted. John Berrien was paralyzed with fear. The APD interview, just two days before, was still fresh in his mind. He was charged with first-degree murder. The detectives had said that he would get the electric chair if he did not cooperate. He resigned himself to telling the police whatever he thought they wanted to hear. By the conclusion of the third interview, John Berrien had named his cousin

George Berrien as the "other Black man" involved in Baker's murder, placing George at the scene along with himself and Juan Melendez.[16]

Bear in mind that, while John Berrien's interview statements included telling details supplied by the detectives, John Berrien never said he saw Juan or his cousin George harm Delbart Baker. His statements were ripe with contradictions, but the distilled version, all lies, amounted to this: He drove Juan and George to Del's Beauty School so Juan could have his hair done and two hours later picked them up; there was no mention of any blood in any of John Berrien's statements, and he had no recollection of seeing a gun on the day he allegedly drove Juan and his cousin George to Mr. Del's Auburndale business; on another day, according to John Berrien, he drove Juan and George to the train station, where Juan gave George two rings, a watch, and a gun to sell, and George boarded a train for Wilmington, Delaware.[17]

The information that Juan Melendez shot Baker and that the "other man" slashed Baker's throat came from David Falcon, who maintained Juan had confessed to him. Police lacked sufficient grounds to bring murder charges against George Berrien, since Falcon had not named the third person involved. But the two Auburndale detectives learned from David Falcon that George Berrien recently had pawned a sawed-off shotgun. After contacting the storeowner and verifying the transaction, police arrested George Berrien for possession of an illegal firearm, a minor offense, and a circumstance wholly unrelated to the Baker murder.[18]

Juan's Arrest

Courtesy of another tip from David Falcon, the Auburndale detectives learned that Juan Melendez was working at the Miller Peach Farm in Harrisburg, Pennsylvania.[19]

Juan had been on the Pennsylvania tree-pruning job for two months, when on Monday, 2 May 1984, strangers in suits appeared in the orchard. FBI agents. Juan sat under a peach tree, eating his lunch. The agents ordered the workers to 'hit the ground.' Face down, on his belly under the tree, Juan raised his arms when the agents called out his name.

"They had a gun pointed at me. They told me to get up. Then they told me to open my mouth to see if I had a missing tooth, which I did. Then they told me to pull up the shirtsleeve on my left arm, so they could see if I had a tattoo. When I showed it to them, they told me I was the man they were looking for."

The agents handcuffed him and took him to Lewisburg Federal Penitentiary. He was wanted for unlawful flight to avoid prosecution with warrants for his arrest, in the state of Florida, for first-degree murder and armed robbery. The next day, he went before a magistrate judge. "The judge was talking about extradition," Juan says, "and I did not know what extradition meant." At this stage in his life, Juan could not read or write English and spoke in broken phrases heavily spiked with "cuss words and slang. The kind of talk you learn on the street."

Day three, Juan spoke with an interpreter.

When the interpreter explained to him what was at stake and that he could either waive extradition or fight it, Juan saw no reason to oppose the process. He was innocent. "As soon as they see my ugly face in Florida, they will know I did not do it"—or so he reasoned. The court-appointed attorney Juan spoke with at Lewisburg Federal Penitentiary concurred with his decision not to resist. "He told me frankly, right from the jump, that they were gonna take me back anyway. You never win in an extradition case."

Juan arrived at the Polk County Jail, in Bartow, Florida, on May 24, his birthday.

Two weeks later, he first spoke with the court-appointed attorney there who would defend him, Roger Alcott. Alcott had entered private practice recently, after serving for four years as a prosecutor for the Florida Department of Law Enforcement and, prior to that, as Assistant State Attorney.

In his preparations for the trial and his conversations with Juan Melendez, Roger Alcott never once enlisted the assistance of an interpreter and no one ever explained to Juan Melendez the complex legal verbiage that Alcott used in these discussions. But encouraged by Alcott's reassurance, Juan resigned himself to trusting this man: "I could hardly understand what Alcott was saying. He told me a lot of things I could not make sense of. I did understand what he was talking about, though, when he would pat me on the back and say, not to worry about it, that I would go home."[20]

David Falcon in May 1984

The same week that Juan Melendez arrived at the Polk County Jail, Auburndale police responded to a call reporting a break-in and shooting at the home of James and Rita Reagan. Two men claiming to be police had barged into the house when Rita Reagan answered a knock at the front door. They slung her around and fired a shot at her eight-year-old son, before kicking in the bedroom door. Alerted by the gunfire and his wife's screams, James Reagan, who had been in the tub, had dashed into the bedroom from the adjoining bath, at the same instant the intruders charged into the room. One of the men, a Puerto Rican, turned a gun on him. James Reagan stopped dead in his tracks, stunned. The two men made eye contact, and then the gunman panicked and fled, apparently realizing that he had been recognized. His accomplice followed.

Outside, the pair of thugs shot three bullets into James Reagan's car and stray bullets into the yard next door, to keep the terrified neighbors away from the windows, not wanting to risk being identified by anyone else.

Auburndale police Detective Gary Glisson responded to the call to investigate the incident. James Reagan was quick to inform Glisson that he recognized the man claiming to be a police officer who had held him at gunpoint—he was a Puerto Rican by the name of David Falcon.

Detective Glisson took Rita Regan aside for a little chat. Glisson said he had good reason to believe the intruders hoped to find drugs. 'The more I look at this, the more charges I could bring against your husband,' Glisson warned her. He went on to stress that David Falcon was dangerous, and she had every right to be afraid. 'If I lock Falcon up, he'll just bond out, and he may come back and get you.'

The Reagans decided to let the matter go. On the advice of Detective Glisson, Rita Reagan signed a waiver of prosecution, and Glisson promised her that Falcon would not be back to bother her.[21]

John Berrien in June 1984

Initially, John Berrien was denied bail. At the end of June, 106 days after his March 15 arrest, John Berrien walked out of the Polk County Jail, released on a meager $250 bond.[22] The State had offered him a deal, and he took it: He would plead no contest to accessory after the fact and would be sentenced to either probation or house arrest, in return for which he would testify against Juan Melendez. He would be tried separately and not until after the conclusion of the Melendez trial. If he refused to testify, the deal was off. The first-degree murder charge would be reinstated.[23]

Original Suspect Vernon James

In October of 1983, just over a month after the murder of Delbart Baker, Vernon James—one of the two men seen at the beauty school just prior to Baker's murder—was arrested for felonious possession of marijuana with the intent to sell and grand theft motor. During the six months that lapsed between his arrest and trial, James was incarcerated in the Polk County

Jail. Shortly after his arrest, James sent word to Assistant State Attorney Hardy Pickard that he had information about the Baker murder case. Arthur Meeks, an investigator for the Office of the State Attorney, paid James a visit. James said he would help them solve the crime, if they got him out of jail, but he did not know who did it. The State Attorney's Office declined the offer.[24]

In early April of 1984, with an April 20 court date pending, James contacted Dwight Wells, an assistant public defender who had represented him in the past. Having gotten nowhere with Meeks, James likely hoped that Dwight Wells might be able to intercede in his behalf. Wells agreed to visit James at the jail, and during the course of their conversation, James confided that he was a homosexual and admitted to being at Mr. Del's Beauty School the evening that Delbart Baker was murdered, portraying the killing as provoked by Baker's inappropriate advances. He had gone to Mr. Del's place to 'have some drugs and have a party.' Mr. Del had come on to him in an overly aggressive way and things got out of hand.[25]

This was probably far more than Dwight Wells wanted to know. He currently was representing John Berrien. John Berrien had refused to accept a guilty plea, insisting that he did not have anything to do with Delbart Baker's murder. According to David Falcon, Juan Melendez had said that he went to the beauty school with the intention of robbing Mr. Del. Vernon James's version of events differed markedly from Falcon's account and appeared to corroborate John Berrien's claim to innocence and to absolve Juan Melendez as well.

Juan Melendez, however, was not Dwight Wells's client, and as an assistant public defender, Wells lacked the resources and means to investigate the veracity of Vernon James's story. James had not given any names, and Wells never asked who else was or was not there. The State had offered John Berrien a plea deal, and Dwight Wells held with his decision that it was in John Berrien's best interest to accept the plea deal and testify against Juan Melendez. Wells never told anyone outside his office about James's confession. The plea deal was a sure thing, a guarantee that John Berrien would receive a minimal penalty, either probation or house arrest, at the worst. The alternative was a first-degree murder charge and possible death sentence. Putting John Berrien's life on the line at a jury trial was not worth the risk. James was a previously convicted felon facing charges for drugs and grand theft motor, both of which would have compromised the credibility of any testimony he gave. There was also the difficult business of the degree of James's involvement in the murder, about which he had been vague.[26]

Vernon James was found guilty on both counts and transferred to

Tomoka Correctional Institution in Daytona Beach.[27] On August 14, Juan's attorney Roger Alcott traveled to the Tomoka facility to interview Vernon James. Alcott had learned, from his review of police records, that Terry Barber had reported seeing Vernon James at the beauty school shortly before the murder and that police had questioned James as a possible suspect. Defense investigator Cody Smith accompanied Roger Alcott when he visited James at the prison. During the course of the interview, James told Alcott about Dwight Wells' visit and that he had divulged the circumstance of the homicide to Wells. In talking with Roger Alcott, James admitted to being at the beauty school on the evening of the murder, but insisted that he was 'outside the door when Mr. Del was shot.' *What about Juan Melendez?* Alcott asked James. *Juan Melendez wasn't there,* Vernon James told Alcott. He didn't even know Juan Melendez.

Alcott recorded the interview. He notified Assistant State Attorney Hardy Pickard, the acting prosecutor for the case, that he had a taped confession in which Vernon James admitted to being at the beauty school when Baker was killed. On September 8, less than two weeks before the trial began, Pickard sent Investigator Meeks to question James a second time. James told Meeks that he went to Mr. Del's with two other men, homosexuals, to help settle an argument. He was inside at first, but then he left. He waited outside while the other two men killed Mr. Del.

James, however, refused to identify the killers by name, unless the State Attorney's Office agreed to help him.

Meeks reported the details of the conversation to Prosecutor Hardy Pickard. In adherence with the rules of discovery, Pickard listed Arthur Meeks as a possible rebuttal witness. Alcott phoned Pickard and asked him what Meeks would say if he put him on the stand. Pickard cleverly dodged the question, mentioning only Meeks' earlier interview with James, when James said he would help them solve the crime if they got him out of jail, but claimed he did not know who killed Baker.[28]

The Trial

A week before the trial, Juan's attorney Roger Alcott took a deposition from John Berrien. Juan was present. Prior to beginning the session, Alcott filled Juan in on the particulars of his case. It was not until then that Juan learned that it was David Luna Falcon who pointed to him and John Berrien as Baker's killers, that John Berrien had made statements to police corroborating Falcon's story, and that John Berrien had agreed to testify against him.

"They are both lying," Juan told his attorney.

Juan had no explanation for why Falcon may have concocted the story. He and David Falcon had scarcely crossed paths in the few months between Falcon's arrival in Lakeland, in December, and when Juan left, in February, for the tree-pruning job. He was in Pennsylvania when Falcon began to lash out at him with threats and accusations and was wholly unaware that Falcon had made threats against his life prior to fingering him in the Baker murder.

As to John Berrien's motive for lying, Juan would not learn the reason why until many years later. "We were friends," Juan says, a hint of sadness in his voice. "They threatened John Berrien with the electric chair. After he got out, John told it in my neighborhood that he had to lie, because if he did not lie, they were gonna charge him with the crime. He put me at the scene, but he did not say I shot Baker. I understand why he did what he did."

During the course of the deposition, in Juan's presence, John Berrien ultimately conceded that the police had promised to protect him and that his statements to the police were mostly false, "except for the incident at the train station," referring to his claim that he took Juan and his cousin George Berrien to the Amtrak station, and before George boarded the train, Juan gave him two rings, a watch, and a gun to sell—but this also was false. Juan Melendez and George Berrien had never ridden in a car together. Juan Melendez and George Berrien had never even engaged in a conversation. For all practical purposes, they were total strangers. Juan recognized George Berrien by sight only and knew he was John Berrien's cousin, but nothing else about him.[29]

In retrospect, Juan believes that the purpose of the encounter was to persuade him to turn State's evidence and testify against George Berrien. Prosecutor Pickard was also in attendance for John Berrien's deposition. Following the session, Alcott asked Pickard if he would consider offering Juan Melendez a deal. Pickard responded with a smile and conciliatory nod. Roger Alcott urged Juan to accept a plea deal and to testify for the prosecution. "They wanted me to say I saw George Berrien slash Delbart Baker's throat, and that after that I left, that I wasn't there when Baker was shot. I did not even know George Berrien. If I saw him walking down the street, I would know he was John's cousin, but I did not count him a friend or even acquaintance." Juan refused to cooperate.

The police investigation failed to recover a firearm or Delbart Baker's missing jewelry. Nor were there any signs of blood in John Berrien's car, amazing given the slaughterhouse of gore that police found when they arrived at the scene. Fingerprints taken from the car did not match those of either Juan Melendez or George Berrien; nor did fingerprints from John

Berrien's car match fingerprints from the crime scene. (Vernon James's fingerprints were never compared to those retrieved from the beauty school.) Roger Alcott petitioned the Auburndale Police Department for the lab work on the blood samples, in the hope that this data might reveal the killer's blood type, since there was evidence of a struggle; but the original chief investigator, Detective John Knapp, had stored the blood samples in an unrefrigerated evidence locker. The samples putrefied, and the lab rejected them as contaminated. A large knife found by police in a desk drawer showed stains that may have been blood, but the knife was never tested for fingerprints or blood. Nor were any of the razors in the barbers' stations submitted to the crime lab.

At the trial, David Falcon testified that he formerly served as an undercover agent in Puerto Rico and was currently a paid informant for the Florida Department of Law Enforcement. He said Juan Melendez had confessed to him one evening at a nightclub when the two of them were drinking and doing drugs. By Falcon's account, Melendez knew about Baker's predilection for expensive gold jewelry and Baker's habit of keeping large sums of cash on the premises, and Melendez and a friend had conspired to rob Delbart Baker. This friend of Melendez's had slashed Baker's throat. Falcon gestured dramatically, telling how Baker scooped up blood and threw it at his attackers. But then, according to Falcon, Baker began to beg for his life, promising "he'd give them one million to take him to the hospital, and Melendez says, 'No, you don't go to the hospital, you'll tell the police,' and he picked up the gun and shot him in the head." Prosecutor Hardy Pickard asked about the type of firearm. "A .38," Falcon replied, adding that Melendez "muffled the sound with a cushion."

Testimony by the medical examiner who performed the autopsy shed doubt on Falcon's story. The surfeit of blood was from the gunshots wounds, not the cut to Baker's throat, the examiner Dr. Francis Drake explained. The throat wound severed a vein not an artery. A severed vein would not cause the victim to bleed profusely.

Roger Alcott attempted to discredit Falcon further when he cross-examined him. In the course of his testimony about the evening at the nightclub with Juan Melendez, Falcon had alluded to a warrant for his arrest for murder in Puerto Rico. Under questioning, Falcon admitted that he previously had been convicted of homicide. But when Alcott asked him about the May shooting and break-in at the Reagan home, Falcon said he did not know anything about it. When Detective Glisson was questioned about the incident, he implied that Mr. Reagan was a drug dealer, and that Mrs. Reagan signed a waiver of prosecution after learning that she could be charged with drug-related offenses. Mr. Falcon, according to Detective

Glisson, took part in the break-in working undercover for the Auburndale Police. The Reagans were presently in New England, Glisson testified. The defense had listed the Reagans as witnesses, and the court had agreed to pay their travel expenses, even though an official subpoena was never issued. The sum effect of this was to paint the Reagans in a very unflattering light, suggesting that they would appear in court only if ordered to do so, and to exculpate Falcon from any wrongdoing in the incident.

The Reagans actually had agreed to testify without being subpoenaed. They delayed making travel plans when Roger Alcott informed them the trial likely would be postponed, due to one of the witnesses being hospitalized. The witness, Detective Glisson, was released from the hospital, and the trial proceeded on schedule, without the Reagans.[30]

When Defense Attorney Roger Alcott asked Agent Tom Roper about the break-in and shooting at the Reagan home, Prosecutor Hardy Pickard objected, and the objection was sustained. Nor would the court allow Alcott to present evidence demonstrating that many of the details contained in David Falcon's account were readily available to the general public from media sources.[31]

John Berrien denied involvement in the crime. He said Juan Melendez had asked him for a ride to Mr. Del's Beauty School, so he could have his hair done and pick up some money, but John Berrien could not remember what day that was—not even whether it was before or after his marriage on September 2. He did remember the time of day, though. At about 4:00 he drove his cousin George Berrien and Juan Melendez from Lakeland to Auburndale. He didn't actually see Juan Melendez or his cousin go inside Delbart Baker's place of business. Juan Melendez had a bulge in his pants that might have been a gun, but John Berrien never saw a weapon. He picked his cousin and Juan Melendez back up at about 5:30 or 5:45. They weren't excited, or scared, or bloody. On the drive back to Lakeland, they talked to one another in Spanish, so he wasn't sure what they said. Sometime later, John Berrien could not remember when, he drove his cousin George and Juan Melendez to the train station, where George boarded a train for Delaware. Juan Melendez gave George two rings, a watch, and a gun to sell on his trip.[32]

When Alcott questioned John Berrien, Berrien admitted that he had a history of prior convictions. As to the fact that in exchange for his testimony John Berrien had made a deal with the State, and like Juan Melendez, initially had been charged with first-degree murder and armed robbery: "I didn't feel like I had nothing to do with it, so I said no contest. My lawyer wanted me to plead guilty, but I wouldn't accept a guilty plea." John Berrien acknowledged that he spent 106 days in jail, and to start with he was denied bail, but after agreeing to testify, "I got a bond and was released."[33]

The only physical evidence corroborating John Berrien's story was an Amtrak record indicating that George Berrien had taken a train to Wilmington, Delaware, on the day after Baker's murder.

The only charge pending against George Berrien at the time of the trial was possession of an illegal firearm, the sawed-off twelve-gauge shotgun, which he had in his possession only briefly before pawning it. George Berrien was employed as a merchant seaman and how he came to have the gun was never clearly established, but there was nothing to suggest the gun was in any way linked to the murder of Delbart Baker.

Following from David Falcon and John Berrien's accounts, the prosecution's case included the assumption that it was George Berrien who slashed Delbart Baker's throat. George Berrien took the stand in Juan's defense and refuted John Berrien's account, down to the last detail. George Berrien testified that he had never been arrested or charged in conjunction with Delbart Baker's murder; he did not speak Spanish; he did not know Juan Melendez, although he had seen him *once*, at his cousin John's house; he had never ridden in a car with Juan Melendez; he did travel to Wilmington, Delaware, on September 14, but it was to visit his children, and he got a ride to the train station from a white man in a pickup truck, because his cousin John's car was in the repair shop that day. He was furious with his cousin for implicating him in the crime, but when he confronted him, and told him to stop lying, John had replied that he was going to stick with his story, because "if he changed his statement, the State Attorney was going to put a murder charge on him."[34]

More than ten witnesses took the stand contradicting and discrediting the prosecution's theory alleging that Juan Melendez killed Delbart Baker. The prosecution had interviewed Dorothy Rivera, presuming that as a former girlfriend of Juan's, she might be forthcoming with information that would shed doubt on his character. Juan had a reputation as a Don Juan. He had fathered three daughters by three different women. "I had a lot of girlfriends, back then," he candidly admits. However, the prosecution's presumption that Dorothy Rivera might be a favorable witness proved to be 180 degrees off the mark. Dorothy Rivera took the stand in Juan's defense. To substantiate her reason for remembering that Juan was with her on the afternoon and evening of Delbart Baker's murder, she produced her marriage certificate, dated 13 September 1982. Dorothy Rivera testified that she celebrated her first wedding anniversary, not with her husband, but with the man she was having an affair with, Juan Melendez. "She put her marriage on the line for me," Juan says, acknowledging Dorothy Rivera's pluck, "I did not recall where I was that day, but she had a reason to remember." Marie Graham and Wilson Angelo Graham, the sister and brother-in-law of Dorothy Rivera, corroborated Dorothy Rivera's testimony. Both remembered that Juan Melendez was at their home that afternoon, and that Marie had spoken with her sister about spending her first wedding anniversary with her lover. Angelo testified that he and Juan watched boxing for several hours, and afterward Juan rode home on his bike, and he gave Dorothy a ride to Juan's apartment in his car. The combined testimony accounted for Juan's whereabouts during the entire time he was allegedly in Auburndale murdering Delbart Baker.[35] By way of further confirmation, Ruby Colon likewise testified to knowing that her daughter Dorothy had spent her first wedding anniversary with Juan Melendez.[36]

Ruby Colon, her husband Angelo Colon, Dorothy Rivera, and Wilson Angelo Graham all testified that David Falcon had told them he either would get Melendez sent to jail or kill him outright. Dorothy Rivera recounted a conversation with David Falcon in which he admitted he was going to testify falsely against Juan Melendez and that none of the accusations were true. Falcon had also bragged to Dorothy and her mother Ruby that he was being paid $5,000 to testify, but Defense Attorney Alcott never elicited this information when questioning the two women in court. Nor did Alcott bring out that Ruby Colon had heard David Falcon rail against Juan Melendez for refusing to take part in his drug dealing and robbery schemes.

If the jury had been told that Juan Melendez refused to help David Falcon with drug deals and robberies, would that have cast Falcon in a bad light? Or would it have made the jury wonder why Falcon would have solicited Juan's assistance in the first place, when, in fact, this never occurred? To introduce Ruby Colon's testimony on the subject successfully, Roger Alcott also would have needed to introduce testimony about Juan Melendez's complex nonrelationship with David Falcon—Juan's refusal to associate with Falcon, based on the inside track information from Falcon's stepsister that Falcon was a drug addict and snitch, and Juan's formerly close relationship with Falcon's family—circumstances underscoring Falcon's antipathy and envy, which were never divulged at the trial. The jury was offered virtually no explanation for David Falcon's hatred of Juan Melendez and may well have found the testimony that Falcon had made threats against Juan Melendez's life hollow and unbelievable.

In the jury's eyes, the credibility of the testimony exculpating Juan Melendez likely was compromised further by racial bias: All of the witnesses called to vouch for Juan Melendez were black; Juan Melendez was a dark-complexioned Hispanic, given to frequent association with African Americans; and the victim was white. Eleven of the twelve jurors were Caucasian.

The only evidence the jury heard that gave substance to Falcon's threats was Ruby Colon's testimony that, following one such outburst, Falcon phoned from her apartment and made arrangements to meet someone at the stadium three blocks away. When Alcott questioned David Falcon about this, Falcon corroborated one aspect of Ruby's testimony: he acknowledged that on the evening of March 6 he phoned Agent Tom Roper from Ruby's apartment. When Alcott questioned Agent Tom Roper, Roper confirmed that David Falcon was the source of the story about John Berrien and Juan Melendez's involvement in Baker's death.[37]

In addition to discrediting the accounts given by David Falcon and John Berrien, Roger Alcott's strategy was to convince the jury that it was not Juan Melendez, but rather Vernon James who killed Baker. Terry Barber, the employee who stopped by the beauty school shortly before the murder, testified to seeing Vernon James and Harold Landrum in the back room and that he contacted the police with this information. Detective John Knapp testified that James and Landrum were the original suspects in the killing. Alcott planned to call Vernon James as a witness. In keeping with what Vernon James had told Alcott during the interview, James had agreed to testify that he was at the beauty school on the evening of the murder, but that he was outside when Delbart Baker was killed, and that Juan Melendez was nowhere in the vicinity. As a veteran informer, Vernon James knew how to play the game, casting himself in the role of a nonparticipating observer. In talking with Roger Alcott—as in his conversations with investigator Meeks and Dwight Wells—James had not named the other participants. This was Vernon James's get-out-of-jail-free card, and he was evidently still hoping to use it.

The trial was already underway when James's cellmate Roger Mims contacted the State Attorney's office saying that Vernon James had confessed to him and admitted to slashing Delbart Baker's throat. (Because he was scheduled to testify, James had been transferred to the Polk County Jail during the last week of August.) When Agent Roper questioned James about his confession to Mims, James stuck with the story he had told Roger Alcott and Investigator Meeks: He was at the Del's Beauty School on the evening of 13 September 1983, but outside when the murder actually occurred.

The State Attorney's office notified Defense Attorney Alcott of Vernon James's confession to Roger Mims, and Alcott subpoenaed Roger Mims as a last-minute witness.

When Vernon James's turn to testify came, Judge Edward F. Threadgill, Jr., instructed the jury to leave the room. Judge Threadgill warned James that his testimony could be used against him. After learning that Mims had been subpoenaed as a witness and was talking with a court-appointed attorney, James said that if Mims implicated him in the murder, he would exercise his Fifth Amendment right and refuse to testify, since by admitting that he was present at the beauty school, he would be incriminating himself.

Of the two potential witnesses, Vernon James and Roger Mims, James as a scene-of-the-crime observer would have been the stronger, far more convincing witness to Juan Melendez's noninvolvement. Mims testimony, at best, would be merely hearsay—although different in one key respect from the testimony James could be expected to give. Mims was prepared to testify that James actually had a hand in the killing. For Defense Attorney Alcott, the question came down to second-guessing the jury: Which witness's testimony would make the jurors more inclined to acquit Juan Melendez? Alcott decided to proceed with his intention to question Mims, knowing that doing so would result in James's refusal to testify.

When Roger Mims took the witness stand, he said that he feared for his life, and he would risk being held in contempt of court and sentenced to an additional six months, to avoid testifying. Aware that Alcott certainly would call Vernon James as a witness if Mims refused to testify, the prosecution congenially agreed to have Mims transferred to another county jail to ensure his protection. In response to Alcott's questions, Mims said that James had told him that he was Mr. Del's lover, and that he was the one who cut Baker's throat; two other men were there as well, also homosexuals, and they were the ones who shot Mr. Del; Juan Melendez and "another man named John" didn't have anything to do with it.[38]

In cross-examining Mims, Prosecutor Hardy Pickard was quick to attack Mims's testimony, discrediting the reliability of his account

PICKARD: How long have you been in a cell with Mr. James?
MIMS: A month, three weeks, maybe.
PICKARD: And Mr. James didn't tell you about any of this until last Friday?
MIMS: Well, we talked about it at various times, but he never did tell me about what happened till that time.[39]

In his opening remarks to the jurors, Roger Alcott had promised them testimony from Vernon James that he was at the scene of the crime when the deadly shots were fired, although outside the building at the time, and that Juan Melendez was nowhere in the vicinity. Vernon James never took the witness stand, and the jurors, not privileged to the behind-the-scenes discussions that took place when they were out of the room, were offered no explanation as to why.[40]

Roger Alcott had just lost what might have proved to be his most important witness—a man who acknowledged that he was at the beauty school when Baker was murdered and that Juan Melendez was not. Alcott questioned Agent Roper about his interview with James following his confession to Mims, but when Alcott asked if James had admitted to being present, the prosecution objected, and the objection was sustained. In the jury's eyes, the only clear-cut testimony implicating Vernon James had come from Roger Mims, a jailhouse inmate.[41] Alcott never attempted to introduce the tape-recorded interview with Vernon James as evidence. He later would maintain that he assumed the recording would be barred as inadmissible hearsay, since, as would have been the case if James had testified, by acknowledging his presence at the beauty school James would be incriminating himself.[42]

During the course of the trial, Juan was questioned by both the prosecution and his defense attorney Roger Alcott. Given his tenuous grasp of the language, did Juan Melendez understand what he was being asked? "I understood that I should answer *no* to everything."

Did you know Delbart Baker? No.

Have you ever been inside Mr. Del's Beauty School? No.

Have you ever been to Auburndale? No.[43]

Alienated and powerless, with only a vague comprehension of the process that was taking place around him, one moment in particular stands out in Juan Melendez's mind. He had put his trust in Roger Alcott, believing Alcott's promise that he would go home. But when Prosecutor Hardy Pickard showed the jury photographs depicting the interior of Delbart Baker's shop taken in the aftermath of the bloody slaughter, Juan was seized by a gut-wrenching fear. "The members of the jury turned to me, and they give me this hate look," Juan says, remembering the point-blank accusation he read in their faces. "I knew then, I was in trouble. This was far more serious than the attorney explained to me."[44]

The prosecution's case against Juan Melendez rested entirely on hearsay. The prosecution called beauty school employees and students as witnesses, and none of them knew who Juan Melendez was; they had never seen him before.[45] Agent Roper testified that there was no blood in John Berrien's car; that fingerprints lifted from the crime scene did not match Juan Melendez or George Berrien; and that Vernon James's fingerprints were never compared to those found at the crime scene. The only physical evidence presented shed suspicion on Harold Landrum: the match between the tread pattern on Landrum's sneakers and bloody footprints in Delbart Baker's shop.[46]

Prosecutor Pickard's closing remarks stressed John Berrien and David

Falcon's credibility. "Somebody's lying . . . You're going to have to decide who to believe and who not to believe. . . . If John Berrien is lying . . . why would he plead guilty or plead no contest and risk going to prison for a crime he didn't commit?"[47] And, "Why would David Falcon lie?" . . . "He had absolutely nothing to gain. . . . Oh, he got a little money from the Auburndale Police Department for helping them out in some drug cases, but . . . he did not agree to testify in return for some deal. . . . The shooting that he was allegedly involved in happened at the end of May of 1984. David Falcon had already gone to the police in March and told them about the crime."—"He went out and developed information himself . . . Now, probably the reason he did that is because he worked for the police in the past. He had been an informant of—he called it the Justice Department."[48]

When Defense Attorney Alcott had asked David Falcon how much he was being paid to testify, Falcon said he couldn't remember. When Ruby Colon and Dorothy Rivera testified, Alcott could have brought to the jury's attention that Falcon told the two women he was being paid $5,000 to testify, but Alcott never introduced this line of questioning during the women's testimony. Alcott's closing remarks to the jury: "The Assistant State Attorney wants you to convict this man and send him to the electric chair based on the word of one person, David Luna Falcon, the murderer, the robber, the cocaine snorter from Puerto Rico who says when I was using drugs and under the influence of drugs and beer, he told me he did it."[49]

The trial had begun on Monday, 17 September 1984. Selecting the death-qualified jury took two days. (The term *death-qualified* refers to the practice of permitting the prosecution to exclude jury members who oppose the death penalty.) On Wednesday, the jury heard the evidence. On Thursday, they retired for deliberation. The twelve-member panel consisted of eleven whites and one African American. The first vote resulted in a tie: six guilty, six not guilty. In order to hand down a verdict of first-degree murder, all twelve jury members had to agree on the defendant's guilt. On the second vote, eleven jurors turned in a "guilty" vote. The single holdout was an elderly woman. On the third vote, the jury reached a unanimous verdict. In just slightly over three hours, the jurors returned to the courtroom: *On the charge of armed robbery, we find the defendant, Juan Melendez, guilty. On the charge of first-degree murder, we find the defendant, Juan Melendez, guilty.*

In capital cases, crimes punishable by death, the trial has two phases, what in effect amounts to two separate trials.* In the first phase, the con-

---

*To counter the 1972 U.S. Supreme Court ruling in *Furman v. Georgia*, abolishing the death penalty because it was unfairly and capriciously applied, all states advocating capital punishment eventually adopted a two-phase system.

viction phase, the jury rules on guilt or innocence. In the second phase, the sentencing phase, the jury decides on the punishment.[50]

From the date of his arrest on May 2 and throughout the ensuing four and a half months leading up to his trial, Juan made no effort to get in touch with his brothers and sisters, or even his mother, with whom he has always been close, "I did not want to get my family involved with it." At the sentencing trial, lacking mitigating circumstances and witnesses to speak out on his behalf, Juan again testified. He says in retrospect, "I think what I did was make the jury mad. I told them in the best way I could, *you people have all the evidence that indicates I did not commit the crime and still you find me guilty. Do whatever you want to do. I don't care*—I probably cursed them, too."

On Friday, 21 September 1984, the jury sentenced Juan Melendez to death.

"I will be back. In the name of Jesus, I will be back," Juan raged, as he shuffled from the room, shackled, chained, and handcuffed, "I will be back, because I am an innocent man."

At one juncture during the presentation of evidence, Judge Edward F. Threadgill had complained that the trial was taking too long. The entire courtroom proceedings, from jury selection through the sentencing phase, had lasted less than five full days.

Thumbs on the Balance Scale That Weighed Juan Melendez's Life

While David Falcon was serving time for murder and armed robbery in Puerto Rico, he escaped from prison. He was recaptured, and earned his release by testifying against the suspects in a New Jersey multiple-murder, for which he, too, was a suspect. The credentials that David Falcon testified to under oath at Delbart Baker's murder trial, to establish his credibility, were wholly false: David Falcon had never served as an undercover agent for the Justice Department in Puerto Rico and David Falcon was not a paid police informant for the Florida Department of Law Enforcement (FDLE).

On the contrary, on March 17, less than two weeks after Falcon contacted FDLE Agent Roper claiming that Juan Melendez and John Berrien had killed Baker, Roper dissociated himself from Falcon and all aspects of the probe related to Falcon's claims. David Falcon's criminal record was an open book, and Agent Roper strongly disapproved of the way Auburndale Police Detectives Glisson and Knapp were manipulating Falcon and the information that Falcon provided.[51]

Detective Glisson's testimony that David Falcon was working undercover for the Auburndale Police Department (APD), when he broke into the

Reagan home, was likewise an out and out lie. From Glisson's perspective, intimidating the Reagans into not pressing charges against Falcon had dual benefits: One, it kept the prosecution's chief witness out of jail, and two, it gave the prosecution leverage to pressure Falcon to testify. Evidently David Falcon had been getting cold feet. Prior to the trial, he confided to Dorothy Rivera that he had tried to leave town, but the police had caught up with him and were forcing him to testify. The APD also made good on the perk they had promised David Falcon, paying him $5,000 for taking the witness stand. Prosecutor Hardy Pickard's closing remarks to the jury that Falcon had "absolutely nothing to gain" couldn't have been farther from the truth.[52]

At the time of the trial, Prosecutor Pickard had information from four different sources pointing to Vernon James as an accomplice in Delbart Baker's murder: James's tape-recorded statements to Roger Alcott; James's virtually identical statements to Arthur Meeks; James's admission to Agent Tom Roper that he was present at the time of the murder; and James's full-blown admission of guilt to his cellmate Roger Mims that he had slashed Delbart Baker's throat. Pickard also knew that David Falcon had lied under oath when he testified that he formerly served as an undercover agent in Puerto Rico and was currently a paid police informant for the FDLE. The inconsistencies and contradictions in David Falcon's and John Berrien's trial testimonies, compared to their earlier statements, were also well known to Prosecutor Hardy Pickard. The information the prosecution had that exculpated Juan Melendez was never presented to the jury. On the contrary, Prosecutor Hardy Pickard clandestinely provided the deliberating jury with damning information of another kind.

In Polk County, Florida, like other areas of the South in the early 1980s, Black neighborhoods were still terrorized by middle-of-the-night cross burnings. In Polk County, Florida, in the early 1980s, KKK members openly gathered for spirit rallies and parades. The jury foreman, Jim Lear, served as a city commissioner in the Polk County town of Winter Haven. Active in local politics, Lear knew Prosecutor Hardy Pickard and Judge Edward Threadgill, personally. Lear, who with his wife owned a beauty salon in Winter Haven, also knew Delbart Baker.[53]

It is telling that the jury did not arrive at anything close to a consensus on its first vote. The jury split fifty-fifty—six guilty, six not guilty. Even this jury chosen from a community prone to ethnic and racial bias, even this jury consisting of eleven whites and only one African American (when the victim was white and the accused was a man of color), even this jury guided by a foreman who had reason to be partial to the prosecution and victim, even this jury had serious doubts about Juan Melendez's guilt. Of the six

Mug photo of Juan Melendez shown to the jury during deliberation. [Polk County Sheriff's Office, 455 North
Broadway Avenue, Bartow, Florida, 33830. Approved by: Cassandra
L. Denmark, Esquire, Director of Legal Affairs & Scott Wilder, Director
of Communications.]

dissenting voters in the first round, one was the African-American man, a
school janitor, and one was an elderly woman. Following further debate
led by the jury foreman, five of the dissenters, including the janitor, came
over to Foreman Lear's side. The elderly woman, the single holdout, remained staunch in her opposition. Pressed to elaborate, she explained that
she simply did not believe that 'nice-looking young man' committed such
a horrible crime. She could not find Juan Melendez guilty. Finally, Lear produced a photograph, obtained from Prosecutor Hardy Pickard, taken ten
years earlier, at the time of Juan's arrest in 1975.[54] Lear supplied his own
caption: 'Someone with that haircut had to have committed the crime.'
The photograph depicted a bare-chested, hollow-eyed young man with a
wild and unruly Afro, wearing an inmate identification placard suspended
from a neck chain: Sheriffs Dept. Bartow Florida—75042—Melendez.[55]
    The mug shot had the intended effect. On the third vote, the elderly

woman came around to Foreman Lear's way of thinking. The jury reached a consensus. The verdict, guilty of armed robbery and murder in the first-degree, sent Juan Melendez to prison for almost eighteen years and nearly cost him his life.[56]

Death Row

Before the trial, Juan was in the bullpen, a communal cellblock with a table and chairs where prisoners awaiting trial were confined.[57] Once the guilty verdict was handed down, everything changed. The guards moved him into a cell by himself. Whenever he was taken out, he wore handcuffs, chains, and shackles. He spent five weeks in solitary confinement at the Polk County Jail. On November 2, he was transferred to Florida State Prison, in Raiford, and incarcerated on death row.

"I was real scared, scared to die for something I did not do. The cell was six by nine, dark and cold. People think Florida is warm, but not North Florida. There was a toilet and bunk. They supplied me with a thin blanket. At night, I covered myself from head to toe, covered my face, because the rats would come out. I could feel them climbing the blanket, crawling on top of me."

And then there were the roaches. "In the morning, they bring the food cart, and they put your breakfast tray through a flap in the cell door. If you stay in the bunk five seconds, the roaches beat you to the breakfast, so you get up fast. The roaches, they were waiting for their breakfast, too."

When Juan had been on death row just nine days, a man was executed. Unfamiliar with the system, thinking he would be next, Juan tore his bed sheets into strips and looped them through the bars, tying his cell door closed. To get to him, the guards would have to undo his makeshift ropes to enter his cell. "I made up my mind I was not gonna walk to that chair. I knew a little boxing, and I would fight them to the end."

When the guard making his rounds saw what Juan had done, he flew into a rage. Juan was on the floor doing pushups, trying to make out like he was a tough guy. "My English was not good, but I knew how to curse, and I reminded him of his mother, the whole family, all the way down. I wanted to scare him, when in truth I was the one who was terrified.

"But then to my surprise, the rest of the condemned men got involved in the argument. They said I was wrong, that all I do is get up in the morn-ing and get in the bar doors and curse and nag and cry about my innocence. I told them the best way I could, that we should fight these damn people. They are killing men every week, and we are doing nothing about it. We

Puerto Ricans don't go out like that, we fight to the end. They still said I was wrong. They told me that was not the way to change things, that I was a fool, 'You do not know how to read, you do not know how to write, you do not even know how to speak English.'

"And then they told me the most beautiful thing I could hear—they told me they would teach me."

The inmates made good on their promise, teaching Juan not only how to speak English, but how to read and write in his non-native tongue, and advising him on the law and the appeals process. It was one of death row's early lessons—the worst of the worst, the men the outside world regarded as monsters, became Juan's mentors and teachers.

But an ugly and hard lesson was soon to follow. One of the death-row inmates who took a special interest in Juan was Melvin Nelson. "He pushed me to study hard, so I could communicate better with my attorneys and understand what was happening with my case," Juan says of the man known to his fellow prisoners as Maddog. Juan and Maddog Nelson formed a strong and fast friendship, a friendship that before long ended in tragedy.

Out in the yard one afternoon, Nelson was shooting hoops, and suddenly fell to the ground, unconscious and foaming at the mouth. Eventually, a nurse responded to the call for help, but empty-handed, without so much as a medical bag. Nelson was not breathing, and the nurse left, returning with an oxygen tank that proved to be nonfunctional.

"Do CPR," Juan yelled frantically, standing with his back to the fence with the others, under the menacing gaze of the guards in the towers whose guns were trained on the prisoners.

The tobacco-chewing nurse spit on the ground next to Nelson's still body and then turned and glared at Juan like he was crazy, 'I'm not puttin' my mouth on that motherfucking nigger.'

"You don't have to. Let me do the CPR," Juan pleaded, "You just do the counting."

The nurse shrugged and spit again. 'All right.'

Juan rushed forward. He took off his shirt, wiped the foam out of Melvin Nelson's mouth, and pressed his own mouth to his friend's lips. The nurse counted, 'One, two, three,' and Juan breathed air into the lungs of the man who had reached out to him with compassion and generosity. 'One, two, three,' and another breath. 'One, two, three' and another.

"My friend opened his eyes," Juan says remembering the moment when he saw a sign of hope. "I thought he was going to live. But then all of a sudden his eyes rolled back into his head, and he made a terrible frown and breathed out hard. It was his soul leaving him.

"I was angry, and I wanted to go after the nurse. The other prisoners

held me back. I got sent to solitary confinement for ninety days for disre-
spect. They let my friend die in the yard like a dog."

A month after his death, Melvin Nelson's conviction was reversed, enti-
tling him to a new trial.*

The Early Appeals

Juan moved relatively quickly through the direct-appeal process. At this
level, the court reviews the trial record for legal error that might have
affected the outcome (for example, improper jury instruction, the prosecution misleading the jury, or the like).[58]

On 11 December 1986, the Florida Supreme Court affirmed Juan's conviction and death sentence, replying that they "found no reversible error in
either the guilt or penalty stages of the trial." One member of the court,
however, expressed reservations. Although concurring with the decision,
Justice Rosemary Barkett noted her concerns in an opinion appended to
the ruling: "There are cases, albeit not many, when a review of the evidence
in the record leaves one with the fear that an execution would perhaps be
terminating the life of an innocent person. . . . After careful review of
the record in this case, I believe that the evidence does not rise to the level
of certainty that should support imposition of the death penalty."[59]

In 1988, Capital Collateral Representative (CCR) began working on
Juan's case. CCR provided public-defender services for individuals sentenced to death in the northern region of Florida. They took over after the
death sentence and conviction had been affirmed on direct appeal.[60]

The post-conviction appeal, filed 16 January 1989, alleged negligence
on the part of Defense Attorney Roger Alcott; error and withholding of evidence on the part of Prosecutor Hardy Pickard; and that the death sentence
was disproportionate and in disparity, since the alleged accomplice,
George Berrien, was never even charged.[61]

Juan's CCR attorneys were wholly unaware that Prosecutor Pickard and
Roger Alcott had documented evidence that Vernon James had confessed
prior to Juan's trial. They had talked with Roger Alcott, but he never mentioned Vernon James's confession or that he had tape-recorded the interview with James.[62]

The appeal cited Alcott for failing to subpoena the Reagans, who would

---

*The Florida Supreme Court recently had heard Melvin Nelson's appeal, but had not yet
handed down a decision. The opinion, delivered after Nelson's death, stated, "We vacate Nelson's
death sentence and reverse his conviction. But for his death, we would remand for a new trial."
Melvin Nelson, Jr. v. State of Florida, Case No. 65279 (1986).

have testified that they were coerced into not pressing charges against Falcon; for failing to inform the jury that Falcon was paid $5,000 for testifying; and for failing to inform the jury as to the nature of Falcon's grudge against Juan Melendez—Juan's refusal to assist Falcon's criminal activities, specifically robberies and selling drugs.

Regarding John Berrien, the appeal cited Alcott's failure to show the inconsistencies in Berrien's pretrial statements and Berrien's pretrial admission that his "statements to police were mostly false" and that the police had promised him he would "get off light."

The appeal cited Pickard for misleading the jury about Falcon's reason for testifying and about Falcon's background and credentials.[63]

On 12 July 1989, the Tenth Circuit Court of Florida denied the appeal without even considering the evidence. No hearing was held. The opinion dismissed the disparate and disproportionate sentence allegations, suggesting that because George Berrien was never charged, there was no justification for comparing Juan Melendez's punishment to George Berrien's punishment, or lack thereof. In denying the negligence, error, and withholding evidence allegations, the court held that the withheld information was available to Alcott, and that this and the other evidence mentioned in the appeal, although not presented at the trial, would not have changed the outcome, since Alcott provided Melendez with alibi witnesses and called into question the credibility of David Falcon and John Berrien in cross-examination.

Juan's attorneys were virtually out of ammunition. They already had presented all the evidence available to them and had little hope of coming up with new evidence. David Falcon had died of AIDS-related complications in 1986, just two years after Juan's conviction.[64] And when CCR investigators tried to find John Berrien and Vernon James, they were equally unlucky. Following two years of house arrest for his part in the Baker murder, John Berrien seemed to have vanished. Family members claimed not to know where he was, and no information followed from public records requests. Efforts to find Vernon James proved even more disheartening.[65] James had also died in 1986. He was found dead in a ditch, shot several times in the head and chest.[66] A CCR investigator requested records relating to James's death but was denied access because the case was still open.[67]

"The Only Way Out Was to Commit Suicide"

"Every time you lose an appeal, you're getting closer and closer to death. The hardest thing for me in there was when they executed a person. When you got a man in the cell next to you, and you've been with him eight or ten years, he knows your whole life story and you know his. You can cry on his shoulder if you need to. Then one day they come and snatch him out of there and put on the handcuffs and shackles and chains and take him to deathwatch. You pray he gets a stay of execution. There were four men they killed, back to back, friends of mine, and I know they were innocent. You can hear when they burn a man's life, when they hit him with the 2010 volts—rrrnnng, rrrnnng—you hear the electricity surging and you see the lights blinking. You know they are killing him, and you can't do nothing about it.[68]

"I wanted out of there, and after a while I started to believe the only way out was to commit suicide. I knew how to do it. I'd seen how my friends did it."

Juan traded four postage stamps for a plastic garbage bag, bartering with the inmate who brought around a cart with supplies from the commissary. The cart tender did not question the transaction. "He knows what you're going to do with it. You use the garbage bag to make a rope, and with the rope you make a noose," Juan explains. "You tie the one end to the bars, and you put the noose around your neck, and you throw yourself down, and then you're free."

The green plastic noose Juan fashioned was ready and waiting, dangling from his cell bars, but then—"I looked at it, and something says to me, I need to think about this a little more.

"I hid the noose under the bunk, and I lay down, and I fell into this deep, deep sleep. When I was a child, I could walk six minutes from my house and be on the most beautiful beach in the world—at least to me. I dreamed I was a little child again, and here I am in this dream swimming in the Caribbean Sea. The water is warm, the sky is blue, the sun is bright. I look up at the palm trees on the beach, and they look so beautiful. And then I see something I have never seen before in my life, four dolphins swimming toward me. Two get on one side of me, and two on the other. Then they start flipping and jumping, and I am playing with them, and I am so happy. I look toward the shore, and I see this old lady waving to me, and she's smiling and happy, because I am happy. It is my mother.

"I woke up and snatched the garbage bag rope out from under the bed, and I looked at it, and said to myself, I don't want to die. I flushed the rope down the toilet.

"I grabbed onto that dream as a sign of hope that one day I would be free, like God was telling me, 'Hey, I know you didn't do it. Hang in there. I control the time. You'll get out when I say you get out.' I prayed it would be in time to see my grandparents alive, my grandmamma and grandpa,

Juan's brother, mother, and a family friend visit him in prison. [Family photo taken during prison visitation]

and I believed God would grant me this. They were old. My grandpa was 103. He was the closest thing I had to a father when I was growing up."

Then, not long afterward, Juan had another dream that proved to be hauntingly auspicious.

"I will never forget the date, because it was a Saturday, and for Saturday lunch we always had chili and rice—what the Mexicans eat. That Saturday after breakfast I went back to sleep, and I dreamed I was with my grandpa. We go to the mountains to get the vegetables for the next day's lunch— tropical vegetables like yams and breadfruit. It was something we used to do almost every day. Coming down from the mountains, I can smell the sweat on my grandpa's shirt and I don't like it. When we get back to my grandmamma's house, she has the table ready for us. Usually the lunch was vegetables and dried fish, but that day it is chili and rice—they don't have that on the island. I eat it, and it is good. 'Everything is going to be all right with you,' my grandpa says to me and he gets up and pats me on the head and blesses me. Then my grandmamma comes and kisses me and blesses me, too.

"And then I woke up, and here comes the lunch—chili and rice, just like in the dream. I tell my friend two cells down, Sammie Rivera, about the dream, and he says, 'Man, they don't cook no rice and chili in Puerto Rico.' And I say, 'Who am I to control the dream—it's a dream,' and we both laugh.

"Monday I got a letter from my mama, saying that my grandpa had passed the Monday before and grandmamma died Thursday, just three days later.

"I was angry with God and threw the bible out through the bars of my cell.

"In the yard, everyone would gather around me to keep me from doing something crazy. You can tell when somebody is going to commit suicide. They stop eating and quit speaking to people. I had all the symptoms. I was very depressed.

"I stayed in that stage for a week or so. Then one day I am sitting on my bunk and the dream is right there again in my mind and I went back into it—it was so real. I could smell the sweat on my grandpa's shirt. If I had not had that dream, I would have had nothing to hold onto when I got the news they had died. God did let me see them again. Who am I to tell God how to fulfill his promise? The promise had to be fulfilled in his way, not my way.

"Every time I think about that dream, I see Sammie Rivera's face. Sammie hanged himself. It was the same year my grandpa and grandmamma died, 1992, not long after the dream. The condemned men who don't find something spiritual either go crazy or commit suicide. I would always tell myself not to look when they wheeled the body out. But then something in the back of my mind would say, 'Don't you want to see your friend one last time?' So I would take the mirror and stretch my arms through the bars, and in the mirror, watch them roll the body down the row. They never take the noose off the neck, and all you see is a blue face that doesn't look like your friend."

When Juan's post-conviction appeal was rejected, his CCR attorneys filed a petition for a writ of certiorari with the U.S. Supreme Court and a petition for a writ of habeas corpus with the Florida Supreme Court.*

If a writ of certiorari is granted, the higher court asks the relevant lower court to inform them of all records in a case, to make "certain" they contain no errors. As at the direct-appeal level, the court considers only errors in the procedure of the lower court and does not concern itself with weighing the evidence, old or new. However, while everyone convicted of a

---

*Florida is somewhat atypical in providing for habeas corpus review before the state supreme court. See the introduction for a discussion of the appellate process.

criminal offense is automatically entitled to have questions of error reviewed at the direct-appeal level, the U.S. Supreme Court considers only those cases that they conclude merit their attention. Writs of certiorari are rarely granted. A writ of habeas corpus, the right to which is a provision of the U.S. Constitution, orders that an imprisoned person be brought before the court to determine if the petitioner is being lawfully detained. In reviewing a request for a writ of habeas corpus, the court petitioned (regardless of whether it is a state or federal court) considers violations of the right to a trial by jury as defined by Article VI of the Constitution, which includes the right "to have the Assistance of Counsel for his defense."[69] Juan's habeas petition alleged that he was denied effective assistance of counsel at the direct-appeal level.[70]

Juan, though, has this to say about his appellate attorneys. "All my appeal lawyers, they were all good. I had more than twelve by the time it was over with. Every one of them was a good lawyer, and every one of them fought hard for me. The problem I had was the judges, the courts. They did not listen."

Certiorari and habeas corpus petitions are generally desperate, last-resort efforts to save a defendant's life when other avenues of appeal have failed.

Juan's petition for a writ of certiorari was denied on 18 October 1993. The habeas petition was denied on 8 September 1994.[71]

Second Post-Conviction Appeal: A Breakthrough, Almost

Following up on a tip from a member of John Berrien's family, CCR investigators found John Berrien in a New Mexico prison. Meanwhile, Vernon James's murder files had been released. The records led to interviews with three women who knew Vernon James, as well as containing references to John Berrien's attorney Dwight Wells. Talking with Dwight Wells about the Baker murder required a release from John Berrien, and Berrien agreed. When Wells was questioned, he told CCR investigators about Vernon James's confession to him. James also had confessed his involvement to the three women. And when John Berrien was questioned, he gave a detailed account of the police coercion and threats and recanted his entire testimony at the Baker murder trial.[72]

Based on this new evidence, a second post-conviction appeal was filed on 13 September 1994, the same day the murder had occurred, ten years prior. On 23 and 24 May 1996, an evidentiary hearing was held in the Tenth Circuit Court of Florida, presided over by Judge Dennis Maloney.[73] May 24,

1996, was Juan Melendez's forty-fifth birthday, and the twelfth anniversary of his extradition to Florida to face charges for the Baker murder.

CCR's subpoena list included Juan's original trial attorney, Roger Alcott; David Falcon's initial contact, FDLE Agent Tom Roper; social psychologist Dr. Richard Ofshe; John Berrien; Dwight Wells; and the three women to whom Vernon James had confessed: Deborah Ciotti, Sandra Kay James, and Janice Dawson.

Deborah Ciotti testified that a few days before Baker's murder, Vernon James told her "about this drug deal going down up at the beauty school," and that "he was going to rob Mr. Del, him and a couple of his buddies." The day after the murder she ran into him, and when she asked, "Did you get what you went for?" James "pulled a wad of money out of his pocket and unrolled this big bag of cocaine."

Sandra Kay James, Vernon James's sister, testified that she had heard rumors that her brother killed Mr. Del, and at a family gathering at their mother's house, she asked him point-blank. He broke down and started crying, and confided in her. Sandra James quoted her brother as saying, 'I set up the robbery, and I was there, but I didn't kill him.'

Janice Dawson and Vernon James lived together in 1985. "He used to brag about it to other people in the neighborhood," Janice Dawson told the court. One night, "He said he had something for me. He went out to the shed and brought back these two rings, that he said had belonged to Mr. Del."

Dwight Wells testified that Vernon James had confessed to him when he visited him at the Polk County Jail, recounting for the court James's admission that he was a homosexual and that Mr. Del had come on to him in an overly aggressive way, which was what led to the homicide. Dwight Wells also testified that, to the best of his recollection, he never told anyone outside his office about Vernon James's confessions.

Roger Alcott denied knowing that Vernon James had confessed to Dwight Wells. Alcott told the court that, had he known about James's confession to Wells, he would have used Wells' testimony at the trial, which certainly was "more credible" and would have carried far "more weight" with the jury than James's confession to his cell mate, Roger Mims. Yet, in Roger Alcott's pretrial interview with Vernon James, which Alcott had recorded, Vernon James had told Alcott about his meeting with Wells and said that, in talking with Wells, he had divulged the circumstances of the homicide and admitted to being at the beauty school when the murder took place. The tape-recorded interview also contained James's statement that Juan Melendez was not present, but Alcott made no mention of the tape-recorded interview at the hearing, and Juan's appellate attorneys remained unaware of its existence.

John Berrien testified that he was "scared from the get-go," referring to the first middle-of-the-night interview at the Lakeland Police Department in the presence of five law-enforcement officers, and that the second interview, conducted by Detectives Glisson and Knapp at the Auburndale Police Department, was even more terrifying: "They would tell me what they wanted me to say. Then if I made a mistake they would stop the tape," and they would say "we're going to stick you with it, or you're going down by yourself, or you can end up like Mr. Del." John Berrien spoke openly about the many lies he told at Juan Melendez's trial: the two rings, the watch, the .38 pistol he had testified to seeing Juan Melendez with in the past, "I was told to say that." By whom? "The Auburndale Police Department." ". . . I said what I thought they wanted to hear." He also testified to being visited, two days later, by Detective Glisson and David Falcon, and how Falcon advised him, 'go ahead, man, help them out . . . Melendez already confessed to doing it.'

The police had recorded both interviews. A portion of the first interview was played for the court. Agent Tom Roper acknowledged being present at the interview and conceded that the numerous "clicks" heard on the recording resulted because the tape was stopped frequently.

Social psychologist Dr. Richard Ofshe, who specialized in false memories, police interrogation techniques, and coerced confessions, testified that the police had used threats to gain control over John Berrien. "Once a serious and credible threat is made, that subject is placed in a coercive situation until the threat is removed." Dr. Ofshe concluded that John Berrien's testimony at the evidentiary hearing was far more likely to be reliable than his trial testimony.[74]

Judge Dennis Maloney denied the appeal. In a decision delivered on 17 July 1996, Judge Maloney said that he "was not sure what to make of attorney Dwight Wells' testimony, since his memory of Vernon James's confessions was sketchy, and he made no notes or tapes of the conversation." Maloney's opinion went on to state that the other four primary witnesses were "not credible."[75] John Berrien's testimony was "completely unbelievable," and as to the three women James had confessed to: "Deborah Ciotti was a prostitute and drug addict at the time of the murder, and is currently incarcerated. Janice Dawson lived with James after both were released from prison on unrelated crimes. Sandra Kay James was addicted to drugs at the time of the murder and is presently serving a thirty-year prison sentence."[76]

In replying to the denial, CCR attorney Gail Anderson submitted a lengthy and detailed brief to the Florida Supreme Court. Anderson stressed that the court should consider "the cumulative effect of the evidence which the jury never heard. . . . Ms. Ciotti, Ms. Dawson, and Ms. James were very close to Mr. James and do not know Mr. Melendez; therefore, they had no motive to lie to help him. . . . [and] Mr. Berrien had a compelling motive to lie at the trial, but no conceivable motive to lie at the evidentiary hearing. . . . Credibility of the witnesses was the central issue at Mr. Melendez's trial."[77]

On 6 November 1998, the Florida Supreme Court affirmed the denial, concurring with Judge Maloney's opinion. The witnesses were not credible, and so there was no new evidence or withheld evidence (with respect to John Berrien's coerced testimony) to consider. Since there was no new evidence, there was no cumulative evidence to consider.[78]

The Sixteen-Year Mark

His fellow inmates had long ago stopped calling Juan Melendez a "fool." He had been studying law and working on an account of his case from prison, which he ultimately sent to every pro-active death-penalty abolition organization he was aware of: the National Coalition to Abolish the Death Penalty, Citizens United for Alternatives to the Death Penalty, Floridians for Alternatives to the Death Penalty, the Center on Wrongful Convictions at Northwestern University, the American Civil Liberties Union, the National Association for the Advancement of Colored People, Amnesty International. "I was at the end of the game. Everything I had was already procedurally barred. You can't bring something up again, once the courts deny it."

The sworn testimony by Dwight Wells and the three women to whom Vernon James had confessed was virtually useless information. Harold "Bobo" Landrum, who was seen with Vernon James at the beauty school on the evening of the murder and whose sneakers matched bloody footprints at the crime scene, had an alibi, and however poorly documented, the court had accepted it as adequate. Although in talking to Arthur Meeks, investigator for the State Attorney's Office, James had suggested there were two other individuals involved, no other documentation as to the possible existence of a third suspect or information as to the identity of a third suspect had ever surfaced. Detective John Knapp—the original chief investigator who neglected to refrigerate the blood samples and who previously had worked closely with Vernon James when he was acting in the capacity of an informer—had been demoted to the rank of patrol officer for mishandling the investigation in the Baker murder case. A few years later, Knapp was fired from the APD for stealing a gun from the evidence room. Former Detective John Knapp might have been able to shed some light on the circumstances surrounding Delbart Baker's death, but John Knapp had died of a heart attack.[79]

Juan struggled to keep the dream of freedom in sight. CCR attorneys Martin McClain, Linda McDermott, and Brett Stand were working on another appeal. Brett Strand, a member of the CCR legal team, paid Juan a visit. Against all odds, CCR's diligence and a healthy dose of luck had turned up both new evidence and previously withheld evidence. But Brett Strand cautioned Juan not to be overly optimistic.

"'If you lose this appeal, you'll be lucky if you live another three years,' Brett Strand told me. I flat told him right back, 'No, you are wrong. If I lose this appeal, I'll be lucky if I live a year and a half. You know who the governor in Florida is, Jeb Bush, and he would not hesitate to execute me.'"[80]

"Vernon James Was There and Juan Melendez Was Not"

In the summer of 2000, CCR investigator Rosa Greenbaum had contacted Cody Smith, the defense investigator who worked with Roger Alcott on Juan Melendez's case. Cody Smith was living in Pennsylvania at the time, and agreed to go back to Lakeland, Florida, to see if he could locate his notes and files on Melendez. Smith could not find anything, but since he was in town, he called Roger Alcott, and they got together for lunch. Alcott had just become a Polk County judge for the Tenth Circuit. When Alcott closed his law practice, he moved all his records to a farm that he recently had purchased, storing them in the garage and wherever there was room—boxes upon boxes full of files and notes. When Cody Smith mentioned his reason for being in town, Alcott recalled seeing a few boxes labeled "Melendez" among the files he had stored at the farm.

Alcott and Smith drove out to the farm and started rummaging through the stacks. Although Cody Smith had accompanied Roger Alcott when he interviewed Vernon James on 14 August 1984, at the Tomoka Correctional Center, Cody Smith was unaware that Alcott recorded the interview. In searching through the files at the farm, Alcott and Smith found a transcript of the tape-recording Alcott had made that day—in which James admitted to being at the beauty school when Delbart Baker was killed and stated point-blank that Juan Melendez was not there. The transcript also contained James's mention of talking with Dwight Wells and divulging to Wells information about the murder.

In December of 2000, CCR's Rosa Greenbaum managed to locate Marty Lake, Vernon James's killer. In 1990, Lake received a five-year sentence for manslaughter for killing James, but only served one year before being paroled. CCR investigators had tried to find Lake before, hoping he might know something about the Baker murder, but Lake confided that in the mid-1990s he was hiding out in Tennessee, since there were several outstanding warrants for his arrest. The Marty Lake connection and Greenbaum's persistence in following up on other leads turned up six additional witnesses who were aware of Vernon James's involvement in the murder of "Mr. Del."

Still more evidence surfaced when CCR issued a public records request asking for all of Prosecutor Hardy Pickard's files and notes on the case.

A third post-conviction appeal was filed in the Tenth Circuit Court on 23 February 2001. The motion included allegations of ineffective assistance of counsel, directed against Roger Alcott. All of the judges in the Tenth Circuit recused themselves, since Alcott as a Tenth Circuit judge was a colleague. The Florida Supreme Court issued an order designating Thirteenth Circuit Court Judge Barbara Fleischer a temporary judge of the Tenth Circuit to hear all matters connected with the case.

An evidentiary hearing was held on 29 and 30 May 2001. In addition to ineffective assistance of counsel, the appeal also alleged that Prosecutor Hardy Pickard had withheld exculpatory evidence and that the withheld evidence, together with the transcript of James's taped confession and the testimony of the six new witnesses, raised serious doubts about Juan Melendez's guilt.

Of the six witnesses who testified to James's involvement in Delbart Baker's murder, Janet Conoway's account was especially revealing. One night when she was partying with some friends at their trailer, Vernon James knocked on the door. James was nervous and jittery. "The front of him was splashed with blood." One of the men at the trailer, Henry Davis, told Janet to get James a pair of pants and a shirt, and she did. Davis handed her James's bloodied clothes and told her to burn them. She took James clothes outside to the burn barrel and set them on fire. When she came back in, she overheard James telling Davis about a struggle, and that "he just had to do it, that's all there was to it, he had to do it." During the investigation of Mr. Del's murder, Janet Conoway told a police officer what she knew about Vernon James, but he had dismissed her with a racial slur, calling her an 'unhuman being.'

Prosecutor Hardy Pickard's records contained detailed notes about James's confession to investigator Arthur Meeks; reports indicating that Detective Glisson pressured the Reagans into not prosecuting David Falcon; correspondence that showed police reports were not prepared until six months after the homicide and included data based on leads not discovered until six months after the homicide; Pickard's personal interviews with David Falcon and John Berrien that differed markedly from the two men's trial testimonies; and names of potential witnesses who might have had information about Delbart Baker's murder or otherwise documented Juan Melendez's innocence. One of these potential witnesses had told Pickard about two men, never investigated, who had threatened to kill Mr. Del.[81]

On 5 December 2001, Judge Barbara Fleischer issued her decision in a telephone conference call. Among the participants were Prosecutor Hardy Pickard and Roger Alcott. Juan listened from prison.

Juan was hopeful. "During the evidentiary hearing, Judge Barbara Fleischer never smiled at me. She was looking at me like I was a mad man. She was wondering, 'Who the hell am I gonna let go? I know he did not commit this crime, but he might have become a monster by now.' With Judge Maloney, that man was real nice to me, smiling and saying 'What do you need, Melendez?' Then he sent me back to death row. The Honorable Barbara Fleischer said she wrote a seventy-two-page opinion. When they deny you, they don't have to write much—they just say, 'procedure barred, no merit'—they don't have to explain it. But when you're gonna let somebody go, you've got to explain why."

Judge Fleischer did not criticize Alcott for not introducing the tape at the trial, but she did reprimand him for not interviewing Dwight Wells as a potential witness, to find out exactly what James had told Wells. Judge Fleischer also reprimanded Alcott for not subpoenaing the Reagans as witnesses, but stated that she did not find these errors egregious enough to support the ineffective assistance of counsel allegation.

Prosecutor Hardy Pickard did not fare nearly so well. Judge Fleischer sited Pickard for multiple Brady violations, that is, for withholding evidence that might have caused the trial to result in a different outcome. Judge Fleischer's explanation stressed that the credibility of John Berrien and David Falcon was the central issue at the trial—the issue hammered on by both the defense and prosecution in their closing remarks—as Pickard had instructed the jury "You're going to have to decide who to believe." The withheld information would have undermined that credibility, and supported the defense's argument that Vernon James was the actual killer. Judge Fleischer also pointed out that David Falcon's interviews with Pickard made no mention of blood slinging or Delbart Baker begging for his life, aggravating circumstances from Falcon's trial testimony, which were vital to the State's obtaining a death sentence as opposed to a lesser penalty.

In summary, Judge Fleischer noted that Vernon James's statements to numerous friends and acquaintances, as well as to Roger Alcott, Cody Smith, Arthur Meeks, and Dwight Wells "corroborate that Vernon James was present and Juan Melendez was not," and added that there was "no physical evidence which connected Mr. Melendez to the murder of Mr. Del." Based on a "cumulative examination of all the evidence" Judge Fleischer ordered that "the Defendant's conviction and death sentence from September 20 and 21, 1984 must be set aside. The Defendant is entitled to a new trial."[82]

When Juan heard Judge Fleischer speak these words over the telephone line, he was relieved and happy, but nearly eighteen years on death row had taught him to accept the slow, plodding workings of the legal machinery as the norm, and not to be overly optimistic: "I knew when the Honorable Barbara Fleischer granted me a new trial that I would win at that trial, but I was not looking to get out soon. I expected Prosecutor Pickard to fight, to appeal the judge's decision. He had the evidence that I was innocent a month before my first trial, and he still tried to kill me. I thought to myself, this is another step. I was expecting it to take about three more years, before I would be released.

"The State had thirty days to appeal the decision. In another death-penalty case where the judge granted a new trial, Pickard had waited until the last minute to oppose the ruling. That's what I thought he was going to do with Judge Fleischer's ruling granting me a new trial. But on December 20, the CCR investigator for my case, Rosa Greenbaum, phoned me. Rosa said she heard the State was thinking about dropping the case."

A rumor had leaked to the press that the prosecution would not seek a new trial, but Rosa Greenbaum had cautioned Juan that the State still had two weeks to appeal the decision.

Early on the afternoon of 3 January 2002, one day before the deadline to appeal expired, a guard appeared at Juan's cell and told him he had a call out. "A call out means you are going off death row for legal business. I figured Pickard had appealed the decision, just like I expected. I took off my clothes and passed them through the flap in the door. Any time you leave death row they do a strip search while you are still in your cell. I put my clothes back on and turned my back to the cell bars so the guard could put on the handcuffs and shackles.

"They took me to the information room. This lady started asking me all these questions. What is my social security number? What do I like to do? When she asked me what kind of job I had, I said, 'Lady, they don't have no jobs on death row.'

"She said, 'You don't know what's going on, do you? You're going to be released today.'

"How it is when a cartoon character gets hit in the head with a sledgehammer and stars start circling around his head and he's in a state of shock—that's what it was like. My Mama knew I was going to be released before I did. My attorneys had phoned her. They don't tell you ahead of time, because they don't know how you will react.

"When they were taking me back to my cell, the guards were calling me Mr. Melendez. I liked that.

"At eight o'clock that night, my cell door opened. I was scared. There were three guards and the captain of the prison. I did not trust them. I turned around for the handcuffs. 'No cuffs,' the captain said. 'Mr. Melendez is a free man.'

"Walking down death row, I was smiling, but the tears were streaming down my face. I was happy, but I was sad too, because I was leaving my friends. 'Don't get in trouble out there. Take care of your Mama,' one of the inmates said when I passed his cell. He was crying, too. They were all pretty much telling me the same thing and wishing me good luck. Then someone clapped and then there was another clap and another clap, and then the whole cellblock was clapping. The guards got mad and told them to be quiet, but they kept it up until I was out of the place."[83]

It had been nearly eighteen years since Juan Melendez had been able to look up at the night sky.

"I wanted to see the moon and the stars, and I could not see them because it was a cloudy night. I wanted simple things. I wanted to walk on grass. I wanted to hold a little baby in my arms. I wanted to talk to some beautiful women. I owe the Honorable Barbara Fleischer my life. She looked at the whole pie, not just a piece of the pie. She read everything about the case from the beginning all the way to the end. Roger Alcott becoming a judge got my case out of Polk County, out of the good-old-boy network where they fabricated the case against me. It was a racist county. If I hadn't gotten my case out of Polk County, I would probably be dead by now. . . . I forgive Prosecutor Hardy Pickard, but I do not respect him. For me to respect him, he would need to admit his mistake. The thing about forgiving is that, after forgiving, only then can you start to heal. If you don't forgive, you are filled with hate and anger. The death penalty does nothing to provide that healing. It's about vengeance."[84]

In its official statement to the press, the Polk County State Attorney's Office said that they would not seek a new trial since of its two chief witnesses one, David Falcon, was dead and the other, John Berrien, had recanted. There was no apology or even remote expression of regret from anyone connected with the prosecution of the case and original jury trial.[85]

For the seventeen years, eight months, and one day Juan Melendez spent in prison—on death row—for a crime he did not commit, he received $100, a shirt, and a pair of pants, the same release package given to inmates who have served out their sentence.

"I would have walked out of there butt-naked," Juan reflects, "I was free."

Living the Dream

A few days after his release, Juan got in touch with his daughters. One lives in Pennsylvania and the other two live in Florida. He has six grandchildren. "I cut off relations with my daughters when I went to prison. They were too little to understand."

The only family members he had maintained contact with all those years were his mother and his five aunts, in Puerto Rico. "I couldn't wait to get back there. I stayed in the States just over a week. My attorneys wanted me to do press conferences and interviews."

On 11 January 2002, he returned to Maunabo, his childhood home. He lives with his mother in a house he helped build for her when he was fourteen. He celebrates January 3 as a birthday. "I was born again that day. My mama celebrates it with me, my mama and five aunts."

To commemorate the occasion, in 2003 and 2004, during the week of January 3, Juan's mother and aunts took him on a cruise to the nearby islands. "They are the type of aunts, who, if I did something wrong when I was a boy, they gave me an ass whipping. But they are the type of aunts, who, if I needed a pair of pants or a pair of shoes when I was growing up, they were always there for me. And they were there for me when I was on death row. They believed I was innocent, which helped me a lot. They wrote to me and sent me photos of the new ones born in the family. And, of course, my mama, she would write me many letters. I remember this one. I still have it: *Son, I just built an altar, and I put the Virgin of Guadalupe in it and roses. I pray five rosaries a day. I am looking for a miracle, and the miracle will come. Put your trust in God, and have faith in him. I know you did not commit this crime. We believe you.*"

Juan earns twenty-five dollars a day, working as a supervisor in the plantain fields. He is in charge of the hiring, and he seeks out the troubled kids to work with him in the field. "I tell them my story and try to give them good advice, and hope they change. The young people are the future."

Juan and his mama reunited following his release. [*Chito Arroyo, La Fsquinia*]

Juan frequently returns to the States and has traveled abroad as well, responding to the many requests he receives to speak at schools, churches,
universities, law schools, conferences, and conventions. He was the keynote
speaker at the National Coalition to Abolish the Death Penalty conference in
2002, 2003, and 2004, and at the Amnesty International national conference in 2003 and 2004. He counts some of his most important work as the
talks he gives at juvenile detention centers. "I urge the kids to keep a clean
record and to stay out of trouble. You are at an age when you think you
know everything, but you don't, I say to them. My lifestyle and having the
armed robbery conviction made it easy for the police to fabricate a case
against me. I am very ashamed of it. I know that it was wrong, and I am still
paying for it.

"When I get through talking with the kids in detention centers, sometimes I just go off by myself and cry. I know where some of them are
headed. They'll be in prison or dead."

Shortly after his release, Juan found himself back in court, as a witness.
Jerry Rogers, one of the inmates who helped him learn to read and write,
had been granted a new trial. Juan was convinced of Jerry Roger's innocence, but the jury found him guilty again, and Roger's attorneys asked
Juan to testify at the sentencing phase.

"I told the jury I knew Jerry Rogers very well. He was my neighbor for many years. He was a lovely man, always talking about his family. In prison he studied the law. He was glad to help anyone who came to him, giving legal advice to the other condemned men. If he had not helped me to learn how to read and write, I don't think I would have survived in there. I was able to read law books, and that helped me communicate better with my lawyers. Also, once I could write, I had pen pals, and writing to them, that gave me comfort."

Juan had to fly back to Puerto Rico immediately after he testified. What would the jury decided? He was tormented with worry for his friend whose life hung in the balance. The next day, he received a phone call from Rogers's lawyers. "They told me that I had saved Jerry Rogers's life. The jury recommended his sentence be reduced from death to life in prison. I have hope. Jerry Rogers is alive."

In talking about his objection to the death penalty, Juan is quick to point out, "People need to realize, they're not killing the same person who committed the crime. They're killing somebody who has changed. Most find something spiritual. They become Muslims or Buddhists or good Christians, like I did. And they teach the others, not just how to read and write, but how to respect, how to have compassion, how to forgive, how to love. That person has the right to be saved. You don't need to kill him.

"Execution only causes more pain and suffering. It is especially hard for the murder victim family. For most, the wound has begun to heal and it is ripped open again. The crime is thrown right back in their face as if it had just happened."

Juan has little hope of receiving restitution for his wrongful conviction and the lost years of his life spent in prison. Of the 36 states that have the death penalty, only 14 pay compensation.[86] Florida is not one of them. Juan is working with an attorney who is trying to pass legislation to change the law. Nonrestitution states maintain that they have no legal obligation to death-row survivors who were wrongly convicted. By jurisdiction of the U.S. Supreme Court, prosecutors and investigators are entitled to absolute immunity and cannot be held accountable for wrongful convictions.[87]

"I have problems, and I am quite sure all exonerated [individuals] do. I cannot be still. I lose things. I have nightmares, and I worry about the ones still in there. After nine years in prison, I was transferred to Union Correctional Institution, a newer facility at the same prison complex. There are still condemned men imprisoned in the rat-and-roach-infested death-row unit where I was held for nine years. I suffer from what Viet Nam War veterans suffer from—post traumatic stress disorder. Some of the exonerated [ones] cannot even speak. Some do drugs and are alcoholics. Some end up back in prison. Others have committed suicide. It helps for us to get together every once in a while, so we remember we are not alone. We are the only ones who understand each other. Our families need counseling to learn how to deal with us, to understand what it is like for us. I am very fortunate, because my mama and I, we get along real good. My mama is very smart. She has only a ninth-grade education, but she knows about life.

"Before I was convicted, I never thought about the death penalty. I never thought it could happen to me. I had to go through all this pain and suffering before I realized that I should fight against it. I tell the kids, and the students at law colleges, and the people at conferences, don't wait until this happens to you or one of your loved ones. Get involved. Write those letters. We need to let the lawmakers know that going against the death penalty is not political suicide.

"Politicians follow the wind. Our job is to change the direction of the wind."

MICHAEL RAY GRAHAM, JR.

A Woman He Had Never Met Sparked a Chain Reaction of Lies That Nearly Cost Him His Life

After I'd been on death row a couple of months, Janet Burrell wrote me a letter and admitted that she'd lied. 'I fell in love with you at the trial,' she said, 'I want you to be with me when you get out . . . You ought to be clear very soon, and you ought to be very proud of me.' I wrote her back and said, 'All I want you to do is just tell the truth, and we'll see what happens when I get out.' But I was thinking, 'You crazy woman, you put me in here.'

      —Michael Ray Graham, Jr., convicted of first-degree murder and
        freed after fourteen years on death row. All charges against
        him and his co-defendant Albert Burrell were dismissed.[1]

The Crime: 31 August 1986, Downsville, Louisiana

    Delton Frost, age sixty-five, and his invalid wife Callie, age sixty, were among the hundred or so residents of the rural community of Downsville, Louisiana, located in Union Parish, in the north central sector of the state.* The Frosts lived in a two-room house with a tin roof and wooden screen door, the house where Delton grew up. The nearest neighbor was a quarter mile down the road.

*In Louisiana, the administrative divisions within the state are referred to as parishes, that is, counties.

Delton and Callie Frost could not read or write. For income, they relied on their social security benefits and Delton's earnings from the homegrown tomatoes and watermelons he sold at a roadside stand. Callie was partially paralyzed. Delton had to carry her to the car when the couple drove into town to buy supplies and cash their monthly social security checks.[2]

A child of the Depression, Delton Frost did not trust banks and kept his money in a suitcase under the bed, where he could guard it even in his sleep.

On Labor Day afternoon, Monday, 1 September 1986, A. T. McLemore, who owned land adjoining the Frosts, stopped by to borrow a funnel to put fluid in his bush hog. Delton did not come out, as he usually did. McLemore borrowed the funnel, and came back a second time to get water when his tractor overheated, and a third time to bring some corn for the hogs he and Delton jointly owned. He tooted his horn, and still, Delton did not come out. When McLemore saw that the hogs had not been fed since the day before, he knew something was wrong. He drove to the home of Delton's neighbor, James Bearden, and Bearden phoned the Union Parish Sheriff.*

Sheriff's deputies found Delton Frost on the floor, just inside the front door, dead, shot in the head, slightly above and behind the right ear, and Callie Frost dead in her chair, shot in the face, below her left eye. Ballistic tests would confirm that the murder weapon was a .22-caliber firearm, probably a rifle. An examination of the premises indicated that the killer had fired only two shots, shooting into the home from the outside through a window. On the front porch and on the floor inside, under Delton Frost's body, there was broken glass from the front door. Sheriff's investigators speculated that after murdering the Frosts, the killer had broken in, and that Delton Frost was then pulled from the chair tipped over beside his body. The suitcase containing the Frost's life savings was gone, as was Delton Frost's .22 rifle. Delton's wallet, containing his driver's license, social security card, and six one-dollar bills was found on the bed, under a jumble of clothes and other articles, which apparently had been dumped out of the paper sacks on the top of the heap.[3]

New sheriff Larry Averitt had never conducted a homicide investigation and had very little formal education in the law-enforcement field. He had taken a few criminal-justice courses at Northeast Louisiana University seventeen years before and had completed orientation training in conjunction with serving as a deputy in a neighboring parish and, later, as a state trooper—the position Averitt held for the nine years prior to becoming

*The small community of Downsville had no police force.

sheriff. The Union Parish Sheriff's office typically employed fifteen to twenty people. When Larry Averitt took office in the summer of 1984, he replaced all but three of the previous sheriff's deputies and staff, primarily with friends and acquaintances from his state trooper days.[4] The deputies who responded to the Frost murders had problems using the sheriff's office camera and succeeded in making only one viable photograph of the crime scene.[5] The single footprint discovered in the Frost's yard was rendered useless, when the deputy attempting to make a mold flattened it with plaster.

The coroner concluded that the Frosts were killed Sunday evening. Just before dark, neighbor James Bearden and a friend of his visiting from Georgia had stopped by the house. Delton had come down from the porch to speak with them. Bearden and his friend never got out of Bearden's truck. Delton had company, his nephew Michael Rogers and another young man with long, dark hair, whom Bearden did not recognize.[6]

Michael Rogers, however, was no stranger to Bearden. Rogers lived had with the couple until shortly before the murders. Rumor had it that Rogers had asked his uncle to loan him some money, and Delton Frost had turned him down. Rogers previously had been arrested for aggravated assault and found guilty of disturbing the peace and drawing a shotgun.[7] When questioned by police, Rogers admitted that he had stopped by the house on the evening of August 31, but that his girlfriend Naomi Ruth Toney was with him, not another man. Rogers insisted they only stayed a few minutes.

Police interviewed Rogers and his girlfriend on three separate occasions, in a series of interrogation sessions lasting over ten hours, but no concrete evidence was found linking them to the crime.

Neighbor Willie Wilson had passed by the Frosts' home between ten and eleven on the night of the murder and saw a white car parked in front of the house, probably a Buick or Pontiac; Wilson only glimpsed the car from the rear. Michael Rogers drove a blue Datsun pickup truck.

The Two-Week Road Trip That Took Michael Graham to Death Row

In the summer of 1986, Michael Graham lived in Ocean View, Virginia, with his mother and stepfather, Elizabeth and Doug Lam, and his two younger half-brothers. Michael, age twenty-two, had moved back home, lured by employment opportunities in nearby Virginia Beach, where tourist development was booming. He quickly found work as a house framer for Dick Kelly Enterprises, a local contractor. His girlfriend and infant son were in Richmond. Michael hoped to be able to afford his own apartment before long and was eager to bring his girlfriend and son Brian to live with him.

Michael doted on his half-brothers, Chris, who was seven, and Bobby, who was only four. Doug Lam had been the primary father figure in Michael's life. Michael got along well with Doug and called him, "Dad." Michael's natural father was a truck driver. He and Michael's mother Elizabeth divorced shortly after Michael was born. When Michael was nine, his father phoned Elizabeth from a truck stop and said he wanted to meet his son. Michael's first memory of his father stems from that truck-stop visit. "I was in awe of him. *My real father, that was my real father*." After that, Michael Graham, Senior, made an effort to get in touch whenever he passed through. When Michael was seventeen, his father offered him a job at a detail shop he had just opened in conjunction with the mechanic business he then managed. Michael quit school, and joined his father working full time, helping him get the new arm of his business launched.

As a child, Michael was extremely hyperactive, but given to intense passion when the occasion roused his interest. His grandfather taught him to fish at the age of two. He tagged along with his mother when she went to ceramics classes and quickly mastered the techniques. He loved sports and excelled at Little League. In school, though, he struggled and may well have suffered from attention deficit disorder, a stumbling block to learning not widely recognized in the early sixties.[8] In his adolescence and late teens, Michael had more energy than he knew what to do with. Jailed for trespassing, for "hanging out" at a girlfriend's house, he subsequently was charged with attempted arson, when he and the other prisoners threw their mattress in a pile and tried to set them on fire, mattresses which proved to be flame retardant and only created a lot of smoke. "We were bored and just trying to stir up some excitement," Michael says, embarrassed. "I hate talking about this stuff—but I have to."

Michael Graham does not deny or excuse the mistakes that he made—and there were some.

During the later half of the summer of 1986, Michael met the St. Clair family from Choudrant, Louisiana. Paul St. Clair had come to Ocean View for a job interview and had brought his family along with him for a summer vacation. The St. Clairs found lodging in a hotel across the street from where Michael lived. Michael struck up a friendship with seventeen-year-old Kenny St. Clair. Paul St. Clair got the job, and the family invited Michael to ride back to Louisiana with them to pick up their belongings. They planned to manage the move themselves. The St. Clairs owned a truck, which they had left with a local mechanic for repairs before setting off for Virginia. Michael had never been to Louisiana.

Michael Graham, age 19. [*Courtesy of Michael Graham*]

"I talked to my boss Dick Kelly and asked him if I could go to Louisiana for a couple weeks. 'Sure,' he said 'Your job will be waiting on you when you get back,'" Michael pauses and then chuckles faintly, in an effort to infuse a bit of humor into the stark, hard truth. "It's still waiting I guess."

"I got my pay check and we left. When we got to Choudrant, the St. Clairs' truck wasn't ready. We ended up stuck there longer than we anticipated. Albert was doing the repairs on the truck—Albert Burrell. He lived just down the road. Albert owned a junkyard, and he paid me and Kenny to help him pull engines when he had a crusher come in. It was just a couple-day job, though. Nobody in Kenny's family was working, and it wasn't long before we ran out of money."

Choudrant is a small, rural community in Lincoln Parish, Louisiana, located about ten miles from Downsville, and only slightly larger in population.[9]

Strapped for cash, Michael and Kenny St. Clair found another single-day job doing yard work. When Kenny St. Clair went into the house to get their check, the woman who had hired them asked if he wanted some water. He accepted, and when she went to get him a drink, he pocketed her checkbook.

"I didn't know Kenny had taken the checkbook until we got home, but I'm not trying to make myself out like the good guy in this," Michael is quick to admit. "I filled out the checks." Kenny St. Clair didn't know how to write a check.

They successfully passed two checks, totaling $300.[10]

Michael was worried, though. "I knew it had to stop. I told Kenny, 'We can't be writing any more checks.' I knew sooner or later the lady would get a bank statement and figure out what was going on."

On the afternoon of September 4, less than three weeks after Michael arrived in Louisiana, Michael and Kenny St. Clair were out riding the country roads. They stopped at a convenience market so Michael could buy cigarettes. Kenny headed for the market on the opposite corner, when Michael went inside the store where they had parked. Michael bought his smokes and went back to the car to wait.

"All of the sudden, these cops started coming in from every which way, four or five cars. I knew what was up. We'd passed a check before at the market Kenny had gone into. I panicked. I jumped out of the car and ran into a cornfield, the cops right behind me."

A blow to the head with a flashlight brought Michael to the ground. Kenny St. Clair had decided to try his own hand at check writing. The storeowner, already alerted that a check recently cashed at his business was a forgery, was waiting for him. He phoned the police, and made it clear, brandishing a handgun, that Kenny was not going anywhere. When Michael bolted, he remarked, 'I should shoot the dumb son of a bitch.'

Michael and Kenny St. Clair were charged with two counts of forgery and incarcerated in the Farmerville jail, the seat of Union Parish where both checks had been cashed.

Although Farmerville was considerably larger than Downsville and Choudrant and had a local municipal government and police department, the community of several thousand residents qualified as a small town, at best.[11] The jail was on the top floor of the Union Parish Courthouse. Attorney Robert Earle, who had an office across the street, was assigned to represent Michael. Earle had been a member of the Louisiana Bar for less than a year. He was the Indigent Defender for Union Parish and supplemented his income doing small-town legal work—divorces, collections, and the like.[12] When Michael talked with Robert Earle, he accepted full responsibility for the two forged checks. "I told him Kenny didn't know what he was doing, that I wrote the checks. I was hoping Kenny would just get probation. I wanted to get him out of it.

"I'd been in jail six weeks or so, and they brought Albert in. I figured maybe they got him on a DUI or something. 'What are you in here for, man?' I asked him when he walked by my cell. 'Murder,' he said. 'What?' I said back.

"He told me his ex-wife claimed that he'd killed these two people. That was the first I knew of the murders. That same night, they started questioning me. I didn't watch TV at the St. Clairs'. They couldn't pick up anything to speak of, no news channels. They didn't have cable. I'd never even heard of the Frosts."

Albert "Ronnie" Burrell: Michael Graham's Co-Defendant

In the first grade, a school assessment test diagnosed Albert Burrell as mentally deficient. The Choudrant elementary school did not offer special education classes. In 1962, Albert was institutionalized, and from the age of seven to sixteen, he lived at the Cooley Hospital for Retarded Citizens in West Monroe, Louisiana, about thirty miles from Choudrant.[13]

Albert never learned to read or write, but he managed to earn a living by doing mechanic work for local residents and with the proceeds from his junkyard. He married, and in 1981, he and his wife Janet had a son, Charles. Janet became involved with Albert's brother, James, and a year and a half after Charles' birth, the couple divorced. State social workers took Charles away from Janet because, by her explanation, she was "not ready" to be a parent. Albert had custody of Charles until 1983, when Janet's mother filed suit and won custody. With the help of his family, Albert filed suit challenging the decision, and Charles was returned to him in 1985. Janet's mother tried unsuccessfully to regain custody. That was the state of things between Albert Burrell and his ex-wife Janet Burrell in the summer of 1986.

Albert and Charles lived with Albert's elderly mother, and Albert operated his junkyard and mechanic business from there. Janet recently had married Albert's brother James. Charles was five. Janet Burrell wanted her son back. She talked the matter over with her grandmother and came up with a plan.

On Sunday, 12 October 1986, Janet Burrell phoned Sheriff Larry Averitt at his home. She proceeded to spin a tale about two encounters with her ex-husband that allegedly occurred on the evening Delton and Callie Frost were killed.

She and Albert had agreed to meet at 8:30 that night on a side road not far from Choudrant to discuss their son, Janet told the sheriff. When she got there, Albert said he couldn't stay, and asked her come back at 11:00. Albert was late for the second meeting, and didn't arrive until 11:30, according to Janet's account. She said she got in his car, and that when she moved some clothes out of the way, she uncovered a wallet containing Delton Frost's social security card and driver's license. Albert counted out twenty-seven $100 dollar bills and admitted to shooting into the Frosts' house and busting in their door, according to Janet, *and* she saw blood on Albert's boots!

The sleepy community of Downsville was horrified and traumatized by the Frost murders. Six weeks had passed, but no one had been charged with the cruel, vicious killings. The sheriff's office had no viable leads. Sheriff Larry Averitt had refused the FBI's offer of assistance—perhaps afraid an FBI investigation might be too thorough for his liking. Sheriff Averitt had been embezzling Union Parish funds and operating a mail-fraud scheme.[14]

Less than an hour after Janet Burrell's telephone conversation with the sheriff, four deputies appeared at Albert Burrell's home. He had just put away his mechanic tools after a day's work and changed clothes. Among the numerous vehicles in various states of disrepair on the junkyard lot was a white Buick station wagon, a car fitting the description given by Willie Wilson, who saw a white Buick or Pontiac parked in front of the Frosts' house on the night they were killed. The officers took Albert Burrell into custody and charged him with two counts of murder.

When Michael and Kenny St. Clair were first arrested, Kenny St. Clair had been questioned concerning the Frosts. The murders had occurred just a few days before, and being from Lincoln Parish made Kenny St. Clair an outsider by country standards.[15] Ballistics tests confirmed that the Remington .22 rifle the St. Clair family owned was not the murder weapon. The investigators lost interest in Kenny St. Clair and had not bothered to question Michael at the time.

Suspicion turned back to Kenny, and to Michael, as well, following Janet Burrell's phone conversation with the sheriff.

In a subsequent interview with sheriff's chief investigator Monty Forbess, Janet Burrell had mentioned Kenny St. Clair's name, but only with respect to Kenny and Albert being neighbors and friends.[16] The St. Clair family lived in a mobile home a mere one hundred yards down the road from where Albert lived with his mother and son. There were several reasons why sheriff's investigators may have had cause to suppose that Albert Burrell had not acted alone, or, in any case, realized that they needed additional evidence.

For one thing, there were problems with Janet Burrell's story. Janet had said that Albert had Delton Frost's wallet, but during the initial search of the crime scene, the wallet had been found on the Frosts' bed under a pile of clothes. Janet also maintained that Albert confessed to shooting into the Frost's home. Albert Burrell wore thick glasses and had very poor distance vision.

Then there was the matter of Albert Burrell's mental deficiency, of which local law-enforcement officials were well aware. Eleven years before, Albert had been charged with arson and found incompetent to stand trial. The psychiatric examiner concluded Albert's "extremely limited intelligence and limited comprehension make it difficult for him to understand what is going on around him." Albert was never prosecuted and, instead, committed for a short time to the Louisiana State Mental Hospital. The arson charges eventually were dismissed.

Threats, Lies, and Bribes

"They interrogated me two or three times," Michael says remembering back to the bizarre chain of events that led to his being charged with first-degree murder.[17]

"They interrogated Kenny, too. They told him the same thing they told me. Excuse my language—this is how they said it—'If you all don't tell us what's going on or give us some information, you're both going to be in prison fucking each other.' That's what the deputy said, his exact words. He was trying to get one of us to make up something.

"A couple days after they started questioning me, they formally charged me. I thought it was a joke, that it was all going to get dismissed—there was no way they could ever take me to trial. I asked my lawyer, Robert Earle, 'Are you going to handle me in my false arrest lawsuit?' That's how ludicrous I thought it was."

Robert Earle, Michael's attorney on the forgery charge, had been assigned to represent him on the murder charge, as well. Earle had never tried a homicide case.

Michael requested a lie detector test and was denied.

When Janet Burrell realized how much trouble she had caused for her ex-husband, she contacted the sheriff's investigators and tried to undo the damage, insisting that none of what she had told the sheriff when she phoned him was true. The deputies threatened to put her in jail and said they would take away her son, forever. Scared, Janet Burrell agreed to stick with her story.

Evidently, though, guilt hounded her. A few days before Michael's grand-jury indictment, Janet Burrell visited him at the jail. He had never laid eyes on her before. 'I'm not testifying against you,' Janet insisted, 'The St. Clairs are.'

She knew nothing further, only that the St. Clairs would appear as witnesses.

Michael sums up how he felt in a single word: "Afraid."

What had the St. Clairs told the police? And why?

He had no money. He was a stranger to everyone, except the St. Clairs, who apparently had turned against him. His family was nearly a thousand miles away.

Michael had phoned his mother when he was arrested for forgery. She was worried and anxious. And he was ashamed. Now, in addition to forgery, he was facing a murder charge, and Michael did not want his mother to know. It would all blow over, and later they would laugh about it— Michael tried to make himself believe that—later they would laugh.

Caving in to his interrogators' threats, Kenny St. Clair finally had given them something they could use. He claimed that on the evening of the murders, Albert Burrell came by the trailer, and Michael and Albert left together in Albert's car.

Sheriff's investigators also had begun to question Kenny St. Clair's parents, as well as his two younger sisters and brother. From the outset, the St. Clair family insisted that Kenny was home on the night of the murders, but initially they had nothing more to offer. When the investigators persisted, they said they recalled Michael and Albert being at their home that night—it was Saturday, August 30, they were certain, because Michael and Albert watched wrestling and wrestling was only televised on Saturday. For all their certainty, the St. Clairs had the date wrong; the Frosts were murdered on the evening of August 31. Eventually, Kenny St. Clair's mother, Glenda, and his fifteen-year-old sister, Jackie, made statements implicating Michael and Albert. The final official version was that on the evening of August 31, the pair left the trailer at about 8:30, and when they returned later that night, Michael had blood on his arm.

Jackie St. Clair also pressured her fourteen-year-old friend Amy Opal into helping them save her brother. In investigators' early interviews with Opal, she knew nothing about the murders or Michael and Albert's possible involvement. Finally, though, Amy Opal came around as well, saying that she had slept over at the St. Clairs' on the evening of August 31, and that late that night, she saw Michael and Albert sitting on the sofa with a brown suitcase open on the coffee table in front of them, counting stacks of money. Confirming the St. Clairs' account, Opal likewise said she saw blood on Michael.

Soon after investigators had begun questioning Kenny St. Clair and the members of his family, Kenny was transferred from the Farmerville jail to the pea farm, a minimum-security work farm for prisoners.

Michael Graham and Albert Burrell's grand-jury indictment was scheduled for 24 October 1986, less than two weeks after Janet Burrell first contacted Sheriff Larry Averitt. The lack of evidence and doubtful credibility of the witnesses worried the prosecutor, Assistant District Attorney Dan Grady. Grady consulted with his superior, District Attorney Tommy Adkins; but Adkins maintained that to drop charges against the two men would embarrass the new sheriff.* Sheriff Averitt had come under harsh criticism for failing to find the killers, especially after refusing FBI assistance. Adkins instructed Grady to proceed and leave weighing the evidence to the grand-jury.

Michael testified at his indictment hearing, but there was nothing he could say to substantiate his innocence. He had no idea where he was on the evening of August 31, because there was no reason for him to remember. "I know exactly where I wasn't—at the crime scene. There were only two places where I might have been, because there's nothing much in Choudrant. I'd have been either at the truck stop playing video games or at the poolroom shooting pool. Those are the only two places we ever went."

After he testified, Michael was transported via the elevator back up to the third-floor jail. 'Don't let Graham near that cell until we get Brantley out,' the guard on duty ordered when the elevator doors opened. Olan Wayne Brantley, known to the guards and prisoners alike as "Lyin' Wayne," had been Michael Graham's cellmate, but not anymore. "They moved Brantley out and made him a trustee. That's when I found out Brantley was gonna testify against me."

Olan Wayne Brantley had been in and out of Louisiana psychiatric hospitals since 1979. He had a history of arrests for writing bad checks. In 1981, the Ouachita Parish Court found him not guilty by reason of insanity, and in 1982, the same court ruled he was incompetent to proceed.

Charged a third time with writing worthless checks in Morehouse Parish in 1986, Brantley again raised an insanity defense. Medical experts testified that during his manic phases, Brantley was "talkative, 'fractious,'" and able to tell fantastic stories." The Morehouse Parish Court, however, found him guilty and sentenced him to six years without parole.

---

*Adkins denies voicing concerns about embarrassment to the sheriff.

Brantley was then transported to Union Parish to face forgery charges and incarcerated at the jail in Farmerville.

When Michael was arrested, he was placed in an eight-man cell. Wayne Brantley was among his cellmates. Michael remembers him as "nervous and shaky. He was a liar, you could tell that right off, making up stories that were just too grand to be true."

Two days after Michael's indictment hearing, Wayne Brantley repaid the favor of being elevated to the status of trustee. In an interview with sheriff's investigator Monty Forbess, Brantley claimed that Michael Graham had told him that he and Albert Burrell had killed and robbed the Frosts.

By the time of the trial, Lyin' Wayne Brantley had emerged as the prosecution's star witness.

The Trial

The prosecution decided to try Michael first. Winning a conviction against Michael would be easier, since Michael allegedly had confessed. If the jury found Michael guilty, Albert's conviction was virtually guaranteed.[18]

Local attorney John Sheehan, who had some small amount of prior experience in homicide cases, had been assigned to assist Robert Earle in defending Michael. Sheehan met the criterion of five years practicing law, required of an attorney defending a client in a capital murder case, and was designated lead counsel.[19]

According to Graham, Earle and Sheehan requested and were denied a change of venue.

Jury selection began on 18 May 1987. All of the forty-seven prospective jurors knew about the Frost murders, either from the media or local gossip. John Sheehan questioned only one of the candidates, with Robert Earle conducting the rest of the interviews for the defense. District Attorney Tommy Adkins handled most of the jury-selection interviews for the prosecution. Both the prosecution and defense were permitted to strike (that is, excuse) twelve candidates "without cause." The prosecution used only three of its strikes, while the defense was forced to use all twelve. Judge James Dozier excused all seven candidates whom D.A. Tommy Adkins objected to "for cause"—individuals who either believed Michael was innocent or expressed reservations about asking for the death penalty. Early on in the proceedings, Sheehan and Earle objected to two candidates "for cause," and in both cases Judge Dozier overruled their objections. Perhaps intimidated, they raised no additional objections, using "without cause" strikes to excuse candidates who knew the Frosts personally or who had intimate acquaintances in law enforcement.

Throughout the two-and-half-day jury selection process, three uniformed and fully armed sheriff's deputies were stationed in the courtroom, conveying the impression that Michael Graham was a violent and dangerous criminal. Robert Earle raised a formal objection to the deputies' presence, but Judge Dozier overruled his objection, explaining that an officer was needed for "getting the jurors and so forth," an explanation delivered out of the presence of the prospective jurors, who were left to draw their own conclusions about the heavy security—conclusions that likely condemned Michael. When he stepped out of the elevator en route to the courtroom for the evidence portion of the trial, the door to the jury chambers—whether by accident or intentionally—was wide open. The jurors saw him, in the custody of two armed guards, wearing handcuffs, shackles, and leg irons. The restraints were removed before Michael entered the courtroom, but the suggestion that he was hostile and dangerous already had been planted in the jurors' minds by their pre-trial glimpse of him.

Michael wore a shirt, slacks, and dress shoes belonging to Robert Earle's son. The only clothes Michael had were the ones he was wearing when arrested, a T-shirt, jeans with holes in them, and ragged tennis shoes. The next day, Michael again would wear a shirt belonging to Robert Earle's son, and the dress shoes, but ashamed of having been seen wearing the same pants three days in a row, on his fourth day in the courtroom, he wore the jeans with holes. Attorneys Earle and Sheehan received no funds to aid them in presenting a defense, not even money for an investigation. Both men were under contract with the Indigent Defenders Bureau and paid a mere $1,000 a month, regardless of how many cases they tried, and regardless of whether their clients were homicide suspects or DUI offenders.[20]

Earle and Sheehan decided that Michael should not testify. They had interviewed the proprietors of the pool hall and truck stop, who confirmed that Michael was a frequent patron, but they could not say for certain he had been there on the evening of August 31. "I wasn't going to sit there and lie and say that I was at some specific place, when I didn't know for sure, and later have it proved wrong," Michael explains. "I wish I could have gotten on the stand, because I felt like defending myself." But his attorneys saw no advantage to calling him as a witness. In cross-examination, the prosecution could ask him about his past criminal record. While waiting to be tried for the Frost murders, Michael was convicted of two counts of forgery.

Prosecutor Dan Grady craftily alluded to the forgery charges in his opening remarks, noting that when Michael became a suspect, he already was incarcerated for another crime. When Defense Attorney Sheehan objected, Grady argued that the information constituted evidence, and Judge Dozier agreed.

The prosecution laid the foundation for its case by calling Janet Burrell as a witness. She testified to the two alleged meetings with Albert on the night of the murders and that she found a wallet containing Delton Frost's driver's license and social security card on the seat of Albert's car at the second meeting. Albert had blood on his boots, Janet claimed, and a large sum of cash, $2,700 in one hundred dollar bills. She said she had not come forward until six weeks after the murders because Albert had threatened her. She acknowledged that she and Albert had been battling over custody of Charles, and that since Albert was arrested, her mother had been awarded custody again, but Janet insisted that her reason for contacting the sheriff had nothing to do with the custody issue.

James Burrell, Janet's husband and Albert's brother, corroborated her testimony, saying that on August 31 he and Janet were visiting at her grandmother's and over the course of the evening Janet left twice.

Acknowledging that sheriff's deputies found Delton Frost's wallet, containing his driver's license and social security card, on his bed, sheriff's investigator Monty Forbess explained away the contradiction in Janet Burrell's account, theorizing that Albert had later returned to the Frosts' home and planted the wallet there.

The first several hours of testimony had nothing to do with Michael, but lest he was getting too hopeful, jailer John Day made it a point to set him straight. When Michael was taken back upstairs during a recess, jailer Day remarked, 'I can't tell who's on trial here, you or Albert.' Then he led Michael along a catwalk to a window and pointed down to the stump of a tree on the courthouse lawn—what had once been a very large tree. 'The last guy executed here, we hung him from there,' Day said matter-of-factly, 'If you have any inclinations about running, I keep a twenty-two in my boot.'

When the trial resumed, the prosecution linked Michael to Albert with testimony from the St. Clair family and Amy Opal.

Jackie St. Clair claimed that Michael Graham and Albert "Ronnie" Burrell had been at their house between eleven and twelve o'clock on the evening of Sunday, August 31, that Michael had blood on him, and that the next day, "Ronnie had large sums of money . . . big bills like fifties," . . . he "kept on giving out money" to her family and buying things like snacks and toys.

In contrast, Kenny St. Clair said that Michael and Albert left the trailer about 8:30 on the evening of Sunday, August 31, and did not return until three or four in the morning. Kenny saw only "a little bit of blood" on Michael, and offered an explanation: "He said he got in a fight at the truck stop." Kenny St. Clair, however, proceeded to bolster up his not particularly incriminating account, testifying to an incident that occurred later that day or the following day, when he and Michael were visiting at the Burrells'. The Burrells' TV had audio, but no picture, Kenny St. Clair noted, and during a news broadcast about the Frosts, Michael got up and switched off the set, commenting, 'That was easy.'

Glenda St. Clair, Kenny and Jackie's mother, testified that Michael and Albert were at her home on the morning following the murders and Michael had blood on his left arm, but she had not seen them on the previous evening.

When Amy Opal took the witness stand, she contradicted the testimony of all three of the St. Clairs. Opal said she slept over at the St. Clairs' on Saturday night, corrected herself saying, "I stayed until Monday, I think," then returned to the events of Saturday night when she went to the truck stop with Jackie St. Clair, after which she saw blood on Michael's "hand. I think it was the right arm. I ain't sure." She became hopelessly flustered and confused and could not remember what she allegedly saw Michael doing on the evening of the murders. Prosecutor Grady prompted the fourteen-year-old girl with question after question to no avail. "We got up and . . . we went to get some water or sumpin' . . . he was sitting in the living room doing sumpin' . . . I don't know what he was doing . . . I'm trying to think . . . I can't remember . . . I know he was doing sumpin'." After more than thirty memory-jogging questions by Grady, and Amy Opal stammering "I don't know" or "I can't remember" more than a dozen times, the judge recommended she be given a break to compose herself. When Amy Opal returned, Grady had a transcript of her grand-jury testimony in hand. Defense Attorney Sheehan objected to using the transcript to refresh her memory, but Judge Dozier allowed Grady to proceed. Grady: "Go ahead and read page 55. Miss Opal . . . do you now recall what it was that you saw Mr. Burrell and Mr. Graham doing that night?" Amy Opal finally managed to give a halting account of Michael and Albert sitting on the sofa, counting stacks of money from a suitcase on the coffee table.

Star witness Olan Wayne Brantley testified that Michael had confessed to killing the Frosts, recounting a conversation in which Michael allegedly said that he and Albert went to Delton and Callie Frosts' home and from "outside the house, shot through the window, shot Mr. Delton Frost in the back of the head, Mrs. Callie Frost . . . they shot her right under the eye." Brantley's testimony included only details that had appeared in the media, and he admitted that he had seen TV coverage of the murders, but he insisted that his knowledge of the location of the bullet wounds came from Michael.* Brantley, investigator Forbess, and jailer John Day gave evasive testimony about when Brantley was made a trustee. No one seemed to know the exact date. Brantley conceded that his cell was not being locked, a privilege of trustees, at the time of his first interview with Forbess, when he told Forbess about Michael Graham's alleged confession, but, Brantley, explained, that was only so the kitchen trustees could use the restroom in his cell.

Ostensibly making Brantley's dubious past an open book, Prosecutor Grady questioned him about his prior convictions and his mental health history. Brantley testified that he had been convicted of writing worthless checks and acknowledged that he had spent time in mental hospitals, but he said that he was currently taking medication to control his hyperactivity, which made him as "normal as anybody else." "Were you off that medication when you committed [the crimes]?" Grady asked. "Yes, sir, I was," Brantley answered, an outright lie. Brantley was taking the medication when he wrote the worthless checks in Morehouse Parish, which had earned him a six-year no-parole sentence just a year before.[21]

That the courts had declared Brantley legally insane and mentally incompetent to stand trial was excluded from the rap sheet provided to Defense Attorneys Earle and Sheehan.[22] In cross-examination by Sheehan, Brantley gave evasive and confused answers to questions about his past convictions and the reasons for his hospitalization.

To put the matter to rest once and for all, Prosecutor Grady asked Brantley, "But you were never found to be mentally incompetent or legally insane, were you?"

"I don't guess," Brantley replied.

"And you didn't get any favors from the Sheriff or from the District Attorney—" Grady prompted.

"No, sir," Brantley answered, another outright lie.

In January of 1987, four months before the trial, the district attorney's office reduced Wayne Brantley's Union Parish forgery charge to a worthless checks charge, which carried a significantly less-severe penalty (a maximum sentence of two years, as opposed to ten years). Brantley's two-year sentence, as well as his sentences for Ouachita and Franklin Parish convictions, were to run concurrently with the six-years sentence assigned

---

*At Albert Burrell's trial, Brantley would concede that he had seen newspaper clippings about the murders. As an inmate, Brantley did not have access to local papers. It was never determined who provided Brantley with the material. *State of Louisiana v. Michael Graham*, No. 28,734-B, ruling of Judge Cynthia T. Woodard, Third Judicial District Court, 3 March 2000.

to him by the Morehouse Parish court, meaning that Brantley would not serve a single day of time for the Union Parish, Ouachita Parish, and Franklin parish convictions.[23]

In an effort to cast doubt on Brantley's credibility, the defense called Ralph Reppond, currently an officer of the court and formerly a Union Parish deputy. Brantley's penchant for fabrication was well known to Reppond, but when Defense Attorney Earle asked Reppond about Brantley's reputation in the community, the prosecution objected that the defense had not laid the foundation for Reppond's qualification to testify on the subject, and Judge Dozier concurred. Earle went to great lengths to establish that Reppond had had numerous dealings with Wayne Brantley as a law-enforcement officer and had known Brantley since he was a child, but Judge Dozier still refused to allow Reppond to answer the question.

Michael Rogers, Delton Frost's nephew, and his girlfriend Naomi Ruth Toney gave conflicting testimony about what time they left the Frost's home, how long they spent there on the evening of the murders, and even about what sort of furniture the Frosts' had on their front porch, where Rogers and Toney allegedly both had sat and chatted with Delton Frost. Rogers said that there was one chair and a coffee table. Toney testified that there was no coffee table, and that they all sat in chairs. The contradictions were significant in view of the fact that neighbor James Bearden had seen Michael Rogers and another young man, not a woman, at the Frosts' home on the evening of the murders. The defense, however, was never informed of Bearden's statement to the police.[24] The only testimony concerning James Bearden came from A. T. McLemore, who said he went to James Bearden's home when he became concerned about the Frosts and that Bearden phoned the police. James Bearden was not present to testify, the jury was told, because his doctor had advised him not to appear in court due to his heart condition.

In his closing remarks, Defense Attorney Sheehan called the jurors' attention to the numerous inconsistencies in the testimony they had heard. Prosecutor Grady rebutted every point that Sheehan made.

Grady summarized the sloppy, contradictory testimony of the St. Clairs, Amy Opal, and Janet Burrell in a concise, overly simplified statement: Graham and Burrell left the trailer at "around eight P.M." and returned "around midnight" . . . "Graham's got blood on his clothes, Burrell's got blood on his boots, and they are sitting in the living room counting big stacks of money." Addressing the fact that no fingerprints were found on Delton Frost's wallet (or any other articles retrieved during the investigation), Grady argued that the killers had wiped the prints off the wallet before returning it.

Prosecutor Grady also rectified witnesses' differing testimony as to what car Albert drove on the evening of the murder. Janet Burrell said it was a turquoise Chrysler. Neighbor Willie Wilson had testified to seeing a white Buick or Pontiac at the Frosts' home late that evening. Contrary to both these accounts, when Albert's mother Gladys Burrell testified, she had insisted that Albert had sold the turquoise Chrysler the February before and that the white Buick that police had observed at her home did not run. Grady pointed out that Janet Burrell's description of Albert's car as a turquoise Chrysler was supported by Kenny St. Clair testimony that Albert picked up Michael in a blue car. Fitting the white Buick into the picture, Grady speculated that Albert drove the Buick when he returned Delton Frost's wallet.

Gladys Burrell and two men who had come by to see Albert on business had testified that Albert was home all evening on August 31, working on a truck belonging to one of the men. Prosecutor Grady, however, proposed that a small window of time was unaccounted for, when Albert could have left to kill and rob the Frosts.

Grady conceded that it had not been established which man actually pulled the trigger, Albert Burrell or Michael Graham, but he cited the law of "principals" instructing the jurors that "all persons involved in commission of an offense . . . are all guilty of the same offense."

It had taken the prosecution less than two full days to present its case against Michael Graham. The evidence portion of the trial began late on the afternoon of Wednesday, May 20, with closing remarks delivered early on the afternoon of May 22. The jury reached a verdict in less than two hours. "When they came back in, a couple of the women were crying," Michael recalls, "Robert Earle looked at me and said, 'That's not good.'"

The verdict was unanimous: guilty of armed robbery and murder in the first degree.

Defense Attorney John Sheehan nearly collapsed in the courtroom when the verdict was announced. The judge called a recess for the evening meal, after which court resumed to continue with the sentencing phase of Michael's trial. Too distraught to continue, Sheehan informed co-counsel Robert Earle that he would have to handle the sentencing portion of the trial alone.[25]

Earle and Sheehan had been certain that Michael would be found innocent. They had done nothing to prepare for the sentencing hearing and had no witnesses to speak on Michael's behalf—except for Michael. Following the advice of Robert Earle, he talked about his family and how much he loved his mother and his little brothers. His mother and stepfather, as well as his natural father, were still unaware that he had been charged with murder, let alone convicted.

The decision of the jurors was again unanimous: "death by electrocution."

Stunned and momentarily speechless, Michael raised his face to the judge. Stumbling over his words, he asked permission to read the jurors a note that he had written to them during the recess. Judge Dozier granted his request, and he slowly unfolded a crumpled scrap of paper.

"I would like to say I have no hard feelings about any of you," he paused, struggling to steady his voice. "Please do not let this trial haunt you in any way. You have decided for yourself what you really felt was right or wrong in this case."

"They were victims, too," Michael says of his note to the jurors, "I tried to comfort them."

Scared and frustrated, Michael had turned to God in the weeks leading up to his trial. "I was pacing my cell and I said, 'Lord, I don't know if you're real or not. But if you are, I'd like you to come into my life.'

"I needed something to give me peace."

The Trial of Albert 'Ronnie' Burrell

Usually, authorities transported condemned individuals to the Louisiana State Penitentiary in Angola immediately following their sentencing hearing. Michael was sentenced on May 22, but he remained incarcerated in the Farmerville jail until after the conclusion of Albert Burrell's trial, in late August.[26]

Pre-trial, Sheriff's investigators had tried to persuade Michael to implicate Albert, and perhaps they hoped that facing a death sentence might make him more cooperative. The prosecution's case against Albert Burrell lacked one key ingredient instrumental in Michael's conviction—Michael's alleged confession to Wayne Brantley.[27]

Just two weeks before Albert Burrell's trial began, he allegedly confessed to Wayne Brantley as well.

At the trial, Brantley told the jury that Albert had admitted to killing the Frosts and had asked him to contact the district attorney's office and arrange a deal on his behalf. Brantley also testified that Michael Graham had said that Albert was the triggerman, information contained in Brantley's original statement to sheriff's officers, but withheld from Michael's attorneys at the time of his trial.

When Janet Burrell testified, she confirmed Brantley's account, claiming that Albert said he fired shots into the Frost's home. At Michael's trial, Prosecutor Grady maintained it was not known which man pulled the trigger, when the prosecution had in its possession Janet Burrell's statement naming Albert as the triggerman—information likewise withheld from Michael's attorneys. The remainder of Janet Burrell's testimony was virtually identical to the testimony she gave at Michael's trial: the two meetings with Albert, the wallet, the $2,700 in cash, the blood on Albert's boots.

James Burrell testified against his brother, corroborating Janet's account of leaving home twice on the night of the murders.

The testimony of the St. Clairs and Amy Opal completed the picture.

Like Michael, Albert Burrell was represented by two public defenders.[28] They never brought up Albert's mental deficiency, which, if nothing else, might have prompted the jury to mercy in the punishment phase of his trial.*

On 17 August 1986, the jury found Albert Burrell guilty of armed robbery and first-degree murder, and like Michael, sentenced him to death by electrocution.

Disbelief, Terror, and Chaos: 1987–1988

When Michael received a death sentence, attorney Robert Earle went against Michael's wishes and phoned his stepfather, Doug Lam.†

"My husband Doug came in from work one day, and said, 'I need for you to sit down. I've got something to tell you.' I didn't believe it. I—" Elizabeth Lam's voice falters. That Michael had been convicted of murder and sentenced to death defied all reason and logic. "I couldn't understand."[29]

Elizabeth desperately wanted to phone her son, but regulations at the Farmerville jail forbade Michael from receiving calls. Finally, after several days of unbearable agony, he phoned her, collect, the only means of making contact available to him.

"Michael said he didn't want to worry me, that it all went so fast, and the last thing he ever thought was that they'd find him guilty of something like that. He'd asked Robert Earle not to phone us before." Struggling to make sense of what had happened, Elizabeth spoke with a sympathetic guard at the jail. "She told me, 'We know Michael didn't do it—we know who did!'"

---

*Albert Burrell's attorneys, Keith Mullins and Roderick Gibson, were disbarred in the mid-nineties, Mullins for a narcotics offense conviction and Roderick for dishonesty, fraud, and deceit.

†Prior to the trial, Earle had written Elizabeth and Doug Lam a letter, asking them to phone his office, but evidently the letter had never arrived.

"There wasn't a day that went by when I didn't think, *Michael could be killed*. They messed up putting him there, and they could mess up and just take him out."

On August 22, Michael made the journey from Farmerville to the Louisiana State Penitentiary in Angola, a four-hour drive. Midway, they stopped at a gas station so Michael could use the restroom. At the fast-food restaurant next door, people sat outside eating, gazing with curiosity at the van and the two guards armed with rifles positioned on either side of the rear door. The door opened, and the instant Michael stepped out, the guards took point blank aim, *chg, chg,* the bolts clicking into fire position.

"I had so much iron on me, it weighed more than I did." Michael shakes his head. "What did they think I was going to do?"

A few hours later, the door on Michael's cell clicked into lock position—the only available cell on the tier, the cell normally reserved for inmates whose execution was imminent. The cell had been washed down after its most recent occupant kept his date with death.[30] The six-foot-by-nine-foot enclosure contained a toilet and a mattress on a steel slab bolted to the wall. When Michael sat on the mattress, a reddish-brown liquid oozed to the surface, soaking the seat of his pants.

"I thought it was blood. I freaked out and started screaming for them to get me out of there. I thought the cell was haunted.

"Finally they let me throw my mattress out and gave me another one, and I wiped down the slab. I was scared to death. I'd seen movies about prison, these four-hundred-pound monsters. I'm five foot nine, and I weighed about 130 pounds. The guys at the jail in Farmerville told me, 'When you get in there, hit the biggest guy you can find'—no way I was gonna do that.

"I was glad I was locked up by myself."

Food came to him via a slot in the cell door. He had eight minutes to eat, before a trustee snatched the tray away. Three days a week, for one hour a day, he could go to the yard—a cage, thirty feet long, with a basketball goal at one end, and razor wire at the top. In the yard, he could converse with the prisoners in the adjacent cages. Four days a week, he was let out of his cell to walk the tier for an hour, during which time he could make phone calls and shower. Occasionally, he played chess with another inmate through the cell bars. The other twenty-three hours of every day Michael spent pacing his cell, studying his Bible, and reading. He favored thrillers with a supernatural flare, books by Stephen King and Dean Koontz, set in a surreal world—a world, like the world Michael inhabited, outside the realm of reason and logic.

"I'd walk probably six hours a day, every day. I'm not one that can sit still. I couldn't sleep, and sometimes even in the middle of the night, I'd walk—four and half steps, short steps, then I'd have to turn around—going over my case, everything just running through my mind.

"One of the hardest things about prison was being away from my family. I worried about my mom. I missed my little brothers.

"But even harder than that was knowing I wasn't supposed to be in there.

"When I phoned my dad, my natural father, he told me, 'You need to get on your knees and pray.' He didn't give me the benefit of the doubt, didn't ask if I was innocent, nothing. He thought that I was guilty, and he hadn't heard anything about the case."

Albert Burrell was also on death row at the Louisiana State Penitentiary in Angola, but on a different tier from Michael. They had no contact with one another, unless they happened to be in the yard at the same time.[31]

In January of 1988, five months after their arrival at Angola, Albert's ex-wife Janet Burrell recanted her testimony at both men's trials. In a taped interview at the office of Albert's appellate attorney, Bobby Culpepper, Janet said her grandmother and another woman persuaded her to make up the story about meeting with Albert on the evening of the murders to strengthen her position in the custody battle over Charles. Albert's brother James also recanted his testimony.

Substantiated by the new evidence of the recanted testimony, Attorney Culpepper filed a motion for a new trial.

That same winter, Janet Burrell began penning letters to Albert and Michael.

"After they sent you to Angola, I was determined to get you out . . . and to correct my mistake," Janet wrote to her ex-husband Albert. "When you get out, it will because of me. I am so sorry." Her letters to Michael were even more startling: "I fell in love with you at the trial. I want you to be with me when you get out . . . You ought to be clear very soon, and you ought to be very proud of me."

"Janet said she was 'the only one who could get us out,'" Michael paraphrases, in reference to one of the letters, where Janet admitted she had lied. Michael turned the letters over to Robert Earle and John Sheehan, who continued to represent him on appeal. "I wrote Janet back and said, 'All I want you to do is just tell the truth, and we'll see what happens when I get out.' But I was thinking, 'You crazy woman, you put me in here.'"

The court scheduled Albert's new trial motion for a hearing on July 6. A few days before the hearing, Union Parish sheriff's investigators paid Janet

Burrell a visit and informed her they would personally "see to it" she lost custody of her children, not only Charles, but her son by Albert's brother James, as well, if she recanted her testimony in court.

The hearing was a catastrophe. Dorothy Ambrose, a Burrell family friend, had forced to her to take back her testimony, Janet Burrell claimed when she took the witness stand, saying that on the day she and Ambrose went together to Culpepper's office, Dorothy Ambrose had a "gun in her purse. In her very purse." Dorothy Ambrose testified that Janet's version of events was wholly untrue, as did Janet Burrell's own brother Richard Evans. Courts rarely look favorably on recanted testimony, even under the most convincing of circumstances. Not surprisingly, Albert's motion for a new trial was denied.

In August of 1988, Earle and Sheehan filed a motion for a new trial on Michael's behalf. For Attorney Robert Earle, Michael's trial and conviction "was a gut-wrenching" experience. "I'd come to feel like Michael was part mine," he says, sounding more like a father than legal counsel. Earle did the legwork and wrote the brief for the new-trial motion. Through his research, Earle learned that Wayne Brantley had tried to dodge prosecution in the past by raising an insanity defense, calling into question Brantley's credibility. The motion also took issue with the credibility of Kenny St. Clair who, since the trial, reportedly had made statements suggesting that he framed Michael.[32]

After spending just over a year at the pea farm for his part in the forgeries, Kenny St. Clair had been paroled. He moved with his family to Virginia, where his father had taken the job he had gone there to interview for when the family met Michael. If the information that Robert Earle received was accurate, Kenny St. Clair had boasted to a young man by the name of Kenneth Surgeon that he was letting Michael take the 'rap.' Unknown to Kenny St. Clair, Kenneth Surgeon and Michael had been friends. Surgeon's mother overheard the disturbing conversation and contacted Michael's mother. Elizabeth, in turn, had contacted Robert Earle.

Along with the new-trial motion, Earle petitioned the court for funds to bring Kenny St. Clair back to Louisiana to testify. After much haggling, the request was granted, but by then Kenny St. Clair had disappeared.

Ten years would pass before Michael's motion for a new trial was heard.

The Long Wait

Overwrought with worry, Michael's mother verged on physical and emotional collapse.[33]

"For the first three or four years, I couldn't deal with it at all," Elizabeth Lam confides. "I cried all the time. I drank a lot. When I'd try to go to bed, I kept waking up, and the first thing I'd think of was Michael, and then I couldn't go back to sleep. I wasn't getting any rest, and I found that if I drank enough, I'd just pass out.

"It took a big toll on my marriage. My husband Doug said that he understood what was happening, but there was nothing he could do. We stayed together for the kids.

"Only my very close friends knew. When I tried to tell people what they had done to Michael, I felt like I was always on the defensive. I didn't think they believed me. I got to where I didn't want to talk to anyone about it.

"Michael would call three or four times a week. Our phone bill was sky high. He was always upbeat, saying that he knew he'd get off, because he was innocent. Sometimes I could be upbeat, but other times—Michael could tell I was crying, and he'd say, 'Don't cry, mama,' and I'd say, 'I'm not crying,' but I would be.

"Doug would cry, too, every time he got off the phone from talking with Mike.

"Chris and Bobby missed him terribly and always wanted to talk to him when he called, but they never discussed it much, because of where Michael was. People just didn't understand.

"We were saving for a family vacation so we could go down there and spend a week with him, but Michael kept saying, 'No, save your money. Things are looking good, I'm coming home. I'm coming home.'"

Michael listened to his little brothers grow up over the phone. Bobby, only four when Michael left, was too young to grasp what had happened. "Bobby was always asking me 'When are you comin' home? When you comin' home?' and I'd say, 'Soon, dude, I'm comin' home soon.'"

His mother frequently mailed him photographs of Bobby and Chris, and Michael arranged them in chronological order, comparing the most-recent photograph to the one before, and the one before that, marveling at how much the little boys had changed.

Then in a routine search of his cell, guards confiscated the photographs. His mother mailed more, and Michael started a new gallery from scratch. That was the way of life on death row, making do.

He disassembled a set of headphones, fashioning a tool to cut thread and material, so he could design a Redskins logo to sew onto a hat—the Redskins were his favorite football team. In a search of his cell, the guards found the metal strip and labeled it a "shim," an implement for unlocking handcuffs. "I showed them when I went before the Disciplinary Board that I didn't need a key to get out of handcuffs. My hands were so small, I could just slip them off." The Disciplinary Board declined to accept his explanation. The shim earned him ten days in the "hole."

Inmates in "the hole," a solitary confinement chamber, were denied all human contact and all privileges—no time in the yard or walking the tier, no mail, no cigarettes, no radios, no reading material, except a Bible. How did Michael pass the time? "I read and went stir crazy. I pretty much paced the whole time. If you smoke and you're trying to quit, it's ideal." By the small joke, Michael veers away from further discussion of "the hole," a memory he would prefer not to revisit. "I started up smoking again as soon as I got out," he concedes.

"The daily anxiety of being on death row is hard to explain. You know you're not supposed to be there, and there's nothing you can do about it. That's always with you. It's a weird, weird feeling, a helpless feeling."

He numbed the pain with homemade wine, trading the trustees cigarettes and postage stamps for fruit and fruit juice and fermenting the mixture in two-quart plastic jugs he bought from the canteen. During the summer, the temperature rose to 110 degrees inside the steel and concrete compound, speeding the fermentation process along, but the few occasions of wine-induced oblivion cost him dearly. The guards eventually discovered his makeshift still and sent him to the hole for thirty days.

Michael did another thirty-day stint in the hole for looking at a female nurse, what the prison termed "aggravated eyeballing."

"I wanted to go crazy in there, but I knew if I did, I'd never make it back. I saw people go from sane to insane, instantly. Guys you could carry on an intelligent conversation with, play chess with or dominoes, would all the sudden snap and turn violent and antisocial—they wouldn't talk to anybody, total psychos."

For Michael's first seven years on death row, there were no educational or vocational programs of any kind. He made do. He devised a way of playing solitaire Scrabble and created a pool table from a Monopoly game box, using pencils for cue sticks and for the balls dismantling roll-on deodorant applicators. Another inmate gave him a set of watercolors, and he took up painting. During the holidays, he made greeting cards and sold them to the other inmates, at the price of two or three postage stamps each, depending on the intricacy of the design.

He wrote frequent letters to his family in the early years, but as time wore on, he needed to hear their voices to ward off despair, and phoned instead, always calling collect, the only way inmates could initiate calls. His family was not allowed to phone him. When they sent money, it was deposited in his account at the canteen. Inmates' cells had no electricity, and Michael bought a battery-operated radio to keep abreast of current events. He could watch TV on a set mounted on the catwalk wall outside his cell, a set he shared with several other inmates, with the program selection left up to the guards. More often he read, studied his Bible, and prayed. It was his way to "always look for the silver lining around the cloud—I had to," he says, "to keep my sanity and to keep my sense of humor going."

Nothing, however, could meliorate the despair that overtook him when another inmate was executed. During Michael's first five years at the Louisiana State Penitentiary, six men went to their death in the electric chair.

Michael would fast to pay homage to the spirit of the life departing from earthly existence. "I prayed and asked God to please take the energy and the strength that the food would have given me and pass that to the person being executed," he explains, "I wouldn't eat that day or the day before."

When the State of Louisiana set an execution date for Robert Fraley, Michael was faced with the most traumatic decision of his life.*

"They were getting ready to take Rob to the death house, and he came to me and said, 'Will you blind me? They can't execute a blind man.'

"I thought about it and thought about, and finally I said, 'Yeah, I'll do it.'

"Rob and I were best friends. Everybody knew it. We had to come up with a pretend fight, so it would look like I did it to settle the score. When Rob was out for his hour on the tier, I said to him, loud so people could hear, 'Hey, since they're gonna kill you tomorrow, how about letting me have that ring you're wearing?' We started struggling through the bars and kept at it until the guards came and broke us apart.

"When I was out for my hour on the tier, I found a piece of glass on a window ledge from a broken window. I ground up the glass, and I paid a trustee in cigarettes to get me some bleach. The next morning, I put the ground glass and bleach in a Coke can and made a torch by wrapping laps of toilet paper into a cone shape. When they let Rob out for his last hour on the tier before they took him to deathwatch, I started heating up the mixture, holding the can by the tab over the torch. My hands were shaking like crazy. We had it planned out to where when he walked by my cell, he'd turn toward me and pull his eyes wide open with his fingers, and I'd throw the hot gooey mess in his face. I could hear him coming, his footsteps on the concrete, and I'm thinking, 'Oh, my God, he's gonna pass by, and I've got to hit him with this stuff. I told him I'd do it.' He wasn't maybe twenty feet from my cell, getting closer by the second, and all the sudden a guard called out his name and ordered him to the front desk.

*Not his real name. The man Michael speaks of here is still in prison, and Michael is concerned that the prison might take disciplinary action against him.

"He had a message to phone his attorney. The court had stayed his execution and reduced his sentence to life.

"What Rob said about the State not being allowed to execute a person who was blind—I don't know where he got that idea. I found out later it wasn't true."

The U.S. Supreme Court Rejects Albert Burrell's Appeal: An End and a Beginning

"I watched Albert deteriorate when we were on death row. Sometimes I'd be out in the yard with him, and he'd keep saying to me, over and over, 'I didn't kill those damn people. They got the wrong man.'

"Word got back to me that he'd stay up half the night, talking to himself in the mirror, saying the same thing, for hours and hours, 'I didn't kill those damn people. They got the wrong man. They got the wrong man.' I found out from one of the inmates whose cell was near Albert's that when he was out in the yard, the other inmates would steal his stuff, whoever was out walking the tier at the time. They'd tie a shoe or weight of some kind to a sheet, sling it into his cell, snag his box and pull it up to the bars—it was called fishing people's stuff out.

"On most of the tiers, the guards couldn't see down the row from the front desk. Whoever did the fishing would give what he took to one of the other guys to hide in his cell. If the person who got stole from filed a complaint, and the guards searched the cell of the person who was out at the time, he wouldn't have the goods. Later the stuff would be passed from cell to cell, and he'd get back what he took. The guards knew exactly what was going on, but they didn't care.

"Even though Albert was older than me, I felt toward him like he was my little brother, because of his mental capacity. I didn't want people messing with him.

"'Prey on the weak'—that's the nature of prison.

"All Albert knew to do was tell the guards, 'Hey, somebody took my stuff,' but they weren't going to do anything. It meant a bunch of paperwork for them and contacting the lieutenant and conducting a search, which was pointless anyway. I told the captain of the prison what was happening with Albert and talked him into moving me into the cell next to him. That stopped it, for a while.

"There was only so much I could do. In prison, snitching on another person will get you killed, or if not that, hurt real bad. Mainly, it was just me being there, somebody who was looking out for Albert, who understood how things worked—that and because I was quiet and kept to myself. People didn't know how to read me, if I was dangerous or what. I'm very mild tempered, but people didn't know that. In prison you've got to put up a shield and you've got to keep it there—it's like trying to be another person."

"Once I was off the tier with Albert, my hands were tied. They moved us around a lot so you wouldn't get too friendly with somebody and start planning something. I was only in the cell next to Albert for a couple months."

By January of 1991, both the Louisiana Supreme Court and the U.S. Supreme Court had rejected Albert Burrell's appeal for a new trial, affirming the jury's guilty verdict and making him eligible for execution.[34]

Albert learned about the ruling from a cruel, sadistic guard, who stopped by his cell and announced, 'We just got a call from the courts, Albert. Pack up your stuff. You're going home.' Ecstatic, Albert packed his belongings and sat waiting for his cell door to open. When the guard returned, Albert jumped to his feet like an eager child. 'I was just playin' with ya, Albert,' the guard quipped, chuckling, 'Your appeal's dead.'

Albert sat down on the bed and began pulling out his hair.

When Albert's appeal was rejected, Michael wrote a letter to the Loyola Death Penalty Resource Center, at Loyola University in New Orleans.[35] In the letter, Michael insisted that he and Albert were innocent. The Center provided pro-bono legal assistance to capital defendants at the post-conviction level, that is, after the higher courts had affirmed the trial verdict.[36] Albert qualified for assistance from the Center. Michael did not. His case was still on direct appeal, the first stage. The courts had not yet reviewed his motion for a new trial.

Michael's letter, however, sparked the interest of the Center's director, Rebecca Hudsmith. She showed it to attorney John Holdridge, who had office space next door. Holdridge had given up a promising career with a Wall Street law firm and applied for a grant to work on death-penalty cases in Louisiana and Mississippi.[37] When the funds came through in 1990, Holdridge moved to New Orleans and rolled up his sleeves.

Holdridge represented clients on direct appeal. He agreed to take Michael's case pro bono, serving as co-counsel with Robert Earle. Soon afterward, Holdridge drove to Angola to meet Michael. He harbored no illusions. Although Michael had proclaimed his innocence, that was common among condemned men. Michael was his client, now, and he would do what he could for him, innocent or guilty. Top priority with John Holdridge was saving Michael Graham from execution.

Michael, however, saw things differently. "Michael wasn't concerned with whether or not I was a good attorney," John Holdridge says, recalling their first encounter. "His primary concern was that I believed him."

"I was innocent, and I wanted it understood straight from the jump, no life-sentence deals," Michael insists. "The first things I asked John was, 'You're not going to try to get me a life sentence, are you?'" There were possible grounds for having his sentence overturned, because at the sentencing phase only Attorney Earle represented him, and Earle did not have the requisite five years' experience. Michael adamantly opposed any such strategies. "If you get a life sentence, people lose interest. If I'd gotten a life sentence, I'd still be in there."

Robert Earle filled Holdridge in on developments in Michael's case since the trial. The most promising new angle was Kenny St. Clair's alleged boast to Kenneth Surgeon about framing Michael. Holdridge threw his energy into bringing Kenneth Surgeon to Louisiana to testify. The judge presiding over the jurisdiction in which Surgeon resided refused to order Surgeon to appear, and Holdridge took his request to the Virginia Supreme Court. After much legal maneuvering, the Virginia Supreme Court finally ordered the lower court to produce Surgeon, but by then Kenneth Surgeon had vanished.

Holdridge filed a motion with the Third District Court in Louisiana for funds to hire an investigator to find Surgeon.

When the court delayed ruling on the motion, John Holdridge decided not to push the issue. "You're never eager to move a case along when you represent someone who has a death sentence," he explains.

Holdridge wholeheartedly believed in Michael's innocence, but Janet Burrell's recanting her recantation at Albert's new trial hearing made the case manifestly problematic. Holdridge had a hunch that proving Michael's innocence hinged on finding Amy Opal.

And meanwhile, the clock was ticking. Louisiana had abandoned using the electric chair in 1991, and after a brief hiatus from the distasteful business of death, resumed executions in 1993 by the method of lethal injection. The first inmate executed by the allegedly more humane tactic was mentally retarded, like Albert.[38]

Albert Burrell Comes within Seventeen Days of Keeping a Date with Death

Ironically, although eligible for execution, Albert Burrell was no longer automatically entitled to assistance of counsel. The U.S. Supreme Court

1989 decision *Murray v. Giarratano* ruled that the constitutional right to assistance of counsel did not extend to post-conviction appeals.

Nick Trenticosta, co-director of the Loyola Death Penalty Resource Center, persuaded several attorneys from the Minnesota law firm Lindquist & Vennum to represent Albert pro-bono.

Chuck Lloyd, Tom Fabel, and Steven Pincus headed up Albert's legal team.* They traveled to Louisiana to visit Albert at the prison and quickly realized he would be no help whatsoever in preparing his defense. All he could tell them was, "I didn't have nothing to do with them two old people. I didn't kill anyone," a litany repeated over and over in conversation after conversation. Records from Albert's arson arrest indicated that he had an estimated IQ of between fifty and sixty. Precedent set forth by the U.S. Supreme Court stated that an individual who was incompetent and unable to assist in preparing his defense could not be subjected to a trial. For that reason alone, Albert was entitled to a new trial. More important, though, Albert's attorneys, like Michael's attorneys, believed their client was innocent.[39]

In April of 1995, Prosecutor Dan Grady gave a sworn affidavit to Albert's attorneys saying that he had advised against indicting Albert and Michael because of the "weak" evidence and "questionable credibility" of the witnesses, but that the district attorney had directed him to present the case to the grand jury "to avoid embarrassment to the sheriff." In an interview a few months later, Janet Burrell recanted her trial testimony a second time and finally spoke up about the sheriff's investigators repeated threats to take away her children if she did not stick with the story she had told Sheriff Larry Averitt on that fateful Sunday afternoon in October of 1986. Her husband James Burrell also recanted his testimony at both trials, saying he had lied because of the deputies' threats to his wife.[40]

John Holdridge had begun working closely with Albert's attorneys, sharing information and leads. Holdridge met regularly with Michael and kept him abreast of new developments. Unfortunately, Janet and James Burrell's repeated flip-flopping had sorely damaged their credibility. Still, Grady's affidavit and the Burrell's recantations were good news.[41]

Inside the prison, circumstance also had taken a turn for the better. The new warden, Burl Cain, had initiated spiritual seminars and promised educational programs in the near future. In the summer of 1995, the prison hosted a death-row inmates' banquet, and Michael's mother and stepfather visited for the first time.[42]

Elizabeth Lam's difficulty in grappling with the horror of having an in-

*Other Lindquist & Vennum attorneys who assisted with the case included Keith Ellison, Candee Goodman, Helen Mary Hughesdon, Ann Kennedy, Joe Maternowski, Pete Michaud, Reuben Mjaanes, Steve Quam, David Sasseville, Loren Thacker, and Jessica Ware.

nocent son on death row had exacted a high price. In 1993, after fifteen years of marriage, she and her husband Doug had separated. They remained friends, though, and drove together to Louisiana to see Michael. "All the way there, I kept telling myself don't get emotional, don't cry. Try to hold back," Elizabeth remembers. "And when I first saw Michael, it was just—I know this sounds hard to believe—but it was like we'd never been apart. I was fine," Elizabeth pauses, "I just hated to leave him again."[43]

Because Elizabeth and Doug had traveled so far, the prison arranged for an all-day contact visit in the prison captain's office, where they could touch and hug Michael with his handcuffs, chains, and shackles removed. Doug was stunned by how small Michael seemed. Compared to most inmates and the guards—large, imposing men—"Michael looked like a little kid," Doug recalls. "It's a terrifying place. The high walls and razor wire and guards in the towers, with their guns following your every move."[44]

Michael sat behind a glass partition, wearing a full complement of iron restraints at the no-contact visits. "It was embarrassing to have my mom and dad see me like that," he says wistfully.

Michael had been selected to address the banquet guests on behalf of the inmates. His handcuffs were taken off for the ceremony, but not his leg irons. Nervous and trembling, he shuffled up to the podium with shackled feet and unfolded the piece of paper on which he had written the speech he intended to read. Then he changed his mind, and spoke from his heart.

He talked about hope, how they all needed to have hope.

The average life expectancy of a death row inmate was nine years. The summer of his parents' first visit in 1995, Michael reached his nine-year anniversary.[45]

Early in 1996, Michael's attorneys learned that Wayne Brantley had cut a deal with the prosecution, receiving a reduced sentence in return for his testimony. "I've been telling them that all along," Michael wrote in a letter to Doug, venting his frustration. "My attorneys are good at what they do, but they are not taking how long I've have been here into enough consideration. The philosophy of my lawyers seems to be: A good client is a live client. They executed another man here March 1st, and every time this happens it spooks the lawyers into wanting to slow the appeals process down."[46]

Baton Rouge attorney Michele Fournet recently had joined Michael's defense team, like John Holdridge working on Michael's case without pay. Fournet had been trained by one of the top criminal-defense attorneys in the state, and Michael was eager for her to become familiar with his case and the issues so they could "get rolling."[47]

He bought a manual typewriter and set himself the task of learning to type, with the intent of eventually helping with the legal work on his case. When GED classes became available, he immediately added his name to the waiting list, eager to finally earn his high school diploma. "This is my goal for now," he wrote in another letter to Doug, "but I understand there will be an opportunity for vo-tech afterwards.

"I hope I am not here that long . . . I know it's best not to let it worry me, but still I can't forget that I have a son in the world. If my memory is correct, Brian will be eleven years old this year . . . I pray that some day I will be given the opportunity to be some kind of a father to him . . . Time stands still in here."[48]

In June of 1996, Elizabeth and Doug visited again. That same month, the state of Louisiana set an August 29 execution date for Albert.[49]

Michael learned about Albert's pending execution from John Holdridge. "It hadn't come to that, yet, John told me. He was certain Albert would get a stay." Still, for Michael, it was sobering news. "If it had been me, I would have been worried. I don't think Albert understood how serious it really was."

Judge James Dozier halted Albert's execution on August 12.[50]

The brief requesting a stay argued that Albert had not received a fair trial and that he was innocent. Nick Trenticosta, who recruited Albert's attorneys, had continued to work with them in representing Albert. On a recent trip to Farmerville, Trenticosta had obtained the prosecution's files on the case, which contained crucial documents withheld from Albert and Michael's trial attorneys: the investigators' notes from the initial interviews with the St. Clairs and Amy Opal. In sharp contrast to the testimony they later gave at the trial, the St. Clairs and Amy Opal did not say anything derogatory about Michael or Albert in their early statements and in no way linked them to the murders.[51]

Trenticosta provided John Holdridge with copies of the interview notes—information Holdridge would not have had access to otherwise, since under the tenets of Louisiana law, the State was not required to turn over the prosecution's files until a defendant had arrived at the post-conviction level.[52]

That the prosecution had not provided the trial attorneys with the initial interview notes constituted a Brady violation. In the 1963 decision, *Brady v. Maryland*, the U.S. Supreme Court ruled that failure to disclose evidence favorable to the accused entitled the defendant to a new trial.

Michael wanted action. Responding to his impatience, John Holdridge talked with him about the possibility of negotiating an Alford Plea in exchange for his release based on the time he had already served. By the provisions of an Alford Plea, the defendant does not admit to committing the act, but admits that the prosecution likely could prove the charge. In a letter to Doug, Michael expressed his dilemma over what he would do if offered such a deal—in essence, an admission of guilt. "If I'm offered a time-served plea and . . . I don't make the right decision, I could die. I won't by any means take a life sentence . . . I would make them execute me before I would take life in this place."[53]

By the close of 1996, though, all discussion about securing Michael's release under the provisions of an Alford Plea had come to an end.

John Holdridge had found Amy Opal.

Opal had married and now went by the name Amy Hutto. In an interview with Holdridge, she conceded that she had been and still was afraid of the St. Clairs, and that they had persuaded her to lie to protect Kenny. In October, Amy Opal-Hutto gave a sworn affidavit to John Holdridge recanting her entire testimony at the trial.[54]

Heartbreak and Tragedy

In late March of 1997, Albert Burrell's mother died of a heart attack. Shattered by the news, Albert fell into a state of incoherent shock and despair.

'Please, God, just let me get out before something happens to my mama,' Michael asked in his prayers. Worn down by the stress, his mother had developed a heart condition and already had suffered several minor heart attacks.[55]

Between worrying about Albert and worrying about his mother, Michael's anxiety level verged on the breaking point. Then the unthinkable happened. Water began seeping under the levee that held back the Mississippi River, following days of torrential, nonstop rain. If the levee gave way, the entire prison compound would be underwater—except, ironically, for death row.

In a middle of the night evacuation, the prison relocated the entire non-death-row population to the death-row compound. A tent city set up outside the facility housed 3,000 inmates. Housing the remaining 2,100 inside, guards locked three men in each six-foot by nine-foot cell.

Michael recalls the experience with unabashed horror. "The one guy in with me weighed 300 pounds. And it wasn't just the three of us in there—we had all our belongings. Six feet by nine feet, a space the size of a small bathroom, and part of that taken up by the toilet and the bunk. We literally couldn't move. The guards told us we might have to stay there all summer, and what with the heat at a hundred degrees plus and no running water—people were bound to turn violent, go crazy. It was one of the scariest moments of my life."[56]

After a day and half, the water began to subside, and life on death row returned to normal. Michael again had some small modicum of privacy—if you could call it that.

Inmates used the toilet in full view of a guard who might be walking by. The incessant din from hundreds of men's voices echoed night and day inside the steel and concrete tomb—a noise barrage compounded by radios and TVs, and, during the summer, the whir from huge industrial fans. Michael bought ten-cent earplugs from the commissary and concedes that he preferred the fans to the alternative. During a heat wave, with temperatures pushing the 107-degree mark, the fire marshal ordered the fans removed, because of an overload on the electrical circuits.

It was so hot and humid the concrete sweated.[57]

Progress at Last

In August of 1997, John Holdridge was in Farmerville doing research on Michael's case, and Robert Earle suggested they go across the street to the pharmacy for a cup of coffee. At the popular town gathering spot, Robert Earle introduced John Holdridge to the mayor and the former Farmerville police chief, George Cothran.

When Holdridge and Cothran struck up a conversation about the Frost murders, the former police chief goaded Holdridge with an intriguing challenge: 'Ask me the right questions, and you'll like the answers, but you've gotta ask the right questions.'

Holdridge fired away. Cothran, it turned out, knew Deputy Monty Forbess quite well. Prior to becoming lead investigator for the Union Parish Sheriff's Department, Forbess had served on the Farmerville police force. Forbess had an established practice of threatening to take away the children of female witnesses who refused to provide him with the testimony he wanted, Cothran confided—insider information about Forbess' tactics that fit hand-in-glove with Janet Burrell's account of the deputies' threats.

Holdridge pressed on, asking Cothran about the murder investigation, and learned that a few days after the murders, a local resident gave Cothran a .22 rifle that he had found in a dumpster near the Frosts' home. Cothran had passed the firearm along to the Union Parish Sheriff's Department. To the best of Cothran's knowledge, the rifle had since disappeared and was never tested for comparison to the .22-caliper bullets that killed the Frosts.

Investigators' reports given to attorneys Earle and Sheehan made no mention of the firearm recovered from the dumpster.

From Cothran's description, it may have been the .22 rifle owned by Delton Frost and discovered to be missing from the house after the murders—a rifle that Delton Frost's nephew Michael Rogers would have known about and had easy access to.

In December of 1997, John Holdridge filed an amended motion for a new trial. Although by then the funds had come through to pay for an investigator to locate Kenneth Surgeon, and Surgeon had been found, Holdridge decided not to pursue that line of defense, testimony that would have been hearsay, at best. The amended new-trial motion argued that the police and prosecution had withheld critical evidence supporting Michael's claim to innocence and that the withheld evidence along with newly discovered evidence totally unraveled the State's case against him.[58]

In early March of 1998, Michael traveled back to Farmerville for the hearing, his first time outside the penitentiary walls in ten years. The new Union Parish jail had electrically operated cell doors. During the middle of the night, with the hearing scheduled to begin the next morning, Michael's cell door mysteriously opened. His mind flashed back to jailer John Day's cautionary advice ten years before, when Day had led him to the jail window and pointed out the hanging tree on the courthouse lawn: *If you have any inclinations about running, I keep a .22 in my boot.*

Michael ducked his head out of the cell, looked up and down the empty corridor, leaned back inside, and pulled the cell door manually closed.

Newly elected Judge Cynthia Woodard presided over the hearing. In office less than a year, she had unseated Judge James Dozier, a fixture in Union Parish, serving as Third District Court judge for more than a decade. An underdog candidate who came from behind to win the election, Judge Woodard risked coming under sharp attack if she granted a new trial to a convicted murderer whom 12 jurors saw fit to sentence to death.[59]

Following the hearing, Michael went back to death row to wait for Judge Woodard's decision, a decision it took her two years to make.

Michael paced, and waited, and paced. Finally admitted to the literacy program he had signed up for in 1996, Michael applied himself to studying for his GED, and in the fall of 1999, scored grade level 12+ on a preliminary screening. His instructor scheduled him to take the GED at the next testing session in December.

On Thanksgiving night of 1999, four men escaped from death row, sawing through the bars of their cells with hacksaw blades smuggled into the prison in books. They made it as far as the Mississippi River before the dogs caught up with them.

Outraged, Warden Burl Cain called an immediate halt to all educational programs and seminars.

Michael never got to take his GED test.

And worse, still, Cain initiated a new spiritual reform program called "Be your brother's keeper," which, as Michael describes it, meant, "snitch on another person."

"In prison, you can't do that," he says shaking his head, "It gets people killed. After Cain started up with the 'My brother's keeper' stuff, the situation started getting really, really bad."

An aura of dashed hopes and distrust permeated the death-row compound.

On 4 March 2000, Michael was in the shower when a guard poked his head in and said, 'Call your attorney.' "On a Saturday?" Michael answered back. He made the phone call, still dripping, wrapped in a towel.

"John was hollering and screaming and crying. I couldn't understand him at first. He was saying, 'We got a new trial, man, we got a new trial.'"

The Last Nine Months

Judge Cynthia Woodard explained her reason for granting Michael a new trial in a carefully worded and meticulously documented thirty-eight page opinion. She cited both new evidence and nine instances of "Brady material," withheld evidence favorable to proving Michael's innocence.[60]

Had the defense known about the .22 rifle found in the dumpster, it would have bolstered their contentions about other suspects, Woodard said. Similarly, withheld pre-trial statements of James Bearden—who told investigators he saw Michael Rogers and an unidentified male, not a female, at the Frosts' home on the night they were killed—may have prompted the defense to investigate further their theory that Michael Rogers killed the Frosts.

Regarding the withheld statements of the St. Clairs and Amy Opal, Woodard pointed to the numerous contradictions when compared to their trial testimony. Jackie St. Clair initially said she saw Albert with one $100 bill and that he used the money to buy a car part, not, as she testified, "large sums of money . . . a whole lot . . . big bills"; Kenny St. Clair initially told the investigators that Michael's remark 'That was easy' pertained to his turning off the Burrell's malfunctioning TV, in no way connecting the murders with the comment; Kenny's mother Glenda St. Clair initially told investigators she did not know what day she saw blood on Michael's arm; and Amy Opal, in her initial interview, made no mention of seeing Michael and Albert counting money and said she had not seen any blood on Michael or anyone else.

Conceding that recanted testimony was usually suspect, Woodard maintained Amy Opal's recantation appeared reliable, especially given that her false testimony was prompted by fear of the St. Clairs.

Woodard, however, refused to give credence to the recanted testimony of Janet and James Burrell who had repeatedly changed their minds. That Deputy Monty Forbess threatened female witnesses was "disturbing," Woodard acknowledged, but there was no proof that it had occurred in Janet Burrell's case.

Woodard devoted nearly a third of her opinion to the doubtful credibility of Olan Wayne Brantley's testimony, prefacing her remarks with Prosecutor Dan Grady's admission that Brantley's "testimony played a major role in Mr. Graham's conviction."

"The true nature of Brantley's mental illness is highly exculpatory," Woodard stated, noting five circumstances that precluded that information from being forthrightly introduced at the trial: the "rap sheet" the prosecution provided to the defense did not include the information about Brantley's prior criminal insanity rulings; Brantley gave false and misleading testimony about his medications; the court refused to allow testimony by law-enforcement officer Ralph Reppond about Brantley's long-standing reputation for untruthfulness; and the prosecution "affirmatively misled the jury by its questions" to Brantley, asking, "You were never found to be mentally incompetent or legally insane, were you?" to which Brantley replied, "I don't guess."

Woodard also took issue with the prosecution's failure to disclose that, in return for testifying, Brantley's charges and sentence for pending crimes were reduced, information that might have affected the weight the jury gave to his testimony. Further calling into question Brantley's credibility, Woodard cited the new evidence that that, since Michael Graham and Albert Burrell's trials, Brantley had claimed that two other capital defendants had made jailhouse confessions to him, suggesting a pattern of snitching "to cut better deals for himself."

Other new evidence that Woodard regarded as significant was testimony confirming that, eight months before the murders, Albert Burrell sold the blue Chrysler Janet Burrell said he was driving that night.

Not only was the jury misled about "many of the facts of this case," Woodard concluded, "this jury was misled about certain areas of the law." In instructing the jury, the prosecution incorrectly argued the Law of Principals, by suggesting "all persons involved in commission of an offense . . . are all guilty." For the standard to apply, Woodard explained, the jury must find that the defendant "had specific intent" to commit the crime.

"We can have no confidence in the outcome of this trial," Woodard wrote in summary. "The defendant has met his burden of proving that he is entitled to a new trial."

The Union Parish district attorney's office had long since withdrawn from Michael's case, claiming conflict of interest because John Sheehan, Michael's lead trial attorney, was now an assistant D.A.[61]

Would the state of Louisiana retry Michael or would they dismiss the charges?

The decision rested with the office of the State Attorney General, which had taken over as acting prosecutor.

For Michael, the months dragged by—April, May, June . . . November. "After Judge Woodard granted me a new trial, I knew I was going to be released. The months after that were the hardest time I did in there. That's when the anxiety really kicked in. Across from my cell was a window, and I could see the front gate in the yard—I was supposed to be walking out of there. I wish I hadn't been able to see that gate."

Michael paced. Four and a half steps to the bars, the window view, turn, four and a half steps to the toilet, turn, four and a half steps to the bars, the view through the window, the gate.

On 11 December 2000, the Attorney General's office announced that it had decided not to retry Michael. Judge Woodard insisted, however, that before he could be released, the Attorney General's office needed to prepare a written explanation for its decision.

Home for Christmas, Almost

The report subsequently prepared by the Attorney General's office stated that there was "a total lack of credible evidence linking Graham and/or Burrell to the crime." Charges against both men were dismissed.[62]

"A few days before Christmas, John phoned me and said it was just a matter of getting everybody lined up to sign the paperwork," Michael recalls. "I couldn't sleep knowing I was getting out in just a couple days. I was supposed to be released Christmas day—they couldn't find the judge. She was on vacation."

Holdridge was scheduled to leave for a long overdue vacation, as well. With the certainty of Michael's release imminent, and yet unconfirmed,

Holdridge considered canceling his plans, but Michael, ever confident, insisted that he go.

Judge Woodard signed the document on December 27.

On the morning of December 28, Louisiana TV and radio stations broadcast the announcement of Michael's release, set for later that same day. He would be the first man in the history of the prison to walk off death row onto the streets (as opposed to being freed following a court decision at the district level and released from a local jail).

Talk buzzed among the inmates. Even though Michael had known since early December that he would be freed, he had kept the news to himself. "I was gonna be leaving all those guys behind, and I didn't want to seem too excited. That just makes them miserable, knowing someone else is getting out, and wishing it was you."

Albert's attorneys had hoped the Attorney General's decision to drop charges meant Albert would be released, as well. Legally, though, Albert's circumstances differed from Michaels. Albert had passed the deadline for introducing new evidence—in Louisiana, one year after the verdict was affirmed on direct appeal. Judge Woodard insisted on conducting a hearing to review Albert's case. Albert's attorneys phoned him and tried to explain. Distraught and babbling incoherently, the only thing Albert understood was that Michael was getting out, and he was not.

In the final hours in his cell, Michael wrote Albert a letter. The letter passed from hand to hand within the prison and reached Albert, where another inmate read it to him. 'You'll be right behind me,' Michael promised, telling Albert not to worry, he would be freed too, and soon. Michael's reassurance put Albert at ease and lifted his gloom. He smiled as he watched Michael walking out the prison gates on TV.

In return for the nearly fourteen years he had spent on death row for a crime he did not commit, the state of Louisiana gave Michael ten dollars for transportation and a denim jacket that was four sizes too big. His attorney Michele Fournet was there to oversee his release. An enfilade of reporters waited just outside the gate. Fournet advised them that Michael did not have anything to say, but they fired away with questions. 'How do you feel?' "Good," he answered. 'What was prison like?' "Bad." 'Where are you going?' "Home."

'We're going to the airport,' Attorney Fournet chimed in, hurrying Michael into her car. They shared a laugh, watching the reporters speed off in the direction of the interstate, and headed for the bus station in Baton Rouge. On the way there, Michael talked to his mother on the speakerphone in Fournet's car. He was unaware that kind of technology even existed. Fournet bought him a bus ticket to Roanoke, Virginia, where his family now lived, gave him $100 traveling money, and hugged him good-bye. She had offered to buy him a plane ticket, but Michael declined, un-easy about flying. He had never been on a plane.[63]

At a layover in Atlanta, Michael cashed the ten-dollar prison check and gave it to a homeless man asking for spare change. He tried to use the pay phone to call his mother and let her know the bus was running late, but the electronic voice prompt insisted he enter his credit card or phone card number. Unable to bypass the instruction, he finally called collect, some-thing he had promised never to do again.[64] Further unnerved by the talk-ing vending machine when he tried to buy a Coke, he gave up on the new-fangled machines and made the entire 988-mile trip, which took over twenty-four hours, without food.

When the bus finally pulled into Roanoke at ten o'clock the following evening, a vanload of people waited to greet him—Elizabeth, Doug, his half-brothers Chris and Bobby, and other close family friends. They drove to Doug's house and celebrated with Christmas presents and a welcome-home dinner prepared by Elizabeth, featuring her son's favorites, shrimp scampi and lobster tail.

Michael ate too fast, accustomed to eight-minute meals, and finished before the rest of his family had barely sampled their vegetables.[65] Loud noises terrified him. In the bathroom, he could not bear to close the door—the fear of being confined in a small space would be with him for some time to come.

He could not climb a flight of stairs without stopping to catch his breath. He did not know how to use a cell phone or how to operate a CD player, and computers utterly baffled him. He could not make eye-contact with women—a legacy from the month spent in the hole for "aggravated eyeballing"; and the mere sight of uniformed law-enforcement officials caused him to panic. He was afraid to leave the house, afraid people could tell from his pale complexion that he had been in prison, afraid people would wonder why he was not wearing shackles and chains.[66]

Life on the Outside

Early on the morning of 2 January 2001, Judge Woodard reviewed Al-bert's motion for a new trial. His attorneys pointed out that, even though Albert had passed the deadline for introducing new evidence, Louisiana law allowed judges leeway in granting a new trial, if "the ends of justice would be served." Judge Woodard signed the motion, and Albert was re-leased later the same day.[67]

His sister Estelle Branch and brother Larry met Albert at the gate. Estelle arranged for a reunion with his son Charles in Shreveport. Charles was nineteen now. Father and son exchanged warm hugs, their first physical contact in fourteen years. Then Albert rode with Estelle to her home, a small cattle ranch in northeast Texas. He has lived there ever since. He has no means of supporting himself. During his long sojourn on death row, Albert Burrell lost the knack he once had for repairing cars.[68]

Still, according to Michael, Albert's doing "100 percent better" than he was in prison. Michael and Albert were reunited in Chicago at the 2002 National Gathering of the Death Row Exonerated, sponsored by Northwestern University. Their paths crossed again in Louisiana, in 2004, when they returned to give depositions for the wrongful conviction civil suit they have filed against Union Parish officials.

Aside from the ten dollars in traveling money the prison provided, neither man has received a penny for the nearly fourteen years they spent wrongfully incarcerated, waiting to die.

For the first several weeks following his release, Michael found himself caught up in a whirlwind of activity. He gave interviews one after the other, and in late January, addressed the Virginia General Assembly, speaking out against Virginia's twenty-one-day rule. By the rule, defendants had only twenty-one days to discover and introduce new evidence following sentencing. "If this would have happened to me in Virginia, I would have been dead," Michael told the legislators.[69] Later that year, he spoke before the United States Senate Committee on the Judiciary in support of the Innocence Protection Act. "I never figured this could happen to an innocent person before it happened to me . . . I ask you to listen to my story and to the many others like mine, and do what you can to fix the process."[70]

Michael adamantly supports abolition of the death penalty and speaks publicly about his experience whenever asked, but when the stage lights dim, he goes back to what he calls home, a small trailer he bought from his brother, located in a mobile-home park where there is scarcely enough room to park a car between his unit and the one next door. "Money has been my biggest struggle since I got out. It's hard to start over at thirty-seven."

With his past experience as a house framer, Michael found a job as a roofer soon after his release, a position that only lasted a few months. The business failed, and he put in an application with the employment service Manpower. Confronted with the question, *Have you ever been convicted of a felony? If yes, explain* and a two-inch line allotted for an answer, he answered 'no.' When a computer search turned up his conviction and death sentence, Manpower rejected his application, because he had lied. He has had many jobs since then, but most of them have been limited-term positions, acquired through temporary-employment services. "In my mind, I wasn't convicted," he says, "because I was later exonerated. I've lost a few jobs for not putting it down. When I did answer 'yes' to the felony question, after I tell them what happened, people are just fascinated. They get on the computer and find out what I'm telling them is true. But I don't like having to sit there and explain it, time after time." Michael hesitates and uncharacteristic annoyance flares in his voice, "I ain't got the time for that."

Michael is still extremely hyperactive. "He can't sit still for five minutes," says his stepfather Doug Lam, "I don't know how in the name of God he ever stood it in prison. He told me he did a lot of pacing—he must have worn a path in the concrete. And now, he's trying to recapture all those lost years. It's so sad. For me, my twenties and early thirties, those were the best years of my life—he missed all that."[71]

Michael had a girlfriend within a month of being released, and six months later he was engaged to be married, to yet another woman, another relationship that never reached fruition.

His current relationship is more stable. He met Cheryl Milton through his mother. The two women were friends and coworkers.[72]

"Sometimes I get depressed," Michael concedes. "The other women I was with, they didn't understand. Cheryl does. It means a lot. She's really been there for me."

When Michael slips off into thinking about his son Brian, as he frequently does, the tears come.[73] Cheryl suggested they look for Brian on the Internet, and she helped him do a preliminary search, but then Michael called a halt to the process. "Brian could be calling somebody else 'Dad.' Before I interrupt their lives, I want to be on my feet. He'll—" Michael's voice trails off, then he collects himself and continues, "He'll turn twenty-one in August."

Michael has learned to use a cell phone, but admits that he is "intimidated" by computers. "I've got people who are willing to teach me," he shrugs. "I just don't have the time or the patience."

The word time recurs repeatedly in his conversation. "I don't have the time to focus on religion, like I did in prison . . .when I have the time, I want to get back into watercolor painting. I haven't done it since I got out.

"It just seems like everything has got a lot faster paced. Just life in general."

Michael served out his full ten-year sentence for the two counts of forgery. Under normal circumstances, he would have been paroled within two years or less.

During the nearly fourteen years he spent on death row, his hair fell out

Michael at Smith Mountain Lake, the site of his dream home. [*Courtesy of Michael Graham*]

and his teeth rotted, from lack of preventative dental care.[74] The best a condemned man could hope for was to have a decayed tooth pulled. Michael cannot afford the remedial dental work he needs, probably in excess of $40,000, and he has never had a job that offered medical or dental benefits.

He liked his most recent job as an order clerk for a marketing firm, but was laid off during a slow period. His longest job, just over a year, was at a Frisch's Big Boy where he "cooked, washed dishes, whatever needed done." He talks about brushing up on his math and science, and taking the GED test, when he finds "the time."

"If I had one wish, it would be for my lawsuit to come through, so I could look after my family." His mother and stepdad both struggle with chronic health issues. "And Cheryl and I could get married," Michaels add, smiling. He wants to buy a lot on Smith Mountain Lake, a forty-five-minute drive from where he and Cheryl now live in Roanoke. He still loves to fish. "I wish you could see the lake—it's just beautiful." A house on the lake would cost at least $600,000, he points out. His dreams are modest—he would buy a doublewide mobile home or a manufactured home.

Michael believes there should be an Innocence Fund to help the wrongfully convicted get back on their feet, but he insists, "The people that did it to you should have to bear the financial burden, not the tax payers." Michael would like to see the prosecutors and law-enforcement officials responsible for his wrongful conviction do jail time, although he realizes that will not happen, since the U.S. Supreme Court has ruled that public officials are immune from criminal prosecution for their part in wrongful convictions.[75]

Michael and Albert's civil suit names more than forty individuals, former Sheriff Larry Averitt among them. Asked in a deposition if he was concerned about the "miscarriage of justice" that resulted in Michael and Albert spending nearly fourteen years on death row, Averitt replied, "I could care [less] what happened between then and now to them. All I care about is what's happening to me." Convicted in 1991 of conspiring to defraud Union Parish of funds and mail fraud, Averitt served two years in federal prison.[76]

Michael wants Delton and Callie Frost's murderers to be found and brought to justice, but acknowledges the unlikelihood, given the shoddy initial investigation and highly suspicious disappearance of the .22 rifle recovered from the dumpster.

As he did when he was in prison, Michael Graham clings to hope. "My attorneys are always telling me it's going good, that it takes a while. I've got to be patient out here, too. It's a lot easier being patient out here. At least I've got my freedom."

MADISON HOBLEY

Tortured by Racist Police and Sentenced to Death by Lies

I was raised in a pretty integrated neighborhood. Before taking me to that interroga-tion room, no one had ever called me a "nigger." I knew the odds about the Black man, how easy he can end up in the penitentiary. I walked the straight path. I did all the things a person would do to avoid being in that situation. I went to school, had a job, settled down. But still, I'm taken into custody by these narrow-minded, evil, wicked men. We pay them to uphold the law, and these men looked me in the eye and told me that they hated me because of the color of my skin and that they didn't care about the people who died in the fire, including my wife and child, that whoever set that fire did them a favor, because "nothing but niggers" died.

People ask me, "Are things back to normal?" I don't know what normal is. Take those sixteen years away, bring me my wife and child back, and give me back my name, the way I was—it will never be normal. I'll never regain the life I had.

—Madison Hobley, convicted of seven counts of felony
murder and aggravated arson and incarcerated for
sixteen years, nearly thirteen of those years on death
row. In January of 2003, Illinois Governor George Ryan
granted Hobley a full pardon based on innocence.[1]

The Crime: Tuesday, 6 January 1987, Chicago, Illinois

Located in the predominantly African-American community of Avalon Park, on Chicago's south side, the apartment building at 1121-23 East 82nd

Street was tidy and well maintained.[2] Less than a block away, however, on the other side of the viaduct, a neighborhood of a different character showed itself. Once a thriving business district, only a laundromat and two liquor stores remained on the thoroughfare known as "the Strip." Drug dealers stood in front of condemned buildings openly plying their trade. Periodically an unmarked police car pulled up, the street vendor extended his hand through the open window, and then the officer continued on his way. Neighborhood residents assumed police were "on the take."

Once inhabited mainly by upwardly mobile African Americans—doctors, lawyers, business owners, and other professional people—by the mid-1980s the character of the Avalon Park community was changing. The neighborhood had fallen to the purview of the urban gang the Black Gangsters. A rival gang, the Black Peastones, had branded the back of the 82nd Street apartment building with their insignia, marking it as their territory. The janitor sold drugs through the window of his first-floor apartment.

At 2:00 on the morning of 6 January 1987, a fire was reported at the 82nd Street apartment complex. The three-story building had seven units on each floor and a garden-level basement apartment. With the interior front staircase engulfed in flames, the only exit from the building for tenants on the upper floors was via the exterior rear staircase. Two women on the second floor threw their children out the window into the arms of people on the ground. A tenant on the third floor climbed out her window and clung to the roof, finally dropping onto the windshield of a car. When firefighters arrived, they rescued some tenants with ladders and entered the building to drag both the living and the dead from the toxic blaze. Seven people perished, among them a seven-year-old girl and a fifteen-month-old boy. The coroner listed the cause of death as acute carbon monoxide poisoning. Many more were seriously injured.

Chicago Police Officer Virgil Mikus, with the Bomb and Arson unit, arrived at the scene at 3:10 A.M. His initial report indicated that the fire started in the front stairwell on the ground level and traveled up. Tests of charred debris revealed the presence of gasoline.

"My Family Is Like the United Nations—Dominican All the Way Down to Dutch"

Madison Hobly was born in 1960 and raised in the middle-class neighborhood of Chatham. The city of Chicago was the only home he knew before being sent to death row. His parents were both of "mixed" race: Native American and Dutch on his mother's side and African American and

Madison, age 23, and his mother Myra Hobley at a family wedding. [*Courtesy of Madison Hobley*]

Dominican on his father's. He jokes about having a cousin who could double for John Travolta.

Madison's mother worked as a nurse and his father was an engineer employed by the Chicago Housing Authority. Madison was the couple's third child and first son. Devout Catholics, the family attended mass regularly. Madison went to Catholic school through his sophomore year in high school. He remembers the nuns' "strict discipline, the rulers on the hands," but also their praise, getting "stars for what we accomplished." The school hosted the Officer Friendly Program, encouraging respect and trust for the police. A good student and an outstanding athlete, he pitched a no hitter at his first game in Pony League baseball. Being a left-handed pitcher earned him the nickname "Lefty." But Madison's "first love" was football. He set his sights on a football scholarship at the University of Illinois or Colorado, until he was seriously injured during his sophomore year. After that, his father urged him to pursue a career in baseball instead. "I moped a little, then pulled down all the football pictures, put up baseball pictures, and convinced myself that baseball was the sport." During Christmas break of his senior year, he attended a baseball conference in Florida. Scouts for the Kansas City Royals and Atlanta Braves had their eye on him.

Madison invited a friend's younger sister to his senior prom, a match-making arrangement by the friend; but when Madison learned he needed to formally ask the girl's mother's permission, he balked, "Forget it. I'm not asking her to marry me." With the prom just days away, and unable to sell the tickets, on a whim Madison phoned a girl from a rival high school whom he had met briefly at school functions and when she was visiting a neighbor of Madison's. Two years younger than him, Anita Johnson was cute and petite—short like him—and judging from what she had worn to the prom the year before, "she knew how to dress." 'Sure,' Anita answered when Madison asked if she just might be interested in going to the prom, 'What color are you wearing?' They made a stunning couple, attired in beige and brown. Madison and Anita fell in love that night. They so much favored one another in appearance, people often mistook them for brother and sister.

Southern Illinois University offered Madison a partial scholarship, but his dream of playing major league baseball had dampened his enthusiasm for college. At the major league scouting tryouts, though, he failed to make the cut—hampered by his height, only five foot seven, so best suited to play second base, a right-handed position.

To add to Madison's despair, his father recently had died of an ulcer. Anita's grandfather sat him down and gave him some fatherly advice. 'There are lots of blacks in sports. If you want to do something special with your life, you should be trying to be a doctor.' Madison seized on an idea—*I can't play the game, but I can still be in the game*. He enrolled in the pre-med program at Northeastern Illinois University with the goal of becoming a trainer or a physical therapist. A first-year course certified him as an Emergency Medical Technician, qualified to administer EKGs and draw blood for testing. Anita, meanwhile, had graduated from high school. In 1981, the couple married, and Madison accepted a job with Foster Medical Home Health Care Service. "Delivering hospital beds and medical equipment wasn't exactly what I wanted," Madison says, reflecting on the decision. "My intention was to go back to school, and they knew that. The company had physical therapists on the staff."

Anita worked as a salesclerk in the hat department at Marshall Fields. The couple lived in an apartment building on Michigan Avenue owned by Anita's father. Madison moonlighted as the manager, which earned them a substantial reduction in their rent. They waited until they were financially stable to have their first child, Philip, born in October of 1985. Then, just over a year later, the couple's life took an unexpected turn.

Invited to a birthday celebration for a co-worker of Madison's, Anita encouraged Madison to go without her, since she had a cold. At the party, he

met Angela McDaniel, a woman the same age as him, and by Madison's account, "a real go getter." That same night, they had intercourse in the back
seat of Madison's company car.

Madison did not plan to see "Angie" McDaniel again, but she took note
of the company phone number displayed on the car's exterior and phoned
him at work. Madison began stopping by her place on his way home. Angela lived with her grandmother and invalid father in a cramped, squalid
apartment, not conducive to intimacy, so the couple frequented a nearby
motel. On November 12, three weeks into the relationship, Angela and
Madison went to look at an apartment in Avalon Park on 82nd Street. 'It's
a very nice building, very clean, very quiet,' the manager Louis Casa told
them, mentioning off-handedly, that 'A lot of these people don't work.'
'Drugs,' Madison thought, his suspicion alerted. Nonetheless, Apartment
301 was large and spacious, a vast improvement over Angela's current
lodgings. Angela, however, had a poor credit rating, and Casa would not
rent to her. To resolve the issue, Madison signed the lease contract. Angela
paid the $590 deposit and, not long afterwards, moved in.[3]

Later that same week, Anita found a complimentary pass to an *Ebony
Magazine* fashion show—inscribed with the name Angela McDaniel—in
Madison's coat pocket. Angela's employer had given her the invitation,
and she and Madison had attended the event. Anita confronted Madison.
When he admitted to the affair, Anita demanded he leave and not return
until he ended the relationship.

Madison moved in with his mother. Miserable, missing his wife and
child, on the third day he returned to their apartment, but there was no one
there. On a hunch, he phoned Anita's girlfriend, Patricia, and found his
wife, but Anita refused to talk with him. After several more unproductive
phone calls, Madison walked over to Patricia's. When Anita refused to
come out, Madison threw a rock at the window and broke a pane.[4]

Frustrated, uncertain what to do, he went back to their apartment, and
twenty minutes later, Anita and Philip arrived. Madison promised never to
see Angela again. The relationship was "purely physical," he insisted, he
loved them and wanted to be with them. Anita accepted his apology, and
the couple reunited. At Thanksgiving dinner with Anita's grandparents the
following week, he publicly apologized to the entire family.[5]

Confused by Madison's unexplained absence, Angela McDaniel phoned
him at work. He agreed to meet her at a lounge on his way home. When Angela learned that Madison had reconciled with his wife, she complained
that she could not afford the apartment on her own and that she had expected him to move in eventually. "I did give her that impression," Madison concedes, "to get what I wanted. The physical thing." He suggested

her family move in with her. Furious, she walked out on him. 'You'll pay for wasting my time!'

Troubled by the encounter, Madison confided in Anita. Anita, though, refused to believe that Angela had contacted him and, again, demanded Madison leave. Taking Philip with him, he spent the night at his mother's house, but returned the next morning. Anita had calmed down and accepted his explanation. The couple settled back into family life.

In mid-December, the manager of the 82nd Street apartment building phoned Madison and informed him that Angela McDaniel had moved out, leaving Madison liable for the rent. Unable to find a sublease tenant, he discussed the dilemma with Anita's parents. Anita's father proposed a solution. Madison and Anita planned to move from their basement apartment to a third-floor apartment that would be available in September, very nearly coinciding with the end of Madison's lease obligation at the 82nd Street apartment. Why not stay there in the meantime? Says Madison, "It made so much sense."

The week before Christmas, Madison, Anita, and Philip moved into to the apartment on 82nd Street. During the holidays, they shopped for new furniture, sharing in the fun and excitement of outfitting their new home. Then on New Year's Eve day, a fire broke out on the third-floor landing, just a few feet from their apartment door.

Madison was at work. Anita and another tenant put the fire out. The damage was minimal—a burn hole in the landing carpet—but Anita was anxious. She believed that Madison's ex-girlfriend had set the fire. She had threatened him, after all.

The day after New Year's, Madison phoned Angela McDaniel. They met at the same lounge. He mentioned the fire, and Angela asked, 'Was it on the third floor?' Madison's suspicions flared. She proceeded to confront him about moving his family into the apartment, and when Madison acknowledged, that yes, he and Anita and Philip were living there, Angela slapped him and stormed out.[6]

Madison has poignant memories of the evening of January 6. "My dream was that Phil would be a be a second baseman, so I was hoping he would be right handed—and Anita knew this. Her grandparents had bought Phil a training spoon. At dinner that night, we put the spoon on Phil's plate, and he grabbed it with his left hand. Anita started laughing, and she said, 'Matt, I think that Phil is left handed.' And I said, 'No, no, don't tell me that. We've got to start giving it to him in his right hand.' I'll never forget that." Madison's voice trails off. "That was our last discussion."

After dinner, Madison worked on assembling their new dining room

Madison's son Phillip, killed in the fire. [*Courtesy of Madison Hobley*]

chairs. Philip soon had his tools scattered everywhere. Madison gave him a piece of candy and took him into the living room with his mother. Minutes later Philip was back. "I don't have any more candy," Madison said. Philip grinned and pointed up at the candy dish on a high, out-of-reach shelf.

Madison fell asleep on the couch with Philip curled in his arms. Anita woke them at 11:30 and hustled her two men off to bed.[7]

At 2:00 A.M., Madison woke to a beeping sound. "At first I thought it was my watch. Everything in my day was based on a beep. Using the equipment we had—liquid oxygen tanks, a concentrator timed on a beep, the Motorola car radio. So, I respond to a beep right away. I realize, it's not my watch. It's not the clock. It's coming from the hallway. 'Nita,' I said, 'I think there's a fire. I'm going out to check.'"

The third-floor apartment stayed too warm, so they often left the bedroom window open several inches. Madison slept in his briefs. He grabbed Anita's purple gym shorts and a T-shirt from a pile of laundry. When he opened the apartment door, he saw smoke lingering at floor level in front of the next apartment down. He started down the hall to alert the tenants, leaving the door to his apartment open. His hand raised to knock, he heard a clamorous popping sound.[8]

The glass had exploded from the stairwell door. Black smoke surged into the hallway.

"There were waves of black smoke. I try to run back into this black smoke, and I'm cursing because it's blinding, and I yell, 'Nita, there's a fire. Close the door. Close the door. Go to the bedroom window.' I think she's in the bedroom, because that's where I left her. I remember her getting up and putting on her socks."

Flames engulfed the doorway and hall leading into his apartment. He knocked on the wall and rattled the security bars to the secondary entrance, a door to which they had no key, calling to Anita to "go to the window, close the door." Then the smoke overtook him. "I started choking, and crouched down. I could feel the heat on my back. I tried to run, stooped over like that. All I could see was smoke." His head swimming, he nearly lost consciousness. He held his breath, to keep from inhaling the fumes and intense heat. Finally, he saw what appeared to be a hand fumbling with the doorknob on the exit to the rear stairwell. The hand opened the door. He followed the person, a woman, down the exterior staircase and ran to his apartment window.[9]

Smoke surged out through the opening. He called for Anita, but she never appeared. He ran around to the front of the building to find help. A man gave him a pair of pants, so large he had to hold them up with his hand. Fire trucks drove past, and Madison chased them as far as the viaduct, then ran back to the rear of the building. A man was trying to coax a woman on the second floor to throw her son out the window. Madison helped the man catch the child, and the man agreed to help Madison catch his son and wife, but flames began shooting out from the apartment window.

Madison ran back to the front of the building, and from this point, his memory has the quality of snap-shot images in a grisly collage. "People lying out on the sidewalk with broken limbs. People screaming. People throwing covers on them, giving people clothes." He asked to use the phone at the house next door, where a woman gave him a pair of gym shoes to wear. He phoned his mother and asked her to bring clothes for Anita and Philip. Back at the apartment building, firefighters had arrived, and he asked a fireman to help him rescue his wife and son. The fireman advised him to go around back, that several people were rescued from the third floor. At the rear of the building, a policeman advised him to check the trauma unit in front. "I'm going around and around, just total chaos." A woman came up to him and draped a coat over his shoulders, a short peacoat-style woman's jacket. When his mother Myra and sister Robin arrived, Madison was shaking and crying uncontrollably. Robin suggested that their mother take Madison home, and she would stay to look for Anita and Philip.

Unable to learn anything from the firefighters and paramedics on the scene, Robin returned to her mother's house. Many relatives had arrived and franticly phoned area hospitals hoping to find Anita and Philip. Robin phoned for an ambulance for her hysterical brother. She escorted the ambulance to St. Bernard's Hospital. The examining physicians found soot in Madison's nostrils and diagnosed him as suffering from smoke inhalation. Robin asked the physicians to give her brother a sedative, but when they insisted on doing still more tests, she took him home.[10]

Fearing the worst, Madison's sister Penny offered to go to the morgue, where she identified her brother's wife and son. Firefighters had found their bodies in Apartment 301, lying to the right of the window, up against the wall. Questioned by two police detective, Penny said her brother was at their mother's house and gave them the address.[11]

"I Didn't Do It. They Got the Wrong Person. I Didn't Do It"

Chicago Police Detectives Robert Dwyer and James Lotito arrived at the home of Myra Hobley at 9:00 A.M. Penny had not yet returned. The detectives asked to speak with Madison, who sat in a chair rocking and crying, still unaware of his wife and son's fate. More than a dozen family members had congregated at the house, and the detectives recommended that they talk outside in the police car. On the suggestion of his mother, Madison had showered and changed clothes. He left the house wearing attire ferreted from his mother's closets—a tweed derby-style hat, an orange terry cloth shirt, and overly snug pants belonging to his petite female cousin.[12]

Sitting in the car, the detectives told Madison that the fire was set intentionally with a liquid accelerant and asked if he knew of anyone who might have had a reason to burn the building. Madison immediately suspected Angela McDaniel and mentioned his suspicions to the officers, recounting her anger and threats when he ended the relationship. He agreed to go to police headquarters to make a full statement. Before leaving, the officers returned to the house, and at their request, Myra Hobley gave them the clothes that her son had worn at the fire scene.[13]

At Area Two Headquarters, the officers took Madison to an interrogation room. The instant the door closed, Officer Dwyer knocked off his hat, hit him in the chest, and handcuffed him to a ring in the wall. After the manner of a dealer in a poker game, Dwyer threw an array photographs on a bench—burned, scorched corpses—saying they were the fire victims.

"One of the pictures I thought was my son. I didn't know for sure, but I later learned my son burned. They threw down the pictures just long enough for me to see them and picked them right back up, and they were saying 'Why'd you do it?' And I said, 'You got the wrong person. I didn't do it. I don't know what you're talking about.' Then Robert Dwyer pulled up a chair in front of me, and he says, 'You're a nigger. I'm a white man. You're a nigger. I'm a police officer. You're a nigger. It's a known fact that black and white don't get along. Call me a honky. Isn't that what you want to call me? Call me a honky.' He's looking at me. He had blue eyes—his eyes, this guy had hatred, 'Call me a honky.' He sticks his thumb in my throat and kicks me in the shins, 'Call me a honky.' And I'm wondering, this guy is nuts, this guy is crazy. 'You're a nigger,' he says, 'And as far as I'm concerned, you're the nigger that did this. You're the nigger that did this. And in fact, whoever who set that fire, that was a favor to us. There wasn't nothing but niggers that died in that fire.'"

When Madison asked to speak with an attorney, the officers refused. More questions followed. They accused Madison of lying when he said that he did not know where Angela McDaniel worked and that he worked for a company located in Bridgeport. "Bridgeport is a community that was known to be very, very unfriendly to Black people," Madison says, second-guessing the officers' reason for doubting him. "Everything I told them was true. To this day, I don't where Angie worked." Madison gave them Angela McDaniel's home address and phone number, and they left.[14]

Concerned when the detectives did not bring Madison back home within the hour, his family phoned Steven Stern, the civil attorney they relied on for any legal business that arose. Stern was Madison's first cousin. Stern had court that morning and sent his colleague Terry Stallings to check on Madison. Area Two officials informed Stallings that Madison had never been there. Stallings waited ninety minutes, returned after lunch, and again was told they had no information on Madison Hobley. Mid-afternoon, Madison's mother received a phone call from a family member who worked at the police headquarters located at 11th and State. 'Matt's here.'[15]

Much had transpired in the interim.

While Dwyer and Lotito went in search of Angela McDaniel, two other officers had transported Madison to 11th and State to take a polygraph test.[16]

A polygraph instrument collects physiological data from at least three systems in the human body: respiratory activity, sweat gland activity, and blood pressure. The officer conducting the procedure, Sergeant Patrick Garrity, attached a single sensor to Madison's wrist. There was no evidence that the apparatus was even operational. 'It shows here that you're lying,' Garrity insisted, not only in response to Madison's firm 'no,' he did not set the fire, but in response to Madison's answer to basic questions like what name he used. Frustrated, Madison finally asked, "Can you read it to me? Isn't the machine supposed to be plugged up? I run EKGs, and I know one thing, you have to plug up the machine." 'You're a smart-assed nigger aren't you,' Garrity fired back and kicked Madison in the shin.[17]

Garrity left and returned with Dywer and Lotito. Garrity informed the detectives that Madison failed the polygraph test, and Dywer replied, 'We don't need him. We have Angie.' Madison took the remark to mean that Angela had confessed, but that was not the case. The detectives had taken Angela McDaniel into custody, but nothing she told them indicated that she or Madison had any part in setting the fire.[18]

Handcuffed again, with the cuffs so tight they cut into his wrists, the detectives escorted Madison from the polygraph examination room, and Officer Daniel McWeeney joined them. The worst was yet to come.[19]

"They took me into a utility closet. There were these old rusty cabinets—I'll never forget, they were light green—and old typewriters with covers over them. The minute they close the door, Dwyer hits me in the stomach, hits me some more, and somebody kicks me in the groin from behind. I'm laying on the floor. Dwyer pulled me up by my handcuffs and said, 'You're gonna say you did it.' 'You got the wrong person. I didn't do it,' I said. Then Lotito says, 'I've got something for him right here,' and he gets this plastic typewriter cover and places it over my head and smothers me while Dwyer's whaling into my stomach. I feel myself dying. I've never been in a fight. At the time, I'm only 135 pounds. These guys, much heavier than me, are hitting me and kicking me and suffocating me, and I'm saying to myself, 'I'm dying. I'm being killed.' I feel myself going out.

"The next thing I know, I feel slobber dripping down, and I'm slumped over in a chair."

Steven Stern had arrived at the 11th and State headquarters, but waited 30 minutes before he was allowed to see Madison. Stern immediately noticed scrapes on Madison's wrists. Madison told his cousin that the police had beaten and "bagged" him and were trying to force him to confess. Stern refused to allow Madison to be questioned further.[20]

Before leaving 11th and State Headquarters, Madison participated in a line-up. Police had located a gas station attendant, employed at an Amoco station near the 82nd Street apartment building, who allegedly remembered a man purchasing a dollar's worth of gasoline, which he pumped into a one-gallon can, less than an hour before the fire. The attendant, Kenneth Stewart, did not recognize any of the five line-up subjects. Hearing them ask for $1.50's worth of gasoline was no help.* Police pressured Stew-

---

*The inconsistency between the alleged amount of gasoline purchased, $1.00's worth, and police ordering the line-up subjects to ask for a $1.50's worth of gasoline raises a question as to why. In 1987, gasoline cost approximately one dollar per gallon.

art to reconsider—was it possible one of the subjects *could have been* the man he sold gasoline to? The short man "favored" the gasoline purchaser, Stewart said, but he could not identify him with "any degree of certainty."[21]

The short man was Madison Hobley.

Madison walked out of the building, handcuffed, escorted by Dwyer and Lotito. Cameras flashed in his face and reporters fired questions at him. 'Why did you do it?' one reporter asked. "I didn't do it," Madison pleaded, "They got the wrong person. I didn't do it."[22]

Dwyer and Lotito ushered him into the back seat of a squad car. The detectives made the return trip to Area Two driving on the highway's skirt, sirens blaring and blue lights pulsing. Motorist stalled in rush-hour traffic gawked at the spectacle. Inside the car, Dwyer entertained his partner with Elmer Fudd impersonations, and Lotito mimicked Blacks. 'Maybe we'll stop and get you some beer and barbecue,' he chuckled, glancing at Madison over his shoulder.

Incarcerated in a holding cell at Area Two, Madison literally believed the entire ordeal was a nightmare. "I remember going to sleep, and before that everything was fine. I was pinching myself. I thought I was dreaming." An officer walked by his cell, and he asked, "Officer, is this real?" There was no sink, only a toilet. Madison flushed it and splashed the water on his face, hoping to wake up.

The following day, Madison talked to Julie Harmon, a public defender. He asked her the same question he had asked the officer, "Is this real?" He also asked if his wife and son were dead. 'They said you confessed,' Harmon informed him. "Confessed to what?" Madison asked.

By the account of the police, Madison had told them he doused the floor outside his apartment door with gasoline, struck a match, setting the hallway ablaze, and exited the building by the rear staircase, on his way out, pitching the gasoline can down the hallway on the second floor.[23]

Substantiating the veracity of the confession, police maintained that, in a search of the second floor, Officer John Paladino found a gasoline can under the kitchen sink in Apartment 206.[24]

The police also claimed to have a second witness to the gasoline purchase at the Amoco station. The witness, Andre Council, allegedly came forward voluntarily after seeing Madison's photograph on TV.[25]

Gangland "Enforcer" Andre Council

No stranger to Area Two police, Andre Council had received probation for several minor offenses and, by the time he turned 20, singled himself out as a leader in the street-gang culture. In his role as the Enforcer, he saw to it that the gang's demands be carried out—a position for which he was well suited, over six feet tall and weighing over two hundred pounds, hence his nickname, Fat Boy. Council lived just a block away from the 82nd Street apartment building. His gang, the Black Gangsters, claimed sovereign authority over the neighborhood.[26]

On 17 March 1987, just two months after the 82nd street apartment building fire, the apartment building at 8216 S. Dobson burned. Andre Council lived at 8212 S. Dobson. The fire started on the basement steps and traveled up the staircase. Neighborhood residents reported seeing Andre Council in the alley adjacent to the building just before the fire broke out. They also told police that they suspected Council was responsible for a fire at 8204 S. Dobson, which occurred the day before. Following a five-hour interrogation, Bomb and Arson Unit officials released Council, claiming there was no evidence linking him to the fires.[27]

On March 30, Council was charged with criminal damage to property for smashing a car window with a tire iron. Lt. Jon Burge, Commander of the Bomb and Arson Unit, interceded in Andre Council's behalf. Property Crimes was not Lt. Burge's purview, but Burge ordered Andre Council's release and waived the results of a fingerprint check on Council, effectively suppressing information linking Council to other crimes.[28]

Jon Burge only recently had assumed the position of Commander of the Bomb and Arson Unit, taking the post in September of 1986. Prior to that, Burge supervised detectives Dwyer and Lotito as Commander of the Violent Crime Unit, a position he had held for more than a decade.[29]

Not long after Andre Council's difficulties in March of 1987, the police helped him secure legitimate employment as a tow-truck driver for the City of Chicago.

Andre Council would become the star witness at Madison Hobley's trial.

'Right to a Speedy Trial'?

A woman whose daughter had died in the 82nd Street apartment building fire told police that she suspected her daughter's boyfriend, because the couple recently had argued. A neighborhood resident reported seeing a man drive up in a white car, walk to the building, and throw something in one of the windows, just before the fire broke out. Police ignored all leads pointing to suspects other than Madison Hobley.

Madison was charged with seven counts of aggravated arson and seven counts of felony murder, and incarcerated without bail in the Cook County Jail.[30]

He requested permission to attend Anita and Philip's funeral and was denied. The jail captain learned from the guards how frightened and emotionally devastated Madison was and called him into his office for a consultation. He arranged for Madison to be put in a cell by himself for a night. After that, Madison spent a month in what he calls "the crazy place," receiving drug therapy for his anxiety. The prison captain gave him a Bible, and he joined a Bible study group led by a minister from a Chicago area church. "I never owned a bible before. When you're Catholic, you're not given a Bible. In high school, if we wanted a Bible we had to sign it out [of the library]. I have that Bible to this day—my notes and everything—the pages are falling out."

Madison cites Proverbs 3, verse 5 and 6, "the first verse I ever learned. It goes like this: 'Trust in the Lord with all thy heart. Do not lean on your own understanding, but acknowledge God, and in all ways he shall direct your path.' That was my guideline on how to make it doing time.

"People would try and challenge me, and I stood my ground. I thank God that being an athlete I was able to adjust. If you show any kind of weakness, you're doomed. I saw a lot of things at the Cook County Jail—a guy get stabbed, he's hollering for the officer, holding his intestines. A guy slam another guy's head on the floor over a cup of coffee. A guy get hit across the head with a mop ringer and drop to the floor dead. A guy get stabbed with a homemade knife, it looked like an ice pick, while he was holding his lunch tray. He crawled, tried to crawl, to the officer inner-lock, and he died right there."

Madison shared a cell with two other prisoners, sometimes three, with one man forced to sleep on the floor. To introduce a modicum of normalcy into his life, he put in daily requests for permission to go to the law library. "I wanted to get away and be in an atmosphere almost of the outside, *and*," he adds with due emphasis, "I was interested. When your life is on the line and you know that you're innocent, you're gonna go all out. I learned how to look up cases and how to make a case by pulling cases that are similar by the arguments. The only way to be victorious was to learn the system."

During the first month of his incarceration, Madison made several appearances in court, for the routine matters of being indicted and arraigned. The protocol on court days shocked and appalled him. "They get you up at four in the morning, and call you for court about six. They put you in one holding cell, then they take you to another holding cell—you're slowly making your way to the courtroom. These holding cells are real small. They can only hold comfortably five people, but they put like seventy guys in a holding cell. Guys just stacked in there—it reminded me of slaves in a boat—most of them black, young."

Some of the men first met their court-appointed public defender in the holding cell, talking through the bars, standing shoulder to shoulder with other prisoners. Madison describes a typical encounter: 'Jamie Jones, how are ya man? My name is such and such, and I'm a PD [public defender]. Listen here, they'll give you four years. Cop out.' 'Wait a minute, I haven't talked to you about my case.' 'It doesn't look good. Read here, it'd be best to cop out. You cop out, you do the time now, or you might be doing thirty years. If I was you, I'd cop out, right now. Otherwise you might be here for a long time. Now come on, what do you want to do? I'll give you five minutes, and I'll be back.' 'But I didn't do it.' The more seasoned prisoners advised the novices to take the plea-bargain offer and most did, guilty or innocent.

The prosecution offered Madison a thirty-year sentence in exchange for a guilty plea. Madison's answer: "No way."[31]

Madison's family considered hiring private counsel to represent him, but the attorney they consulted insisted that the family put up homes and business property for collateral, and Madison had high regard for his public defender, Julie Harmon. "Julie was fighting for me, she believed in me."

At his first interview with Julie Harmon on the day after his arrest, Madison had recounted the abuse he suffered at the hands of officers Dywer, Lotito, and Garrity. Harmon had Madison examined at an area hospital and took photographs of the scrapes on his wrists and bruise on his chest. She also lodged a complaint with the Police Department's Office of Professional Standards (OPS). In an interview with the OPS, Madison described the physical and verbal abuse in detail.[32]

Not long afterward, Madison was visited by a woman who said her son had been brutalized by Area Two police, caved into the torture, confessed, and was sentenced to death. Madison's experiences had made him wary. "I didn't say much of anything. I didn't know who she was, and I didn't trust her." He cautioned his family against talking to the woman, afraid that she may have been someone from the state attorney's office.

The woman, in fact, was the mother of death-row inmate Stanley Howard. Following Madison's interview with the OPS, Julie Harmon had begun receiving phone calls from police officials, who refused to give their names, recounting other stories of torture and abuse at Area Two. Julie Harmon researched Stanley Howard's case. Like Madison, Howard was slugged, kicked in the shins, suffocated with a typewriter cover, and suffered wrist wounds from tight handcuffs. The prosecution intended to introduce Madison's alleged confession as proof of his guilt. Harmon filed a pre-trial motion to suppress the confession on the grounds that it had been coerced, by way of proof offering Madison's statement to the OPS, the photographs of his injuries, confirmation from the hospital examination, and Stanley Howard's abuse by officers from the same Chicago precinct, Area Two.[33]

The sixth Amendment to the U.S. Constitution guarantees the right to a "speedy trial," in Illinois defined as a no longer than ninety days from the formal declaration of charges at the arraignment. However, each time the judge granted the prosecution or defense's request for a continuance— whether to allow for further investigation or to accommodate an official's vacation—the ninety-day period began again.

Patient, Madison had accepted Julie Harmon's explanation that they needed more time, but by the summer of 1989, Madison still had not been tried. The guards liked and respected Madison, and many believed he was innocent. A guard escorting him to an attorney visit struck up a conversation. When he learned Madison was represented by a PD, jail lingo for a public defender, the guard shook his head and said, 'Man, you have a Penitentiary Deliverer, Hobley. You need to get a private attorney.' Waiting two and half years for a trial date was too long, the guard insisted.

At the visit, Madison pressed Julie Harmon for an explanation. Even in retelling the episode, his voice sounds pleading, "Julie, how come we're not going to trial yet? How come we don't demand trial?"

They did not want to go to trial now, Harmon had reasoned, it was the middle of the summer, and the jurors would be gazing out the windows, wishing they were outside. She promised him, though, that it would be soon.

The prosecution's requests for continuances delayed the proceedings another full year, with Madison finally receiving a trial date of 16 July 1990, the middle of the summer. The 82nd Street apartment-building fire had received national media coverage in January of 1987 and was once again headline news. Mayor Richard M. Daley was in the midst of a heated campaign for re-election, and a conviction would showcase his tough-on-crime stance.

The media praised the Chicago Police Department for finding the man responsible for setting the fire in less than twenty-four hours. An inflammatory article in a leading Chicago paper falsely claimed that Madison's son Philip died sucking his thumb, something the child had never done. One emotionally charged video segment showed fragments of an interview with Anita's grandmother, Niomi Rivers, and a quick pan to Commander Jon Burge and his entourage.[34]

The Trial: "The State Attorneys Were Like Devils to Me"

Defense Attorney Harmon went into the trial disempowered on multiple fronts. The prosecution claimed that the gasoline can recovered from the 82nd Street apartment building was never analyzed for fingerprints, even though a police report that Harmon received indicated that the can was negative for prints—evidence pointing to Madison's innocence that she could not confirm. And Harmon knew nothing of Commander Jon Burge's order to release Andre Council without a fingerprint comparison to see if he was linked to other crimes, a document the prosecution neglected to turn over when she filed a discovery request.[35]

However, Harmon did receive police reports revealing that Andre Council was questioned in conjunction with two Dobson Avenue arson fires in March of 1987. Speculation naturally followed that Council may have set the 82nd Street apartment building fire and implicated Madison to exonerate himself. The fact that police released Council without charges, disregarding the statements of witnesses who saw Council at the Dobson Avenue fire scene, suggested at the very least that Council received the special treatment to ensure his trial testimony.[36]

To pursue that theory, though, meant calling into question the motives and actions of Area Two police, and Harmon was having no success whatsoever in that arena.

Judge Christy Berkos had decided that the jurors would be allowed to hear the polices' account of Madison's alleged confession.* Berkos gave no credence to Madison's claims of police brutality. Implying that Madison routinely consorted with ex-convicts, Berkos conjectured that Madison heard Stanley Howard's story of abuse from men who had known Howard in prison and borrowed from the details to fabricate a similar tale.[37]

An attitude of blatant mockery prevailed in the courtroom. During jury selection, Judge Berkos and the prosecuting attorneys scoffed when a prospective juror said that he did not believe he could vote for the death penalty if Madison was convicted. Another prospective juror openly ad-

*Judge Christy Berkos was formerly the mayor of Cicero, Illinois, a suburb of Chicago with a legacy of hostility toward African Americans. When Dr. Martin Luther King visited Cicero, he suffered head wounds inflicted by protestors throwing stones. "To Remember Martin," 2007 Community Faith Celebration address by Rev. Canon Henry L. Atkins, Jr., 14 January 2007 http://www.dartmouth.edu/~tucker/news/highlights/mlk-2007.html, retrieved 24 April 2007.

mitted that he did not like 'Black people,' and the prosecution joked that they thought he was a fine candidate for the jury.

Of 114 prospective jurors, only 16 were African Americans. One woman begged to be excused to care for her daughter, recently released from the hospital after being comatose for three months due to an automobile accident. Pressured to do her civic duty, she became the only African American on the final jury panel of 12. Both the prosecution and the defense were allowed to dismiss 14 prospective jurors without cause. With only one without-cause challenge remaining, the defense was forced to choose between two police officers, a white suburban policeman and a Black officer on the Chicago police force. Madison's defense team chose the white suburban policeman, as the lesser of two evils.*

The defense's strategy included proving that the Chicago police had brutalized Madison, thereby discrediting the police's claim that he had confessed.

The strategy was doomed. To reinforce Madison's credibility, Harmon hoped to introduce Stanley Howard's account of abuse and accounts of abuse from two other individuals who were brutalize by Area Two police. The prosecution raised a motion requesting that the jury be prohibited from hearing the accounts, and Judge Berkos granted the request.†

For the jury, it would be a matter of weighing Madison's word against the word of the police.

Presentation of evidence began on 18 July 1990. Madison wore a suit for his daily appearances in court. His handcuffs and shackles were removed out of the presence of the jury, but he entered the courtroom with the sheriff shadowing his every step, "following me, right behind me, like I'm gonna run or something." The subliminal messages conveyed by the courtroom ambience troubled him. "Why was the State sitting right there by the jury where they could see them and touch them and see that they were real? They've got me way on the other side of the room, where I can't even look at them, like I'm a dangerous man, and they don't want me near them." And then there were the prosecution's carefully labeled evidence folders and "giant exhibits. And here we are, we've got stuff made with crayons, handmade stuff."

---

*A few weeks before the trial began, two young attorneys had been assigned to assist Julie Harmon, Clyde Lemon, Jr., and Jeffery Howard. Barbara Brotman, "The Verdict," *Chicago Tribune*, 30 December 1990; Hobley interviews; *The People of the State of Illinois v. Madison Hobley*, no. 71184, 31 March 1994.

†Judge Berkos opined that the abuse Stanley Howard allegedly suffered was too "remote" to be relevant because it occurred more than three years before Madison allegedly was abused, a paradoxical rational in view of Berkos' pre-trial opinion that street gossip about Howard's abuse story may have reached Madison. Conroy, "The Magic Can."

Portraits of the victims were displayed in the courtroom. The fire survivors testified first, telling how they jumped from windows and threw their children to people on the ground. Those who lost family members described their loved ones. Anita's grandmother Niomi Rivers took the witness stand to identify Madison, in the emotionally charged setting leading jurors to suppose she believed he was guilty, when, in fact, in a TV interview she had insisted she did not think Madison set the fire. In court, her opinion on Madison's innocence or guilt was never sought.[38]

Andre Council identified Madison as the man who purchased a dollar's worth of gasoline at the Amoco station located just a few blocks from the 82nd Street apartment building. According to Council, Madison wore jeans, a hat, and a navy blue or black pea-coat—the hat Madison wore when taken into custody, and the coat his mother gave police. Council said that he was at the service station visiting with the attendant Kenneth Stewart. When fire trucks drove past headed in the direction of his house, Council allegedly left, stopped briefly at home, and then went on to the scene of the fire, where he again saw Madison, dressed in the same attire.[39]

Refuting Council's testimony, the mother who dropped her son from a window testified that, when Madison helped catch her child, he was wearing only a T-shirt and pants—no hat, no coat, and no shoes. Another survivor of the fire noted that the coat buttoned on the left and was a woman's coat. When she saw Madison, he was wearing the coat, but no hat and no shoes.[40]

To raise doubts about Council's motive for testifying against Madison and point to him as a possible suspect, Julie Harmon asked Council if he was arrested for arson in March of 1987. The prosecution objected to the question, and a conference in the judge's chambers followed. The prosecution produced a police report indicating that Council was questioned about the Dobson Avenue fires, but never charged. Judge Berkos sustained the objection. The trial proceeded with the jurors wholly unaware that Council had been questioned as a suspected arsonist and may have received special treatment in exchange for his testimony.[41]

Service-station attendant Kenneth Stewart acknowledged that, when he viewed the line-up, he could not identify Madison with "any degree of certainty." On the occasion of the gasoline purchase, he only saw the man's face for three or four seconds, Stewart said. The prosecution, however, pressed Stewart to make an in-court identification and insisted that Stewart assign a percentage to the degree to which Madison "favored" the gasoline purchaser, and Stewart answered, "99 percent."[42]

Another non sequitur in the testimony of Andre Council and Kenneth Stewart was their description of the gasoline can used by the individual who bought gas. Both Council and Stewart said that they believed it was a one-gallon can. The gasoline can recovered from Apartment 206 was a two-gallon can.[43]

Officers Garrity and Dwyer testified that Madison confessed to purchasing the gasoline and setting the fire so he could be with his girlfriend; but the only record of the alleged confession was Dwyer's typewritten report dated January 31, three weeks after the interrogation. Dwyer claimed his handwritten notes got wet, the "ink was running," and he threw them away. Garrity's notes from the polygraph examination stated that the subject made "admissions," but contained no specifics. By the officers' account, Madison said he poured gasoline on the stairwell and outside his apartment door and threw the gasoline can down the second-floor hallway as he was leaving the building.[44]

Shown the two-gallon gasoline can recovered from Apartment 206, the apartment's residents testified that it did not belong to them, adding that they kept the door to their apartment locked and eventually were rescued via ladder by firefighters. Firefighters testified that they broke in the door of Apartment 206 when searching for survivors. Accounting for how the gasoline can came to be under the sink in a locked apartment, the prosecution speculated that firefighters might have kicked the can into the apartment, or it might have been blown into the apartment by high-pressure fire hoses.[45]

Officer John Paladino testified that he was contacted late on the afternoon of January 7, just as his shift was about to begin, and that Detective Dwyer instructed him to go to the apartment building and search for a gasoline can on the second floor; he subsequently found a gasoline can under the sink in Apartment 206. Paladino's testimony confirmed what was already known from police reports, except for one alarming detail. Asked about the black dust on the outside of the can, Paladino said it appeared to be residual fingerprint powder, from when the can was dusted for prints.[46]

Defense Attorney Harmon requested a mistrial, arguing that the prosecution's failure to provide her with the fingerprint report constituted withholding evidence. The prosecution, however, contended that there was no fingerprint report, opening its files for Judge Berkos to examine, and Judge Berkos subsequently denied Harmon's request.[47]

Blocked at every juncture, midway through the trial Julie Harmon decided to hire consulting engineer John Campbell, a former NASA employee who specializing in aircraft fire and explosion research, to refute the prosecution's theory that the fire started on the top floor from gasoline that Madison allegedly poured outside his door and ignited. With her limited budget, Harmon could only afford to pay for a single day of Campbell's time. As Campbell sat waiting to testify, he surveyed the neatly tagged displays and exhibits and reviewed the photographs from the fire scene. It quickly became apparent to Campbell that the two-gallon gasoline can could not possibly have been in the second-floor hallway during the fire. The reason was obvious: The can on display and shown in the fire-scene photographs was clean and in excellent condition, while photographs of the second floor hallway showed severe fire and smoke damage.[48]

Campbell informed Defense Attorney Harmon of the anomaly before taking the witness stand, and she planned her questions accordingly. She first asked Campbell about the origin and path of the fire. Citing a police report confirming the presence of gasoline in charred debris from the ground-floor stairwell, Campbell explained that the fire had started there, traveled up the staircase, and "mushroomed out" on the top floor as a result of the superheated gases expanding. Madison's description of the fire was consistent with the "chimney effect" phenomenon that occurred, Campbell said. The blowtorch-like force of the flames when they exploded into the hallway caused the severe damage to the area just outside Madison's apartment, he insisted, not an accelerant poured on the hallway floor.[49]

Attorney Harmon then showed Campbell a fire-scene photograph of the two-gallon gasoline can and a photograph of the second-floor hallway following the fire, and asked if the gasoline can could have been in the hallway during the fire. The jury, however, never heard Campbell's answer. The prosecution objected that Campbell's opinion was mere speculation based on photographs, that he had only been hired the day before, and that he had not even visited the fire site. Judge Berkos concurred and refused to allow Campbell to answer the question.[50]

Campbell was an older gentleman, and in cross-examination, the prosecution taunted and humiliated him, holding a photograph that he had made reference to just a few inches from his face, then jerking it away, with the admonition, 'This? Can you see it.'

In part supporting Campbell's theory of the fire's origin and path, Fire Marshall Francis Burns testified that if the door to and window in Apartment 301 were open, the fire would have been drawn to that location, but Burns said that the severe damage to the door and hallway outside Apartment 301 led him to conclude that the fire started there.[51]

Bomb and Arson Investigator Virgil Mikus agreed. Acknowledging that his original report stated that the fire started in the ground-floor stairwell, based on traces of a liquid accelerant detected in the charred debris, Mikus said he now believed the fire started outside Apartment 301. He illustrated his position with photographs, pointing to a circular burn pattern on the hallway floor, as indicative of a flammable liquid being poured there. Explaining why tests did not detect gasoline in the third-floor hallway, Mikus proposed fire hoses washed away the residue.[52]

Says Madison of the state witnesses and state attorneys, "They were like devils to me. We didn't even come close to bringing out the truth."

When Madison testified, the prosecution repeatedly objected to his account of events. 'He's pleading with the jury, he's reasoning with the jury. Just answer yes or no.' "I'm trying to explain," Madison would reply, begging to be allowed to tell the jury what really happened, only to be cut off, 'Just yes or no.' Several times during the course of his testimony, Madison wept. At one point, he turned to the jurors and raged in frustration, "I'm not a murderer. I didn't kill my family." To the extent that he was permitted to, Madison recounted the affair with Angela McDaniel, his reconciliation with Anita, the horrific night of the fire, and his battery and abuse at the hands of the officers who claimed he confessed.[53]

The woman he had followed down the rear staircase testified to escaping from the burning building by that route, but she was not aware of anyone being behind her.

The jury viewed the photographs taken on the day following Madison's interrogation, showing scrapes on his wrists and a bruise on his chest. Detective Dwyer countered that the wrist injuries were caused when Madison resisted, tugging at the handcuffs. According to Dwyer and the other three officers who participated in the interrogation, Lotito, McWeeney, and Garrity, the abuse Madison described—the racial slurs, being kicked, slugged, suffocated with a typewriter cover—never happened.[54]

In closing, Julie Harmon argued that the prosecution had failed to produce any physical evidence linking Madison to the crime—no hair or fibers, no fingerprints, no gasoline on his clothes. In bold disregard for the earlier assertion that there was no fingerprint report, the prosecution responded that the defendant had "chosen not to leave his fingerprints anywhere on the can," leading the jury to surmise that Madison wiped the can clean before discarding it. As for there being no gasoline on his clothes, the prosecution speculated that Madison deposited his clothes in a dumpster after setting the fire, likewise explaining inconsistent accounts of his attire at the fire scene.[55]

The jury of six men and six women retired to deliberate on the evening of August 1. Reports vary on what took place in the jury room, but according to several jurors, the suburban police officer Mathew Evans appointed himself jury foreman. Allowed to view the morgue photographs of the victims, not displayed at the trial, one juror would later comment, "They were like charcoal. The skin was completely gone."[56]

On the first poll, all six men and one of the women turned in a guilty vote. Discussion followed. Two of the women believed that the police had physically abused Madison. Evans, in uniform and wearing his gun, talked about the difficulties police encountered when dealing with hostile subjects, arguing that the conduct of the Area Two detectives was entirely acceptable. The next poll resulted in a vote of nine guilty, three innocent. At 9:00 P.M. the jurors were driven to a nearby hotel to be sequestered for the night.[57]

They dined together at the hotel restaurant. The two-week trial had received daily media coverage, and when diners at a nearby table realized that the group was the Hobley jury, they began to call out advice. 'Hang the motherfucker . . . You know he's guilty . . . Give him the death penalty.'[58]

When deliberation resumed the following morning, one of the three hold-out jurors switched sides immediately. The two dissenting votes came from Alice Coward and Nancy Crandall, who remained convinced that the police had brutalized and beaten Madison. Coward, the sole African-American juror, had spent four hours riding public transportation every day for the past two weeks, and her mother had been forced to move in with her to care for her invalid daughter.[59]

A first-degree murder verdict required jury unanimity, and jury foreperson Evans informed the group that their 'decision was going to be unanimous.' By some accounts, Evans laid his gun on the table during the course of the heated debate. Alice Coward switched sides, but juror Nancy Crandall held out for six hours. Crandall finally gave in and then went to the bathroom and cried. In convincing herself to vote with the group, Crandall reasoned that perhaps Madison was beaten, because "he did it."[60]

Back in the courtroom, all of the woman jurors wept. The jurors were polled individually. Sobbing uncontrollably, one woman could not answer and another juror answered for her, but Judge Berkos insisted she speak for herself, and finally she managed to say, "guilty." When Nancy Crandall's turn came, she hesitated and whispered a silent prayer: *God help me, and God help him.* After a seemingly interminable delay Crandall, too, answered, "guilty."[61]

Madison gazed silently at the teary-eyed jurors passing tissues around and comforting one another. "I was devastated. I could not believe it. But, by the time the verdict came down, I already knew I was doomed," he says, resignedly. "I remember looking out the window, looking up, saying, 'Lord, I don't believe this is going on. I do not believe this is happening to me.'"[62]

. . .

Court resumed the following week, for the sentencing hearing. Twenty-seven character witnesses appealed to the jurors to spare Madison's life—family members, former teachers and coaches, co-workers, the Presbyterian pastor who led the Bible study class at the Cook County Jail, and even jail personnel spoke on Madison's behalf.[63]

The prosecution, however, presented a police report stemming from the incident when Anita had refused to come out to talk with Madison, and he threw a rock and broke a window at her friend's apartment. The woman had filed a police report, but the charges later were dropped. According to the account of events related at the sentencing hearing, police had set up telephone surveillance at the woman's apartment, and Madison allegedly had phoned and threatened to burn the building.[64]

Although farfetched to suppose that the beleaguered Chicago Police Department dispatched an officer to monitor phone calls because a window was broken in a domestic dispute, the jurors had already implicitly avowed their willingness to believe the police over Madison by their guilty verdict. After deliberating only two hours, they reached a decision on his punishment: death.[65]

Death Row

Madison was taken straight from the courtroom to a solitary confinement cell and hustled off to the death-row unit at the Pontiac Correctional Center later that same week.

He rode handcuffed and shackled in the rear of an armored security van, escorted by state troopers in patrol cars. After two and half hours, the van left the expressway. Madison peered out the small window. "I know I'm going to a penitentiary, so I'm looking for a penitentiary. We go down this side street and I'm seeing houses, and I'm thinking, I hope they're not gonna take me in an alley and shoot me or something." And then he saw the facility that would be his home, "the fence and the tower and the barbwire. They pull you right up to the dungeon, right up to the doors, like dungeon doors, that said Condemned Unit."

In his cell, with his arms outstretched, he could lay the palms of his hands flat against both walls. An aluminum toilet, sink, and steel bunk with a two-inch mattress lined one wall. "You could move like this"— Madison demonstrates walking in a shuffling gait with his arms pressed to his sides. "I was in there for twelve and a half years.

"I got used to drinking spoiled milk. Or sometimes I'd eat cereal with water. Whatever was supposed to be cold was usually warm, and whatever was supposed to be hot, was usually cold. There were times where they served raw chicken"—what the inmates called "slick-back" chicken.

Anytime an inmate left his cell, he was subjected to the humiliating indignity of a strip search, then handcuffed and shackled once he redressed. The restraints were not removed unless he was locked inside a shower cell or locked inside a recreation area.

Madison saw an inmate get stabbed on the way to the showers. "You're handcuffed behind your back and you're walking with a chain, so you're completely helpless," he explains. "A guy reached out of his cell and stabbed him with a homemade knife."

Inmates had less than an hour of exercise time, Monday through Saturday, with a limit of fifteen men in the yard, and the rest taken to the indoor recreation area. If an inmate skipped his turn in the yard, the opportunity fell to the next man on the list. Madison counted inclement weather a blessing. "When it was cold, nobody wanted to go out. I went out every chance I could get, when it was freezing, subzero, when there was a tornado warning—the sky got dark, leaves were blowing, squirrels running. I even went out in the rain. I had to get some air. That was my therapy. I went out when it was 106 [heat index], really hot, record breaking. I put my shirt over my head and just sat."

Troublesome inmates were placed in segregation, behind a steel door in a cell with virtually no light, denied all human contact, and permitted only one shower and one exercise session a week, alone. Madison tells about an inmate in segregation who cut himself with a chicken bone, "so he could take a walk to the hospital—he was that desperate."

Under routine conditions, inmates could have five visitors a month and make one collect twenty-minute phone call a day, provided the guards brought the phone, which they sometimes refused to do. With the phone rates exorbitantly expensive, Madison limited his calls home to one per week.

Something so trivial as new packaging on a commissary item evoked great excitement. "'Did you see that, they changed the package on the cookies? How about that?'" Madison says in mock illustration. "Guys would talk for hours about the cookie package," anything that broke the tedium of the day-in-day-out sameness.

Under lockdown conditions, all privileges were curtailed for the entire cellblock—no showers, no exercise, no commissary requests except necessities, no visitors, and no phone calls, even though forbidding prisoners to phone their attorneys was a violation of prisoners' rights. Madison considered it an outrage that he was punished with lockdown for other prisoners' infractions—sometimes even when those infractions occurred outside the Condemned Unit or at another penitentiary. He nonetheless managed to keep his anger in check. Madison never caused trouble and never received a single disciplinary "ticket." Surviving as a victim of injustice had become a way of life for him. "I had to tell myself this is prison, what do I expect. This is death row. My goal was to get out. My goal was to prove my innocence."

The Angel of Death Row

Not long after he arrived on death row, a representative from the appellate defenders' office advised Madison it would be at least two years before an appellate attorney was assigned to his case; but a few weeks later Madison received a "call out" (that is, an order to be taken from his cell) for an attorney visit.

His visitors, Kurt Feuer and Jon Stromsta with the law firm Ross & Hardies, offered to represent him pro bono. "Why would you want to take my case," Madison asked, skeptical. "There are other guys sitting here waiting, that were here before me?" Their answer was simple and straightforward—they believed he was innocent—but Madison no longer trusted anyone. At one point during his interrogation, Officer McWeeney had said that he believed him. The Chicago Police Office of Professional Standards (OPS) purported to believe him, but in court, the prosecution had picked apart his statements to the OPS implying that they contradicted his trial testimony. And what was *pro bono*? Madison was unfamiliar with the term. He eyed the two men warily. "Let me think about this."[66]

Madison phoned the representative from the appellate defenders' office who explained that *pro bono* 'wasn't a gimmick' and meant that the Ross & Hardies attorneys would represent him as a public service, without charge. "He told me it was a great opportunity," Madison says, recalling the conversation, "that they were a private law firm, and they have the resources and the money." Julie Harmon had believed in him. Madison never doubted that. But lack of resources and funds had hampered her efforts to prepare his defense from the outset.

Madison accepted the offer.

A few months before Madison went to trial, a small Chicago-area newspaper published an article titled "The House of Screams," recounting tales of torture and brutality by officers from the Area Two Violent Crime Unit acting under the direction of Commander Jon Burge. Some of the victims described abuse even more horrific than what Madison suffered. One man was burned on a radiator; others had electric shock applied to their testicles with a cattle prod. As a consequence, the OPS launched an investigation and concluded that, for more than a decade, detectives under Burge's supervision had engaged in "systematic" abuse and "planned torture." The City of Chicago attempted to suppress the investigation's findings, but a U.S. District Court judge ordered the results be made public in February of 1992.[67]

The following year, the Chicago Police Board terminated Commander Burge for his active role in condoning and inflicting torture.[68] Significantly, two key items of false evidence presented at Madison's trial were linked to Commander Burge: Madison's alleged confession to officers whom Burge had schooled in the use of coercive tactics and the alleged gasoline purchase testified to by Andre Council. Remember that Burge had pulled rank to prevent Council from being fingerprinted which may well have masked Council's link to criminal activity and kept Council from being discredited at the trial. However, in 1993 Madison's attorneys remained unaware of Burge's intervention on Council's behalf.

In March of 1994, the Illinois Supreme Court affirmed Madison's conviction and death sentence. The appeal drafted by Madison's legal team raised forty-five issues and the court rejected them all.*

Among the court's conclusions: the "jury venire of 114 prospective jurors, of which only 16 were black, did not violate the defendant's right to jury drawn from a fair cross section of community," because the defendant had not shown "that the low number of black on venire resulted from anything other than pure chance"; the trial court had not erred in limiting the testimony of the defendant's expert witness, because "Campbell's expert opinion was not necessary to facilitate the jury's understanding of the facts"; "the contents of the fingerprint report, if a fingerprint report ever existed, are unknown . . . [and] would not be available" even if the defendant were granted a new trial, since the prosecution had opened its files to be examined, and no fingerprint report was found; allowing the jury to view "the morgue photographs" of the charred corpses was "admissible to establish the identity and cause of death of the victims"; and perhaps most shocking, the trial court had not erred in refusing to allow the accounts of abuse by the three other individuals brutalized by Area Two police, as these accounts were "irrelevant," since the allegations of two of the individuals "were dissimilar to allegations of defendant," and although the allega-

*In preparing the appeal, Feuer and Stromsta were joined by Ross & Hardies' attorneys Kelly Bugle and Michael King. *The People of the State of Illinois v. Madison Hobley*, No. 71184, 31 March 1994.

tions of Stanley Howard were similar, "there was no evidence that either Howard or defendant sustained injuries consistent with their claims."[69]

The Supreme Court justices may well have been aware that the OPS investigation revealed Area Two police officers routinely engaged in "systematic" torture and abuse, but the justices were under no obligation to take that information into consideration when arriving at a decision, and they did not.

The Illinois Supreme Court set Madison's execution date for 21 September 1994.[70]

"In the system, when you file eligible for the death penalty, they give you a date of your execution. When you get close to an appeal, that date is erased. When you lose the appeal, they put down another execution date. Each time you get near that date, they come get you, you get a physical, they clean your teeth, and they make sure you're in good physical shape for them to kill you. If that's not premeditation, what is? This can mess with a person's head. You have a date to death. And it continually changes. You only have nine stages of appeal. If you don't have an attorney that's really on the ball, and you miss putting in that motion for appeal, they will be happy very quick fast in a hurry to put you to death." So said Madison, in talking about what it was like living with a death sentence.

His attorneys' motion for a rehearing of the Illinois Supreme Court decision was denied on 27 May 1994. They next filed a motion for a Writ of Certiorari in the U.S. Supreme Court. The court refused certiorari (that is, to review the record of court proceedings from the lower court) on 28 November 1994.[71]

By the close of 1994, having exhausted his first three stages of appeal, Madison was one-third of the way to finalizing his date with death.

Then, by an uncanny coincidence, a second "great opportunity" presented itself.

Following a legal visit, one of the other inmates told Madison that the investigator he was working with had asked him to 'Tell Lefty I said, Hello.' The investigator, Robert Jones, said he had gone to school with Madison, hence his use of Madison's nickname, Lefty.*

But Madison did not recall knowing anyone named Robert Jones.

Other inmates began coming back from legal visits with the same greeting. Tell Lefty I said, Hello. The investigator spoke highly of Madison. 'Man, that guy didn't do that. I went to school with him. We played ball together.'

*Robert Jones is not his real name.

A month or so after the first Robert Jones greeting, Madison had a visitor, and when he walked into the visiting room, he noticed a man sitting with another inmate who looked strikingly familiar. The man came over and introduced himself. "So you're Robert," Madison laughed. In high school, everyone called him "Bobby."

Madison and Bobby Jones struck up a conversation. Jones had been following Madison's case. He worked for the Capital Resource Center, a group that provided pro bono legal assistance for condemned inmates. "Do you think you can do some work for me, some work for my law firm, my team?" Madison asked.

Jones said he would talk to his supervisor. Not long afterward, Jones and the Director of the Capital Resource Center, Andrea Lyon, paid Madison a visit.

The Hobley case was already on Andrea Lyon's radar screen. Madison's trial attorney Julie Harmon had contacted her, adamantly insisting that Madison Hobley was innocent—a departure from the norm for Harmon, who tended to be cynical and believe most of her clients were guilty.[72]

Madison greeted Andrea Lyon with an apology, embarrassed that he could not offer her coffee or water since death-row inmates had limited commissary privileges. "I absolutely understood after I met him why Julie felt the way she did," Lyon says. "You develop a sense about these things after you've done them for a while. It was clear to me he no more did it than I did."[73]

Andrea Lyon gave the green light for Bobby Jones to act in the capacity of Madison's investigator and said that she intended to work closely with Jones to monitor developments in his case.

Following the visit, Madison filled out a library research form with Andrea Lyon's name in the subject line. The search yielded up an article that had appeared recently in a national newspaper. Andrea Lyon's stellar reputation as legal counsel and her crusade to save the lives of condemned men had earned her the sobriquet "the Angel of Death Row."

Julie Harmon had passion, but no resources and no money. Madison's Ross & Hardies attorneys had passion, resources, and money, but they had never handled a capital case before. They presented well-written and carefully documented arguments, but the courts were not listening to them. Andrea Lyon had clout, legal muscle.

Madison phoned Lyon and asked if his attorneys could "contact her from time to time to get some legal advice." Not only did Lyon agree to act in an advisory capacity; she said that Madison could petition the court to add her to his legal team.

Madison talked to his Ross & Hardies attorneys about the possibility of Lyon coming on board, and they enthusiastically championed the idea.

. . .

With his conviction and death sentence affirmed, Madison's case entered the post-conviction phase. His first motion requesting a new trial, filed 30 May 1995, ultimately was amended twice as data continued to surface that strongly suggested that the case against him had been fabricated from the outset.[74]

Madison's investigators had found Angela McDaniel, the woman he had a brief affair with the fall of 1986, and McDaniel gave a sworn affidavit sharply contradicting the information Madison's attorneys had received from police. According to the police's version of events, McDaniel willingly participated in a short thirty-minute interview during her lunch hour on the day after the fire. Her statements from that interview indicated that Madison tried to re-establish a relationship with her in early January. The State subpoenaed McDaniel to testify at the trial, but she never appeared, and her whereabouts then were unknown.[75]

In the affidavit taken by Madison's legal team, McDaniel said that the police came to her place of employment and threatened to humiliate her in front of her employer and co-workers if she refused to accompany them to headquarters. Once there, they handcuffed her to a ring in the wall, asked if she knew how to play the card game fifty-two pickup, and threw down photographs of the victims' burned corpses. They called her a 'bitch' and 'ho' and told her that a witness, who saw her at the fire scene, was watching from behind the tinted window in the interrogation room. At that point, according to McDaniel, she broke down and cried. Police held her in custody from noon until midnight. They accused her of lying when she took a polygraph test. She finally answered satisfactorily, after several repeat tests, and police released her.[76]

In another affidavit, service-station attendant Kenneth Stewart recanted his "99 percent" certain identification of Madison at the trial, saying he "felt pressured" by the prosecution. Stewart acknowledged that he picked Madison in the line-up solely on the basis of his height—he was the only short man.[77]

Madison's legal team also interviewed the jurors. Several said they felt bullied by police officer Mathew Evans, who had elected himself foreperson, routinely brought his gun into the jury room, used his influence as a law-enforcement official to defend the tactics of Area Two police, and proclaimed that the group was going to reach a 'unanimous' verdict of guilty, making the others reluctant to dissent. Recounting the incident at the restaurant, jurors spoke about the unsettling and intimidating remarks of other diners: 'Hang the motherfucker . . . You know he's guilty . . . Give him the death penalty.'[78]

Most revealing of all, Madison's attorneys gained access to intentionally concealed police documents, a scheme discovered by Investigator Lee Smith.[79]

Smith had replaced Madison's high-school friend Investigator Bobby Jones, who was transferred to another department. When the Chicago Police Crime Lab insisted there were no files logged under the record department (RD) number assigned to Madison's case, Lee Smith made a personal visit to the crime lab. A laser-unit staff person provided Smith with several inventory numbers related to Madison's case and advised him to contact the Evidence and Recovered Property Section (ERPS) for specifics. At the ERPS office, the staff person researched the numbers for Smith. One number referenced the two-gallon gasoline can introduced at trial. Another number also referenced a gasoline can. On 7 September 1995, Madison's attorneys issued a subpoena requesting permission to examine the second gasoline can.[80]

The second gasoline can was logged under a RD number different from the number officially assigned to Madison's case. When Smith followed the numbers trail on the alternate RD number, he found a host of previously undisclosed police records related to the fire. The data filed under the alternate RD number listed the victims of the 82nd Street apartment building fire, but did not include Madison's name. One document proved the lie in the prosecution's insistence that there was no fingerprint report on the two-gallon gasoline can, stating that the can was tested for fingerprints on 6 January 1987, the day of the fire, and the three forms of analysis performed showed the can negative for prints.[81]

Madison's attorneys never got to examine the second gasoline can logged under the alternate RD number. Three weeks after they issued the subpoena asking the police to produce it, Officer Virgil Mikus, who had retired a year before, ordered the can destroyed—Officer Mikus, who had investigated the fire, concluded it started in the ground-floor stairwell, then reversed his position at trial, saying it started in front of Madison's apartment.[82]

Madison's attorneys subpoenaed a copy of the order to destroy, but the police department refused to release any further information.[83]

To quote Madison, "The jig was up."

The amended new-trial motion, filed 13 May 1996, cited suppression of evidence, intimidation of jurors, misconduct by the jury foreperson, the affidavits from Angela McDaniel and Kenneth Stewart, and thirteen accounts of police brutality committed by officers Dwyer, Lotito, McWeeney, and Paladino documented in the OPS report.[84]

Judge Dennis Porter had replaced Judge Berkos, who had retired. On 1 July 1996, Judge Porter dismissed all the claims raised in the motion without even conducting a hearing to review the evidence.[85]

Madison's attorneys appealed the decision to the Illinois Supreme Court.[86]

In early 1997, Madison was transferred from the Pontiac Correctional Center to the Menard Correctional Center, extending the drive for family and friends who came to visit from two and a half hours to five.

"I Have Very, Very Little Trust in the System. How Can You Trust These Evil, Wicked People?"

Madison's fellow inmates frequently enter into his discussion of his death-row experience. He talks about Walter Stewart, an inmate he met at Menard. Under the influence of crack, Stewart had robbed a jewelry store, killing the proprietors, and then sat down on the curb and waited for the police to arrive. The State offered him a deal: a sentence less than death if he pled guilty. Stewart accepted the deal, but after he had confessed, the State rescinded the offer and sought a death sentence. Not long after Madison arrived at Menard, Walter Stewart was executed.

The man housed in the cell next to Madison dropped his appeals and began writing threatening letters to the governor and courts daring them to kill him. A loner, Lloyd Hampton shunned conversation and interaction, but Madison reached out to him and tried to engage him in Bible study and prayer. "You don't really want to die, Hamp. I don't believe that." Eventually Lloyd Hampton confided in Madison, recounting how he flipped his pickup truck killing his ten-year-old daughter, nursed his grief with alcohol and drugs, and in his chemically induced madness bludgeoned an elderly couple to death.

The courts eventually granted Lloyd Hampton's request. Illinois carried out executions at Tamms Correctional Center, at the southern tip of the state, and transported condemned men to the site via helicopter. On the day before his execution, Hampton wrote Madison a note, asking if his 'Suzy,' his former prison girlfriend, had been coming to visit Madison. "Hamp had lost it," Madison says wistfully. "The next morning you could hear the helicopters outside, *chsh, chsh, chsh, chsh.* And you could hear Hamp whistling. He was getting his clothes together, and he said, 'Well, I'm leaving everyone. I'm on my way.' He was happy. Then you could hear the officers coming, you could hear the chains, down in the gallery coming to get him.

"The next day, there was a little article in the paper like this big," Madison gives a finger measurement, indicating a two-inch column of print. "They called him 'the drifter from Texas.' No one ever knew anything about him. Dead and gone. They execute nameless people."

Madison sits facing the window, a seat he chose deliberately. He pauses to glance outside, and when he begins speaking again, there is a subtle change in his voice.

"I want to tell you this story. The medical health care facility I used to work for was in Bridgeport. They call Bridgeport the 'Back of the Yards.' It's surrounded by stockyards and slaughterhouses. When you get close to there, you smell the stench. One morning going to work, when I was coming off the ramp, there was a trailer pulling this cow. I stopped at a light, and I remember looking at that cow. I can smell the dead animals, and I remember wondering if that cow could smell the death. I could see the nervousness in the cow's eyes. I felt sorry for the cow. They carry them in a trailer, latched in there. So later on, here I am in this cage, on death row, and when they take a person out and execute him, I felt the same nervousness as that cow. I know how that cow feels, because I know there's a chance they're going to slaughter me, just like they slaughtered that cow. When is my time coming? I used to get so frightened, I felt like I couldn't breathe. I was so afraid they were going to execute me without people knowing the truth. It wasn't that I was afraid to die." Madison hesitates. Tears are rolling down his face. He continues in a voice shot-through with grief, "I was afraid to die without people knowing that Madison Hobley did not set that fire. Madison Hobley loved his wife and child."

Lloyd Hampton was executed in January of 1998.[87]

In early March of 1998, Madison's attorneys argued his motion for a new trial before the Illinois Supreme Court.[88]

The opinion was delivered on May 29. The court refused to acknowledge the significance of the thirteen accounts of police brutality, opining that since Madison had maintained from the outset that he had not confessed, it was "inconsistent" for him to argue that his confession was coerced. The information contained in the affidavit from Kenneth Stewart would not have altered the outcome of the trial, the court said, since Stewart had testified to his uncertainty about the identity of the gasoline purchaser when viewing the line-up. Likewise, according to the court, the information contained in the affidavit from Angela McDaniel "does little to help the defendant's case." As to the conduct of the jury foreperson Mathew Evans, the court held that "Evans simply offered his opinion on matters of credibility based on his particular experience as a police officer," and "no improper 'evidence' was interjected into the jury's deliberations."[89]

The court, however, ruled that "prejudicial outside influences were brought to bear upon the jury" by the nonjurors shouting slurs and directives at the jurors while they dined. The court also cited the State for failing "to disclose . . . two pieces of exculpatory evidence: (1) a report that the defendant's fingerprints were not on the gasoline can introduced against him at trial, and (2) a second gasoline can."[90]

"Our confidence in the outcome of the defendant's trial has been seriously undermined," the Illinois Supreme Court stated in conclusion, ordering the Cook County Circuit Court to conduct a hearing to determine if Madison was entitled to a new trial.[91]

Madison would wait in his cell—where with his arms outstretched he could lay the palms of his hands flat against the walls—for two more years before that hearing was held.

Coincidences, Contradictions, and Lies

Madison made daily requests for case files from the law library and routinely discussed strategy with his attorneys. When he discovered that a number of the men incarcerated along with him were, likewise, victims of police brutality and torture, he began to strategize with them, as well. Talking from cell to cell and during recreation time, they came up with a plan. If they banded together as a group, maybe the media would take an interest in their cases. The Ford Heights Four—four Chicago-area men wrongfully convicted in a murder-rape case—had attracted the attention of the media, and in 1996 Governor Jim Edgar granted them a full pardon.*

Madison and his fellow torture victims—convicted on the basis of coerced or fabricated confessions—soon became known as the Death Row Ten. They contacted social-justice activist Joan Parkin, an adamant opponent of the death penalty. After hearing their stories, Parkin took up their cause, co-authoring a pamphlet publicizing their plight. The Illinois-based citizen-activist group the Campaign to End the Death Penalty joined the crusade, staging protests and issuing news bulletins, giving them a voice outside the walls of the prison.[92]

Meanwhile, on the inside, Madison had learned some interesting and valuable information about the 82nd Street apartment building that he

---

*The Ford Heights Four, four African-American men from Chicago's South Side, were convicted of a 1978 double murder and rape. In 1995, a group of journalism students from Northwestern University investigated the case and learned that police knew and intentionally concealed the identity of the actual killer. Subsequent DNA testing confirmed the men's innocence. Ward Larkin, "Ford Heights Four," *Abolish Archives*, 5 August 1997, http://venus.soci.niu.edu/~archives/ABOLISH/aug97/0037.html, retrieved 6 May 2007; Kay Lydersen, "Why Innocent People Land on Death Row," *The New Abolitionist* 2, no. 2 (February 1998), http://www.nodeathpenalty.org/newabo06/dProtess.html, retrieved 6 May 2007.

was convicted of burning. 'Man, that building you lived in was a drug building,' several inmates told him. Madison recalled suspecting that might be the case when he went to see the apartment with Angela Mc-Daniel, and the building manager had remarked, 'A lot of these people don't work.'

Madison passed the information along to his attorneys and investigators. Painstakingly tracking down leads, his investigators discovered the behind-the-scenes story on Andre Council and the gang culture of the neighborhood.[93]

From that, they pieced together a theory of the crime radically different from the one presented by the prosecution at trial. Madison's investigators believed that Andre Council's gang, the Black Gangsters, had burned the 82nd Street Apartment building in retaliation, because a rival gang, the Black Peastones, had taken control of the drug traffic in the building. A photograph showed that the Peastones had branded the building with their insignia. According to sources interviewed by the investigators, the neighborhood was in the midst of a gangland drug war, and Council acted in the capacity of Enforcer for the Gangsters. Streetwise insiders maintained that burning a building to eliminate unwanted drug competition was common practice.[94]

That theory took on an even more disturbing significance when Madison's attorneys received a copy of Commander Jon Burge's previously concealed order to release Andre Council without a fingerprint check when he was charged with criminal damage to property, just two months after the fire. Not only was it now clear that Council received favors from police in exchange for his testimony; neglecting to check Council's prints for possible links to other criminal activity was manifestly suspicious in view of the fact that police chose to dismiss casually Council's possible involvement in the Dobson Avenue arson fires. Among neighborhood residents who had observed the interchange between drug vendors on the Strip and police detectives in unmarked cars, it was commonly assumed that police received payoffs for ignoring the drug traffic. Were police protecting Council to avoid jeopardizing the arrangement? Not long after Madison's trial, Andre Council was convicted of home invasion, but he received a light sentence, and by the summer of 1996, Andre Council was back on the streets.[95]

Madison's legal team had come to believe that the alleged gasoline purchase at the Amoco station was a fiction invented by either Andre Council or Kenneth Stewart, under pressure by police. At trial, Council claimed that he and Stewart were good friends, but when Madison's investigators had interviewed Stewart, Stewart said that he was terrified of Andre Council.

Given Stewart's fear of gangland "Enforcer" Council, Stewart easily could have been pressured into going along with Andre Council's tale about an individual walking up to the service station with a gasoline can and purchasing a dollar's worth of gas on the night of the fire—a story concocted to deflect suspicion from himself.

The entire case against Madison smacked of calculated and planned fabrication. The Illinois Supreme Court ruling ordered "the State to provide the defense with all the information it has concerning the second gasoline can and its destruction." It turned out that the destroyed gasoline can was also a two-gallon-capacity model, confiscated following an arson that occurred on 16 December 1986, just three weeks before the 82nd Street apartment building fire. The youth accused of setting the December 16 fire, Donnel McKinley, pled guilty and received eighteen months in juvenile detention. When Madison's attorneys interviewed McKinley and showed him the two-gallon gasoline can found in the 82nd Street apartment building, McKinley insisted that it was the same gasoline can he had used on 16 December 1986, to set a fire on Paulina Street. McKinley recognized distinctive scratches on the can. Officer Virgil Mikus, who ordered the can from the McKinley arson destroyed, had investigated both the Paulina Street arson fire and the 82nd Street arson fire. The Chicago Police Department had clearly defined procedures for logging and eventually discarding evidence in resolved crimes. Every piece of evidence related to the McKinley arson was destroyed six months after McKinley's conviction, except for the gasoline can, which allegedly had been sitting on an evidence shelf for ten years and was, by utter "coincidence," destroyed three weeks after Madison's attorneys learned of its existence—or so the State had argued before the Illinois Supreme Court.[96]

Was the can destroyed? Or was it actually the same can that was introduced into evidence at trial, a can removed from the evidence shelf ten years before and planted at the 82nd Street apartment building, where Officer Paladino conveniently discovered it. Officer Virgil Mikus had been retired for a year when he signed the order to destroy, creating a paper trail accounting for the police's inability to produce the can. No further information on the can's destruction was available.[97]

In a deposition, former Assistant State's Attorney George Velcich—one of the two prosecutors at Madison's trial—shirked blame for any wrongdoing in regard to the two-gallon gasoline can. Velcich insisted that the gasoline can introduced at the trial was not the gasoline can used to set the fire. Three months later, however, Velcich retreated from that position, in a letter stating that his memory had lapsed since the trial, and, after reviewing the transcripts, he realized that he had misspoken.[98]

. . .

The evidentiary hearing mandated by the Illinois Supreme Court began on 31 May 2000, before Cook County Circuit Court Judge Dennis Porter—the same judge who had rejected the evidence without review in 1996. Madison's attorneys decided against requesting a change of judge, since they ran the risk of further kindling Judge Porter's disfavor in the event the request was denied.[99]

The hearing dragged on for two years, with Judge Porter granting twenty-five continuances.[100]

The Illinois Supreme Court had cited three areas as possible grounds for a new trial: juror intimidation by nonjurors, the withheld fingerprint report, and the withheld evidence regarding a second gasoline can.

In the initial sessions, Judge Porter heard evidence on the jury issue. All of the jurors who could be located testified about the incident at the restaurant. With the exception of jury foreperson Mathew Evans, the jurors agreed on what took place—the other diners making vicious and accusatory comments, shouting remarks such as, 'You know he's guilty, give him the electric chair,' and 'Hang the motherfucker.' Evans, however, said he had no recollection of harassment by the other diners.

Next on the agenda was the issue of the withheld fingerprint report. Madison's trial attorney Julie Harmon testified that she specifically had requested the results from fingerprint tests pertinent to the case, but she was never provided with any such documents. When she received a police report mentioning that the gasoline can was negative for prints, she made a thorough search of the prosecution's available files, but found nothing that she did not already possess. Trial prosecutors George Velcich and Paul Tsukuno conceded that fingerprint tests were performed on the gasoline can, but denied concealing the results. By way of excusing their failure to supply the fingerprint analysis to the defense, Tsukuno claimed there was no formal fingerprint report, merely some notes on a to-from memo.[101]

The State gave an equally farfetched explanation in regard to the gasoline can that Officer Virgil Mikus had ordered destroyed. Echoing their "coincidence in time" argument before the Illinois Supreme Court, attorneys for the State contended that either Investigator Lee Smith or someone from the ERPS office had "transposed" digits for one of the inventory numbers Smith received from the laser unit clerk, and again, by pure "coincidence," the incorrectly transcribed number corresponded to the inventory number for the can confiscated from the McKinley arson, a gasoline can that was in no way connected to the Hobley case—or so the State maintained.[102]

Madison's attorneys countered that the can from the McKinley arson allegedly was destroyed to conceal the fact that it had been taken from an evidence shelf and planted at the 82nd Street fire scene ten years before. To that end, they called Donnel McKinley as a witness.[103]

McKinley began convincingly enough. Rising to his feet, McKinley grasped the gasoline can and demonstrated how he had squeezed it to force out the gasoline. The bend creases in the can corresponded perfectly with the pressure points from McKinley's hands. But then, McKinley went on to say he remembered there being a strip of tape on the can. The State's attorneys were quick to point out that the tape McKinley referred to was attached by the crime lab during testing procedures.[104]

McKinley had never mentioned the tape in his pre-hearing interviews with Madison's legal team. Perhaps the excitement of being in the limelight prompted him to add an unwitting embellishment to his account.

Or perhaps Donnel McKinley intentionally impeached his own testimony, a likely enough scenario, given the Chicago Police Department's history of employing coercive tactics.

One thing was certain: the two-gallon gasoline can found by Officer Paladino had not been in the building during the fire, a circumstance confirmed beyond all doubt by the testimony of Dr. Russell Ogel from Packer Engineering, spokesperson for a team of arson experts who investigated the fire. The can "was simply too clean," Ogel said, showing no traces of melted debris that would have been expected to stick to the surface given the extreme heat; but even more blatantly obvious, if the can had been exposed to fire, the plastic cap would have melted, as had numerous other articles in the apartment where it allegedly was found.[105]

Further alluding to contrivance by police, Ogel noted that the photographs of the alleged circular burn pattern outside Madison's apartment showed debris pushed up against the walls, suggesting that the area was swept clean and what appeared as a circular pattern was created in the process. Echoing the testimony of fire expert Campbell at the trial, Ogel insisted that the fire started on the stairwell lower in the building, explaining that the structure of the staircase drew the fire upward, a phenomenon exacerbated by the open window in Madison's apartment and the vent above the apartment door.[106]

In the final leg of its argument, the defense presented witnesses and police records confirming that police not only neglected to investigate Andre Council as a possible suspect; they took measures to protect Council and granted him special treatment in exchange for his testimony. Under oath, the police detective who investigated the Dobson Avenue fires admitted that the routine procedures for arson suspects were not followed when Council was questioned—no tests were done to detect gasoline or residual fumes on his clothing or person, nor was Council fingerprinted. The defense then introduced the order signed by Commander Jon Burge two weeks later, releasing Council on a documented criminal damage to property charge, again without comparing Council's fingerprints for possible links to other crimes.[107]

Judge Porter received praise from some quarters for allowing testimony and exhibits not directly related to the three areas identified in the Supreme Court order. During the proceedings, Madison was incarcerated in the Cook County Jail, but at his request, during the continuances, he returned to death row, where at least he had a cell to himself and a modicum of protection from the violent and disruptive behavior of other prisoners.[108]

Judge Porter announced his decision on the morning of 8 July 2002. A number of local television stations picked up the story. Madison got the news via a letter delivered with his daily mail. He sat on the thin mattress covering his steel bunk, his eyes shifting back and forth between the small TV set in his cell and his official copy of Judge Porter's ruling.[109]

He vividly recalls his reaction: "When I read it, it made me just want to throw up. A waste of time, I thought, a waste of tax dollars and a waste of time. This guy had already made up his mind before we ever even walked in there."

Judge Porter dismissed the issue of juror intimidation by nonjurors, opining that he did not know who to believe since the jurors gave conflicting testimony, and, even if the incident did occur, there was no proof the diners shouting slurs and directives were talking about the Hobley case.

On the issue of the prosecution's failure to provide the defense with the fingerprint report, Porter held that the defense's not having the actual report had not affected the outcome of the trial since defense attorneys knew from another source that there were no fingerprints on the can.[110]

Although Judge Porter acknowledged that "Burge interceded on behalf of Council," he insisted that Madison had not been harmed by Commander Burge's "intervention." Porter gave no credence whatsoever to the possibility that police were concealing Council's involvement in the fire. "The only reasonable explanation for this intervention is that Council was a witness," Porter concluded.[111]

Ironically, Judge Porter's assessment of the reason underlying Burge's "intervention" pointed to obvious grounds for granting a new trial. Long-established legal precedent held that if jurors were not informed of special treatment afforded a witness—as was the case since the State concealed Burge's order at the time of the trial—the jurors lacked information pertinent to making an unbiased decision, that is, that the witness might be lying to repay the favor.

Judge Porter's opinion chided the defense for what he called their "theory du jour" about various gasoline cans. Porter was not required to rule on the issue of the fire's origin and did not. In denying Madison's petition for a new trial, Porter stated in conclusion, "There is no showing the favorable evidence could reasonably be taken to put the whole case in such a different light as to undermine confidence in the verdict."[112]

Madison's attorney Andrea Lyon had known Judge Porter when he was a prosecutor and did not hold him in high regard. Lyon was outraged by what she calls Judge Porter's "scurrilous ruling," but not surprised. "It was clear to me from the day I walked into court that Porter was going to give us hearing, let us put everything on the record, and then rule against us."[113]

Once the courts rejected an item of evidence, it could not be reintroduced. If the Illinois Supreme Court affirmed Porter's ruling on appeal, the information amassed through years of investigative and legal work would be of no use whatsoever in securing Madison's freedom through judicial channels.

There was, however, hope from another sector.

In 2000, Governor George Ryan had called a temporary moratorium on executions in Illinois and appointed a commission to review the administration of the death penalty in the state. Since the mid-1970s, Illinois had executed twelve condemned individuals and released thirteen who were discovered to be innocent. Ryan was compelled to action by the case of Anthony Porter, in 1999 proved innocent after almost eighteen years on Illinois' death row. In April 2002, the commission recommended eighty-five death-penalty reforms. Disturbed by the commission's findings, Governor Ryan ordered a clemency hearing for every death-row inmate in the state.[114]

Two of the Ross & Hardies attorneys who had worked diligently on Madison's case in the early days had left the team, overwhelmed by the stress and frustration. Kurt Feuer and Andrea Lyon, though, stayed the course. Governor Ryan had stated publicly that he was considering commuting some death sentences to life in prison. For Feuer and Lyon, a commutation for Madison Hobley was not acceptable. He was innocent. With his attorneys' help, Madison wrote to the governor requesting a full pardon.[115]

"Like at the Beginning, I'm Pinching Myself"

Some of Illinois' condemned men adamantly opposed having their sentences commuted to life, afraid the attorneys representing them would lose interest. They preferred the certainty of an untimely death to the prospect of spending the rest of their life in prison. Not long after Governor Ryan announced that he was considering commutation, one of Madison's fellow death-row inmates at the Menard facility hung himself.

The governor's clemency hearings began on 15 October 2002.[116]

In November, a rumor reached Madison that the governor actually might be taking his request for a pardon seriously. A fellow inmate returned from an attorney visit saying that, according to his attorney, several cases had attracted the governor's attention and for those lucky few, not just commutation, but a full pardon was a distinct possibility. The attorney had let slip a few names, and one of those names was Madison Hobley.

"Free Madison Hobley," chanted the Campaign to End the Death Penalty activists in a public demonstration outside the State Attorney's office. Judge Porter's refusal to grant Madison a new trial in spite of the compelling evidence of his innocence soon won him the attention of radio, TV, and print media sources nationwide.[117]

In early December, Madison was transferred back to the Pontiac Correctional Center. By then, rumors that he might go free had begun to circulate in the press. Attorney Lyon had spoken with the governor personally, although he had given her no clear indication of his intentions. "I was thinking, maybe the governor would do something for Christmas," Madison says, speaking of the past as if he were still living it, "that would be a nice Christmas present."

Due to the shortage of guards willing to work, there was no yard on holidays. For Madison who coveted his time outdoors, that doubled the aura of despair. His family had a strong tradition of holiday rituals and celebrations. He describes Christmas on death row as "a slice of ham and a piece of pumpkin pie that looked like it came out of a vending machine." He had spent fifteen Christmases on death row.

When Christmas number sixteen came and went, Madison hung his hopes on the new year. New Year's Eve passed, as well. Then Madison learned from Attorney Lyon that Governor Ryan planned to make a speech at DePaul University in Chicago on Friday, January 10, and the governor had asked Lyon to introduce him. Lyon was an instructor in the DePaul College of Law, and it was well known that she represented Madison. The media speculated that Governor Ryan would announce Madison Hobley's release.

"The night before, it was all over the news," Madison remembers. "My stomach was in knots. I couldn't eat, my food wouldn't go down, I couldn't sleep. Every time it came on, guys were hollering my name, 'Did you hear that? You're going home.'"

As of midnight on January 9, attorneys Lyon and Feuer had received no official word. The governor's speech was scheduled to be aired on the noontime news. On the morning of January 10, Madison, who had been up most of the night, sat in his cell gazing blankly at the TV screen, sick with worry. What if something happened to the governor? What if he changed his mind? At 11:30 A.M., in a pre-broadcast announcement, a commentator said the governor was expected to issue a pardon for Madison Hobley and three other men. Madison held his breath, counting the seconds. He wanted to believe it was true, but he needed to hear the governor say it "live . . . directly out his mouth," to hear the governor say his name.[118]

At DePaul, Madison's sister Robin sat in the audience weeping, reading a copy of the governor's prepared remarks that had just been handed to her by an aide.[119]

Attorney Lyon introduced Governor Ryan, and he stepped up to the microphone.

The governor spoke first of the state's shameful record of wrongful convictions and the Illinois legislature's refusal to enact the death-penalty reforms recommended by the commission he had established.[120] "With the 13th exonerated inmate in January of 2000, we had released more innocent men from death row than those hopefully guilty people we had executed . . . I must share with you some startling information. There are more innocent people on death row . . . Madison Hobley, Stanley Howard, Aaron Patterson, and LeRoy Orange . . . four more men who were wrongfully convicted and sentenced to die by the state for crimes the courts should have seen they did not commit . . . beaten and tortured and convicted on the basis of the confessions they allegedly provided . . . Today I am pardoning them."*

For Madison, listening to those words in his cell on death row, "it just seemed like the sky opened up and all I heard was angels."

Then, literally within moments, he found himself caught up in a whirlwind of activity.

"The next thing I know, they were telling me, 'Let's go.' I'm like, 'What?' And they said, 'You're ready to go aren't ya? Let's go.' They wouldn't even allow me to shake anybody's hand. I'm a risk now. They have to get me out of there, because if something happens to me, I'm a free man."

---

*The following day, Saturday, 11 January 2003, Governor Ryan commuted the sentences of the remaining 167 Illinois death-row inmates to life in prison. It was his last official act. His term of office ended on Monday. He had not run for re-election. Jeff Flock, "'Blanket Commutation' Empties Illinois Death Row," CNN, http://www.cnn.com/2003/LAW/01/11/illinois.death.row/, retrieved 7 February 2007.

"I'd made that walk a million times, always shackled—shackles on your feet, shackles on your hands. How it feels to walk without handcuffs and shackles, I can't believe it. I'd never been able to walk like this." Madison rises to his feet and demonstrates walking, taking long strides swinging his arms.

"They took me to receiving, where they register you, and the officers are saying, 'What are we supposed to do? We never had a guy pardoned before?' One of the officers that escorted me said, 'Man, you're free. When you get home, you need to get you a playstation.' It was so weird.

"Before, they always treated me like a dog, less than an animal. They were so nice and kind to me."

The sergeant overseeing his release warned him that once he was outside, he would be confronted by a blitz of TV cameras and reporters. The sergeant asked if he wanted an escort to the car where his family and friends waited, and Madison accepted the offer.

"When I walked out that door, all these cameras were flashing. They wanted interviews, and I didn't want to talk. I wanted to wait for my attorneys. I remember looking back at the jailhouse where I had been for so many years, and it brought tears to my eyes. There were still guys in there being treated like animals, and I was free to walk away from it."

"I think about that to this day, and I know that I've been blessed."

Madison gave a short interview to a radio broadcaster who had helped publicize his plight. The news had spread across the nation by the time he pulled the car door closed. He talked by cell phone to a cousin who lived in St. Louis, and the cousin's first words to Madison were, 'I saw you on TV!'

The media had descended on his mother's home on Chicago's South Side, guessing that Madison would go there. Helicopters circled the house, and a television station had set up a base unit on the corner of her block. Instead, Madison spent the first night of his freedom just outside the city, at the suburban home of Attorney Lyon and her husband.

"One minute I'm in this cell, and the next minute, I'm at Andrea's house. Like at the beginning, I'm pinching myself. Late that night, it was real quiet, and I got frightened, this feeling of anxiety. I had been in an environment where people stayed up all night, and there was always commotion and banging. I remember looking out the window, and it reminded me of looking out of a cell, and then, I realized, 'Man, I can actually go out there.'

"It put a kind of joy to me. I watched the sunrise."

Later that morning, Andrea and her husband drove Madison to a nearby

Madison Hobley and attorney Andrea Lyon. [*Leslie Lytle*]

outlet store to buy a winter coat. He had no clothes, since he had been in prison for sixteen years. The instant Madison walked in the door, a clerk rushed up and began congratulating him. Andrea had suggested that she hire a bodyguard to accompany him for a week or so. Initially, Madison objected to the idea, but ultimately he agreed. He gave several interviews that first day, to both the national and international media, and the following day, Sunday, the cameras even followed him to church. "They had cameras in my face for at least a week straight," Madison says remembering back to that chaotic time.

In prison, Madison had vowed that he would register to vote as soon as he was set free, so he could "vote the crooks out of office." While he was downtown with his bodyguard to accomplish the task, people stopped their cars in the middle of the street and jumped out to run up and shake his hand.

The other thing that Madison desperately wanted to do was visit the grave of his wife and son. "I didn't know where the grave was, and no one would let me go by myself. I had to wait for someone to be able to go with me and show me. But later that week, I was able to—" Madison pauses, searching for words to describe the experience, then he breaks down and weeps.

Two weeks after his release, Madison left Chicago and moved to Baltimore, Maryland, where he had relatives.

Chicago was not the city he remembered. The landmarks he cherished, like the old baseball stadium, had been torn down. The city was so much bigger, in so many ways foreign, and, yet, paradoxically, there was nowhere he could go where he wasn't recognized.

"Everybody knew me there. I just wanted to get away."

Not long after he moved to Baltimore, he agreed to participate in a speaking tour hosted by the Campaign to End the Death Penalty. He told his story and spoke out against capital punishment at universities and colleges throughout the nation—Northwestern, Columbia, Georgetown, Berkeley, Notre Dame—to name only a few. After nine months on the road, and a brief stay back in Baltimore, he traveled to Rome and addressed audiences on behalf of the anti-death penalty organization Hands Off Cain. Between speaking engagements, he worked part-time assembling radios for an electronics company.

His mother's chronic emphysema compelled him to move back to Chicago in the summer of 2004, to be near her and support her as she had supported him. He took a job with a Chicago area law firm, doing light filing and errands, but being in a confined environment made him anxious and nervous. The firm knew Madison's history and was sympathetic, allowing him to take two-hour lunches and long breaks.

Madison turned in his resignation after just a few months. In the course of an hour-long conversation, Madison frequently will rise from his chair and walk around the room. "I can't stay anywhere for a long time. I start to get itchy and shaky. I have to move." His symptoms are not unlike those of other death-row exonerated men who spent long years locked in a cage smaller than the standard size dog pen at boarding kennels.

Under the provisions of the Illinois wrongful conviction indemnification statue, Madison received $10,000 for each year of life taken from him, a total award of $160,000. "I don't even remember seeing it," Madison says. "It just came and went. That's like one year's salary."

Today, Madison Hobley is a stay-at-home dad with two infant sons. His wife Lisa has a bachelor's degree in business. She works for a major national bank and, privately, as a real estate investor. In addition to caring for the children, Madison does the laundry and vacuuming and most of the cooking. They are a deeply devoted couple. "I go through depressions and mood swings," Madison concedes. "Sometimes I just go silent. Lisa understands." Madison has frequent nightmares replaying the horrors he saw in prison—a man lying on the floor with blood oozing from a gaping head wound, a man holding his intestines in his hands—*and* nightmares replaying the fire. He is a light sleeper and something as insignificant as running water will wake him and cause his heart to race. "Once I wake up, I can't go back to sleep, because of the babies. Milo, he's eighteen months. I lost Philip when he was fifteen months. I never raised a child past fifteen months."

Being back in Chicago makes him paranoid, fearful that he somehow will find himself "caught up in the system again."

"A couple months ago, I saw a car accident—the girl, she was in pain, and the guy was dazed. I wanted to go over there and help them, but I said, 'Nah, I better not, because they'll say I did it.'" He rarely leaves the house, and whenever he does, his sons are with him. "I don't go anywhere alone if I don't have to. If they ever falsely accuse me, they'll have to say he had two babies with him."

Madison has a civil suit pending against the city of Chicago, filed jointly with two of the other men pardoned by the governor. Since Madison's release, still more information has come to light confirming that the police knew he was not responsible for setting the fire. While Madison was in the Cook County Jail awaiting trial, arson fires continued to occur on Chicago's South Side, and the fire department informed police that the MO was identical to the 82nd Street arson fire. Also alarming, according to one source, police took Andre Council into custody on the morning following the fire and detained him until late in the evening. By that account, Andre Council was a suspect from the outset, rather than a witness who came forward voluntarily; according to the source, Council never mentioned Madison Hobley's name or seeing him on TV, until the police brought him home following the day-long interrogation.[121]

In November of 2006, the city agreed to a settlement. His mother's health had improved, and eager to leave Chicago, Madison made a down payment on a house in another state, expecting to receive the first payment from the agreed-upon award in January of 2007. In a public statement issued on 19 February 2007, the city reneged on the deal. The U.S. District judge who mediated the dispute openly criticized the administration of Mayor Richard M. Daley for refusing to honor the agreement, calling the city's behavior "unprecedented."[122]

Madison lost the $2,500 down payment.

"Why me, God?" Madison asks, reflecting on the conspiracy of deception and fraud that stole sixteen years of his life. "I think Judge Dennis Porter is a coward. The same as the judge before him. Berkos. Had they done the job that they were supposed to do, I would have been granted a new trial and wouldn't have been a recipient of Governor George Ryan's pardon. The state's attorneys were crooks, wicked, and just masters of deception. Liars. These are the people that are supposed to be representing good. I can't even imagine still being in prison. I probably would have lost my mind by now. If I dwell on it too long and let myself think back, I get angry. I get frustrated. I'm so grateful that the truth set me free, but I don't have any trust. If you can't trust a police officer, if you can't trust a state attorney, if you can't trust a judge, who can you trust?"

RANDAL PADGETT

Sentenced to Death by DNA Evidence that Led Police Away from the Truth

I'd never been in prison before. I didn't know what prison was, except what I'd seen in the movies. I'd never even been in jail, until they arrested me for my wife Cathy's murder.

They sentenced me to death on my birthday, May 22, and carried me to Holman Prison that same day. It was late by the time we got there, around 10:30 at night. They did a strip search and took everything away from me. I kept thinking, when is the guard gonna come over and kick me in the face. Just the feel of the place, people screaming, all kinds of commotion, and those metal doors sliding and slamming, sliding and slamming. Another one opens up and then it slams behind you. It seemed like a hundred metal doors."

—Randal Padgett, set free by a unanimous verdict of
"not guilty" after five and a half years incarceration,
three and a half of those years on death row.[1]

The Crime: Friday, 17 August 1990, Arab, Alabama

Following Thursday night's revival service at New Brashier's Chapel Methodist Church, Cathy Padgett lingered to chat with some of the other churchwomen. Driving at night and going home to an empty house made her uneasy, but Cathy Padgett put her trust in God. 'If anyone was in my house, I would just bind them up in the name of the Lord,' she declared in a testimony to her faith. Cathy had attended the revival at the New Brashier's Chapel Methodist Church every night that week, at each service going forward to the altar and asking God to help her through this difficult time.[2]

That past May, Cathy and Randal Padgett had separated after sixteen years of marriage. Randal had admitted to having an affair. Although as yet unwilling to take the radical step of filing for a divorce, the couple had discussed it and arrived at an amicable property settlement, as well as agreeing to share custody of six-year-old Heather and eleven-year-old Micah in the event they divorced. Randal continued to see his children on nearly a daily basis.[3]

Randal and his girlfriend Judy Bagwell had a trip to Florida planned for that weekend. Feeling guilty about being away from his children for so long, Randal had asked Cathy if Heather and Micah could spend Thursday afternoon and evening with him, and Cathy had agreed. He took them to a movie and afterward to play miniature golf. Randal was staying in a mobile home on his chicken farm, a seven-mile drive from the couple's other farm on Bridge Road where Cathy lived. Randal tried phoning Cathy several times that evening to make sure she knew he intended to keep the children overnight. He reached Cathy a few minutes before ten. She had just returned from the revival. It was the last time Randal Padgett would speak to his wife.[4]

About two o'clock Friday morning, Jimmy Gullion, a truck driver for Goldkist, was on his way back from making a feed delivery. Gullion saw dust rising above a cornfield that bordered Bridge Road and slowed his rig. Surfaced in gravel, Bridge Road intersected with the highway Gullion traveled. The speeding vehicle causing the dust cloud was a white Ford Fairmont station wagon with a missing rear hubcap, Gullion noted when it came into full view. His lights shone briefly into the car's interior, and he could make out the silhouettes of two people. The driver had slender arms, bushy black hair, and wore a blouse-like top. The event logged itself in Gullion's mind for being unusual—in eleven years of traveling that stretch of highway on a regular basis, he had only once before seen a car on Bridge Road at that time of night.[5]

Randal and the children rose early. After driving into town to Hardee's to buy sausage and biscuits for their breakfast, Randal took the children to the home of his aunt, Lillian Snow. Lillian frequently cared for Heather and Micah. She lived just across the creek from the thirty-two-acre farm where Cathy's house was situated.[6]

Randal and the children unpacked their Hardee's breakfast and ate at Aunt Lillian's table, then Randal left to tend to chores in the chicken houses. He came back at noon and had lunch with his family. His cousin Reba Davis and her daughter, who lived in a mobile home on Aunt Lillian's property, were also there. Ashamed about his affair and not wanting his family to know that he and his girlfriend had plans to leave for Florida that same afternoon, Randal told his aunt and cousin he was going back to finish up chores at the chicken farm.[7]

Randal's hired hand finished up the chicken house chores. By early afternoon, Randal Padgett and his girlfriend Judy Bagwell were on the way to Destin, Florida.

Usually Cathy came by Lillian's to pick up the children between 4:30 and 5:00, after she got off work. When Cathy was late, Reba phoned the house several times, but no one answered. Reba, Cathy, and the children intended to have supper at the church that evening, the final night of the revival. Thinking perhaps Cathy had gone straight to the church from work, Reba phoned there, as well, but no one had seen Cathy.[8]

Looking forward to the evening outing, Heather and Micah suggested that Reba drive them home to change clothes so they could go on to the revival as planned. They knew where a "secret" key was hidden and could let themselves in.[9]

'Mom must be home,' the children chorused when they saw their mother's car in the garage. The door leading into the house from the utility room off the garage was unlocked. Cathy's purse was on the floor just inside the doorway, the contents strewn about. Six-year-old Heather headed straight for her mother's room.[10]

'Something's wrong with Momma!' she wailed and burst into tears.[11]

Micah, Reba, and Reba's daughter Laurie rushed to the back of the house. Horrified, Reba ushered the hysterical children into the kitchen and phoned for an ambulance.[12]

Cathy Padgett lay crossways on the bed on her back, her legs spread with her right foot propped up on the nightstand and her left foot resting on the floor. She was naked from the waist down. The bed linens were soaked with blood. Bloodstains splattered the headboard, nightstand, wall, and windowsill. Cathy Padgett had been stabbed more than forty times. Her left thumb and right pinky finger were nearly cut off, evidently from her desperate effort to wrest the knife away from her attacker. There were cuts on seven of her ten fingers. Her pink sleep T-shirt with the logo "Alarm Clock Shock" was pushed up to just below her breasts. Her blood-soaked tampon had been removed and placed on the pillow. Her panties had been cut on both sides, from the waist to the leg openings, and remained under her buttocks in back, with the front flap dangling over the edge of the bed.[13]

The Marshall County Sheriff's Department and Arab Police Department worked through the night canvassing the crime scene, taking photographs and dusting for fingerprints. Exhausted, the officers and investigators went for breakfast at a local diner early Friday morning. The waitress who served them eavesdropped on the conversation. 'It looked like she was raped after she was already dead,' one officer remarked. Said another, 'The whole thing looked staged to me.'[14]

"If I'd Been Home With My Wife Like I Should Have Been, Cathy Might Be Alive Today."

Randal Padgett has sandy blond hair salted with telltale signs of age. Over six feet tall, with a stocky physique, he looks like a man who might have played football in his younger years. "Nah," Randal says in his shy, soft-spoken drawl, "I played basketball in junior high, but I didn't go out for any sports in high school—you had to stay after school for practice, not enough time for hunting and fishing. I loved to hunt and fish."[15]

Randal was born in 1950, in Arab, Alabama, a small community in Marshall County, a predominantly rural region located in the northeast sector of the state. Marshall County has a total population of 84,000. By comparison, the nearest city of any size, Huntsville, in neighboring Madison County, has a population of 158,000. Except for his college years and his time on death row, Randal Padgett has lived in Marshall County his entire life. "My pop was a farmer. He row cropped, until he got into the chicken business, and eventually, raising chickens was all he did. After high school, I went to Jacksonville State University and got a bachelors degree in business with a minor in economics. That first year after college, about all I did was fish, me and this buddy of mine, every day for nearly a year. My pop started to get on me, 'Don't you think it's about time you do something besides fish, son?' I was in Huntsville at Kmart in the sporting goods section and the manager was talking about needing help, so I hired on as an assistant manager.

"That's where I met Cathy."

A petite, blue-eyed blonde, Cathy Cavanaugh worked as a cashier in the automotive section. Randal had scarcely dated at all in high school. His only prior steady girlfriend was a woman he dated in college, a relationship that lasted less than a year. Cathy Cavanaugh was friendly and easy to talk to, and finally Randal got up the nerve to ask her for a date.

She accepted and suggested Randal follow her home after work, so he would know where her house was. "Huntsville was a big city to me," Randal says sheepishly. It was raining and the roads were slick. When a traffic light just ahead changed from green to yellow, Randal panicked—*I'm gonna lose her.* He sped up, Cathy stopped, and Randal plowed into the back of her car, severely damaging her bumper. They phoned for the police to file an accident report. When the officer arrived, they were sitting in the car holding hands. The officer thought they were strangers who had become intimately acquainted in the short span between the accident and when he had arrived at the scene. In a sense, it was true.

Five years younger than Randal, Cathy still lived with her family.[16] To hear Randal describe their courtship, one might guess it was the early 1950s, rather than the wild and promiscuous early seventies. They went bowling, to movies, and out to eat. "Just the normal stuff a country guy does," Randal says. Cathy indulged Randal's passion for fishing, joining him for long, lazy afternoons on the water, reading a book while he cast his line.

In 1974, after dating for just over a year, Randal and Cathy married. They made Arab their home, and Randal got a job at Cutler Hammer, a local factory that manufactured electrical switches. He started out as a scheduler and received several promotions. When Eaton Corporation took over the company, Randal stayed on, eventually rising to the position of supervisor over inventory control and the production department.

In 1983, Cathy and Randal bought thirty-two acres from Randal's Aunt Lillian and moved into the house located on the property, land belonging to his mother's family for three generations. Cathy and Randal's neighbors across the pasture were Judy and Tommy Smith. Judy came by the house to see the couple's new baby, Heather, and the Padgetts took Judy up on her offer to teach Micah to swim—the Smiths had a pool. Randal also knew Judy from work. Judy held Randal's starting position, scheduler in the production department.

In many respects, the Padgetts were a storybook-happy family. Fond of camping, they made regular holiday excursions to the Great Smoky Mountains and nearby lakes. Cathy stayed home with the children when they were young, later taking a job at another Arab-area factory. Their social life revolved around the church and church community. Cathy was raised a Catholic, but she followed her husband in his faith and joined Randal's church, Shoal Creek Baptist. Randal served there as a deacon. Randal's male friends were predominantly small business owners and professional people, churchgoing men like him.

Every night before tucking his children into bed, Randal read to them.[17] "I had a good life. I loved my wife and two kids. If anybody had ever told me that I would have an affair, I would have laughed at them. If they had said it would be with *that person*, I would have laughed extra hard. She wasn't my type."

That person was Judy Smith. Her speech tended toward the coarse and

Randal, Cathy, and Micah Padgett. [COURTESY OF RANDAL PADGETT]

vulgar. She made frequent use of what Randal calls the "f word," a habit he found "disgusting." Although near Cathy's age—Judy was a year older—the two women were different as night and day. Cathy wore her medium length blond hair in loose, soft curls. Judy was also a blonde, but with a closely cropped, boyish hairstyle, often accented by unmatched earrings of two radically different designs. Tall and leggy, her tight, short skirts were quick to catch the eyes of the men. She courted attention, sometimes coming to work wearing one red sneaker and one blue sneaker. In girl-talk with the other women, she told outlandish stories about saving her husband's semen and using it for facials and to make protein drinks or dipping chocolate in it for a snack. She had cheated on her husband Tommy before and was rumored to have caused the break up of more than one marriage.[18]

Judy Smith was among the employees Randal supervised. He was well liked at Eaton, known for his impish joking and gentle teasing humor. In almost thirteen years of marriage, he had never even fantasized being with another woman. Then, in July of 1986, what started out as a joke changed the course of his life.

"One day at work, a bunch of us were standing around talking and Judy said something about all of us coming over to her house that night to go skinny-dipping. It was in the summer, and we'd all been putting in a lot of overtime at the plant and getting home late. That night I was almost to my house, and I came up behind Judy's car, and when she pulled in her drive I

Randal, Cathy, Micah, and Heather Padgett. [COURTESY OF RANDAL PADGETT]

thought, well, I'm gonna trick her and make her think I'm gonna take her up on her offer to go skinny dipping. So I pulled my headlights into her drive, then backed out, and went home.

"I didn't think any more about it, until the next day at work, when Judy said, 'You chickened out on going skinny-dipping, didn't you?' That night I worked late again, and coming home, almost at the same spot, there her car was in front of me again. She pulled in her driveway, and I thought, well, I'll show her who's chicken. I pulled in behind her and got out and said, 'Let's go skinny dipping.'

"I figured she'd laugh, and I'd go home. But she said, 'Okay, let's get some towels.' Her husband Tommy worked nights, so it was just us. We went out to the pool. I took off my shoes, she took off her shoes, the both of us stripping, one thing at a time, until we didn't have any clothes on. I waded out into the pool. I can't swim. She was wanting to do more than skinny-dip, but I didn't. I put my clothes back on and went home.

"This was on the start of a three-day holiday weekend and all weekend what might have happened that night at her pool was all I could think about. *Just do it that one time and see what it's like, it'll be all right*—that's what the devil kept telling me.

"So the next day we worked, I told Judy I was coming over—we did more that time."

Randal was ashamed and disgusted with himself. "After the first time I met with Judy, I got down on my knees and I cried out to God to help me and forgive me.

"But then, before you know it, I'm back doing the same thing."

Randal makes no excuses for his behavior, and in no sense blames Cathy. But he acknowledges that he and Cathy "had lost our flirting with one another." Things Cathy failed to notice, earned him petting and attention from Judy. *You got a hair cut! . . . There's a Band-Aid on your arm-what happened?* Sensitive to his likes and dislikes, before long she dropped the "f— word" and frequent cursing from her conversation, in his presence. And Randal remade his image of her, forgetting how distasteful he once found her crude speech and ostentatious manner. She made him feel special, made him feel like "this woman wants me."

Judy and Tommy Smith had no church affiliation, favoring a different sort of social life. Judy would tell Randal stories about the swingers club she and Tommy had belonged to for a time, a group of couples who engaged in partner swapping. Before he met Cathy, Randal had only had one sexual partner. Judy Smith was the third.[19]

Soon sensing trouble in his marriage, Judy's husband Tommy became even more suspicious when he noticed his wife sitting in the shade of the back breezeway, ogling Randal Padgett across the field.[20] Bothered with a sinus condition, Tommy came home early from work one night. Through the front window, he saw two people get up from the couch when he pulled in the driveway. Randal dashed out the back door, and Judy met Tommy at the front door.

Tommy Smith did not need to ask to know who his wife's visitor was.

'We're just friends,' Judy hurried to explain.

Tommy slapped her, "You need to find you a place to stay tonight."

Judy left and spent the night at the Holiday Inn.

Randal went home and confided in Cathy.[21] Two days later, Randal called Tommy and tried to smooth things over with his neighbor, parroting Judy's explanation that they were just friends.

"I thought I would stop seeing Judy," Randal says, "but I didn't."

Judy began pressuring Tommy for a divorce. When Tommy succeeded in tape-recording a portion of a conversation between Judy and Randal, he confronted his wife at gunpoint. "If ever I catch you meeting him while you're living with me, I'll blow your damn brains out."

Early in 1987, Tommy Smith consented to the divorce, although still rife with jealousy. He stalked his wife, and just two weeks after they signed the divorce papers, Tommy discovered Judy and Randal at a motel in the nearby town of Scottsboro. Tommy Smith slashed the tires on Randal's car and then drove home and phoned the plant manager at Eaton.

Eaton's code of ethics mandated automatic dismissal for an employee in a supervisory capacity who engaged in an extramarital affair—a policy reflecting the church-dominated ethos of the culture. Individuals in a position of authority instructed by virtue of their example. Tommy Smith's account of Randal Padgett's hotel rendezvous with his ex-wife put the plant manager in a difficult and potentially embarrassing situation. Judy, who had returned to her maiden name Judy Bagwell, reported directly to Randal Padgett. When the plant manager asked Tommy Smith what he wanted done, Tommy Smith answered, "I want his job!"

Randal was asked to resign and did. Judy Bagwell, not part of the management staff, suffered no repercussions. Talk buzzed among the incredulous Eaton employees. Many refused to believe Randal Padgett was having an affair, especially with Judy Bagwell.

Friends tried to persuade Randal to end the relationship, but Randal would hang his head and mumble, 'I don't see the person you all see.' Embarrassed and confused, Randal resigned from the office of deacon and stopped attending services. "I got ashamed to go to church," he confesses, "then I got ashamed to even talk to God."

Conversely, when Cathy learned that Randal lost his job and why, she became even more devout, seeking solace in her faith. Membership at Shoal Creek Baptist Church had been steadily declining for several years. In the summer of 1987, Cathy accepted an invitation to visit New Brashier's Chapel Methodist Church and soon switched her church affiliation, lured by the enthusiastic and energetic congregation.

New Brashier's Chapel Methodist held worship services twice weekly, on Sunday mornings and Wednesday evenings. Following a Wednesday evening service in September of 1987, Cathy opened her car door to discover a woman crouched in the floorboard behind the back seat. When Cathy screamed, the hiding woman threatened to kill her. Most of the church members had left, but the few who remained heard Cathy's terrified shrieks and rushed to her aid. "It's me, Judy," the woman who had accosted Cathy blurted out, and only then did Cathy recognize her. Judy Bagwell wore a gray sweat suit, curly black wig, and white leather gloves. "I love Randal, Randal loves me," she blubbered, explaining to the small crowd who gathered that she just wanted to talk to Cathy. A brief discussion about religion followed. Then Judy left, walking off in the direction of the cemetery, where she apparently had hidden her car.[22]

Cathy told Randal what had happened, and that same night, Judy phoned him, admitting that she had made a "bad mistake." Although Judy's behavior was shocking and unsettling, for Randal, the dividing line between reality and illusion had grown hazy and indistinct. He pushed

Judy away, but he left the door open a crack, telling her that he needed to stop seeing her 'for a while.'[23]

Devastated, Judy Bagwell phoned Cathy repeatedly, and when Cathy refused to talk with her, Judy began leaving threatening messages on the answering machine, telling Cathy that she needed to let Randal go.[24] Eventually, to put a stop to the harassment, Cathy disconnected the machine.[25]

Cathy and Randal settled back into family life, and Randal decided to pursue a long-time dream. "I'd wanted a chicken farm for years, but every time I'd think about borrowing the kind of money it took to get in the business, I'd get scared. After I left Eaton, I had to find a new way to earn a living." The couple enlisted the services of real estate agent Brenda Massingill to help them find a poultry farm.

Randal and Brenda knew one another from his time at Eaton, where she was also employed. A single mother with two children to support, Brenda had taken a second job as a realtor to help make ends meet. One evening at the office, Brenda Massingill received a phone call from Tommy Smith. Smith had heard that the Padgetts were looking for a chicken farm, and he wanted to buy the farm where they were living now.

'You tell Randal Padgett it would be in his and his family's best interest if he'd sell the place to me and left here,' Smith declared in what sounded more like a threat than an offer. 'I'll pay any amount. I want that farm. I want him out of my sight. Tell him to name his price.'

Harboring certain reservations, Brenda Massingill phoned the Padgetts. Cathy answered and the two women talked briefly about Randal's dream of raising chickens. Brenda was touched by Cathy's dedication to her husband. 'Oh, Brenda,' Cathy said, 'If you can do anything to help Randal, I would appreciate it so very much.'

When Brenda talked to Randal and passed along Tommy Smith's exorbitant offer—'Name your price'—Randal answered curtly, sarcastically, "A million dollars."

In March of 1989, the Padgetts bought a farm with six chicken houses, offered for sale privately. The property was located just seven miles from where they were living. To finance the endeavor, they borrowed $200,000.[26]

Randal had begun seeing Judy Bagwell again. She had moved from her mother's to a house in Arab. To make Randal jealous, she invited a male friend over for the evening. He stayed late into the night. Randal drove by the house and saw an unexpected car in Judy's driveway. He knew whose car it was. Randal drove by again and again, and still the man did not leave. Eventually Randal went home, but he was back at Judy's first thing the next morning. The dishes from Judy and her date's dinner were still in the sink.

Tormented, Randal finally told Cathy he had resumed the affair with

Judy, and Cathy replied resolutely, 'I know.' "I still love you," he said, "but I've got to do something." In July of 1989, the couple separated, and Randal moved into one of the two mobile homes on the chicken farm property.[27]

Never one to drink to excess, Randal Padgett's habits began to change. A few weeks later, coming home from a hunting excursion, he was arrested for drunk driving. He phoned Judy, and when she came to pick him up, he asked her to take him to Cathy's house. The "secret" key was not in its usual hiding place in the utility room off the garage, and Randal had to slip the front-door lock with his driver's license. Once when Cathy was out, Judy and Randal had had intercourse at the house. On that occasion, though, Judy did not stay long.[28]

Randal had decided to move back home. He could not have Judy taxiing him around if he lost his driver's license. His aunt, his sister and two brothers, his parents—they didn't know about the affair. And Randal did not want them to know.[29]

However, Randal Padgett continued to see Judy Bagwell. Somehow, he could not bring himself to break away from her. "When I was with Judy, as soon as I'd get there, I'd be wishing I was home. And then, when I was home, I'd be wishing I was with Judy. I was miserable." Cathy, if for no other reason than women's intuition, knew that her husband was still being unfaithful. Cathy never made a scene, but finally she confronted Randal with what she feared was the truth: 'You still love Judy.' In May of 1990, the couple separated a second time. They discussed divorce and jotted down a few handwritten notes about how they might divide their property and possessions. Cathy talked with Huntsville Attorney Claude Hundley, who agreed to represent them both, if and when they got ready to take the definitive step of filing.[30]

Randal never conferred with Hundley or any other legal professional. He refused to confront what seemed for him an impossible choice—perhaps because both choices were hollow and empty. Only vestiges of his former life with Cathy remained. He had alienated himself from the social network of his church, and Cathy now belonged to a different church. He and Judy had no social life. They never went out, not even for dinner. At bottom, Randal did not want anyone to know he was involved with Judy Bagwell. The life he had before, the life he loved, was comprised of people of a vastly different sort.[31]

In late July, Cathy and the children went with her mother and father to Canada for a summer vacation. She returned home to discover a dead dog in the utility room. Cathy had no idea how the animal managed to get in. Maybe she left the door ajar, and it wandered in and became trapped when a breeze blew the door closed. Although possible, the scenario seemed unlikely. The dog had been there for some time and was already in a high state of decomposition. Appalled and distraught, Cathy phoned Randal, and he came over to the house and removed the fetid, rotting carcass.[32]

When Cathy ran out of gas a few weeks later, she again phoned Randal for help. Randal saw his children every day, picking them up when their mother left for work, most days taking them next door to his aunt's home, so she could look after them while he tended to chores in his chicken houses. In many ways, the Padgetts had a model separation, just as theirs had been a model marriage in the early years. Even people who knew about Randal's affair found it hard to imagine Cathy and Randal divorced.[33]

Judy Bagwell, though, was already making plans for her life with Randal Padgett. 'Come here, come here, and let me show you what I got,' Judy beamed excitedly, one day in early August, when Randal stopped by to see her. She ushered him into the spare bedroom, now furnished with bunk beds identical to those in Micah's room at Cathy's house.

Randal had never taken the children to Judy's house. He never saw her when he was with them. Since he and Judy first became involved, the children had been in her presence only once, when they were with their father in downtown Arab and happened upon Judy entirely by chance.

Randal frequently spent the night at Judy's, so it struck him as somewhat odd when Judy suggested he ask Cathy if Heather and Micah could stay with him on the Thursday night before they left for Florida for a weekend outing. That would mean he would not be spending the night with her.

And, in fact, Randal had already arraigned to take the children to a movie Thursday afternoon and for them to sleep over Thursday night. He would be gone from Friday through Monday, and he knew they would wonder when they did not see him for three days. Spending extra time with them beforehand made him feel a little less guilty. Perhaps when he got back, he would make up a little white lie about being busy with the chickens.

"I Can't Believe You're Arresting Me. You're All Messin' Up"

Judy had made the lodging arrangements for the Florida trip, an excursion prompted by Judy's recently acquired passion for scuba diving lessons. The drive from Arab, Alabama, to Destin, Florida, took nearly eight hours. Randal and Judy arrived in Destin late Friday night, and checked into the Harbor View Motel. Shortly after eleven, a motel employee knocked on the door, with a message for Judy to call her sister Peggy Binning. There was no phone in the room, and Judy went outside to use the pay phone.[34]

Randal's memory of the subsequent chain of events has the quality of a surreal nightmare. "I'd just gone to sleep when Judy got the message to call her sister. Judy came back from using the phone and tells me 'Cathy's been killed.' I just went berserk. We went outside to the phone booth, and I called my brother. 'All I know is she's been killed with a knife,' was all he could tell me. I got physically ill and vomited. 'I've got to go home,' I said to Judy, 'I've got to go home.'"

Randal vomited again, and then the phone in the booth rang. Marshall County Sheriff's Investigator Bob Norwood had received the number from Judy's sister. After talking with Judy, Peggy Binning had phoned the sheriff's office with information on how to contact Judy and Randal.[35]

Investigator Norwood informed Randal that his wife was deceased. Randal asked for more information, but Norwood refused to give him any details. Randal said he would leave immediately and come to the police department at soon as he got back to Arab. Norwood's report states that he heard "no emotional distress" in Randal Padgett's voice. Randal scarcely remembers the conversation.[36]

With Randal in no condition to drive, Judy took the wheel, but thirty minutes out from Destin, Judy drifted off to sleep and nearly wrecked the car. Randal drove the rest of the way home, with Judy intermittently dozing and when wakeful, semi-incoherent and seemingly dazed.

"You might be a suspect, because of the incident at the church," he said to her at one point during the course of the eight-hour trip, and a sobering realization followed. "I guess I might be, too—you don't think I had anything to do with it?" he asked, appalled at the thought. 'Oh, no! No!' Judy insisted.[37]

"It was already daylight when we got back," Randal says, and his eyes take on a bewildered, far away look, thinking back to that morning. "I left Judy off at her house and went to the Arab Police Department. The people I needed to talk to weren't there yet—it was about 7:30—so I waited outside on a park bench."

Finally, just before nine o'clock, the three officers arrived who had conducted the preliminary investigation, sheriff's investigator Norwood, Arab Police Lieutenant Billy Stricklend, and Tom Taylor, an agent for the Alabama Bureau of Investigation.[38]

"They wouldn't give me any details. When I asked how Cathy was killed, all they would say was 'brutal, it was very brutal.' I asked was she beat up, and they said 'cut, it was very brutal.' I asked was she raped, and they said 'We can't say.' They told me in a situation like this, they suspect the spouse first, and I said that I understood, especially because Cathy and I were separated, and I was having an affair. I told them about the affair. I told them what all I knew."

In his statement, Randal gave the officers a full account of his relationship with Judy Bagwell, beginning with when they first became involved four years before. He acknowledged that he and Judy had discussed the possibility that they might both be suspects during the drive back from Florida, almost as an afterthought mentioning that Judy had not denied being involved.[39]

But when the investigators asked Randal Padgett, 'Who's the first person that crosses your mind who might have killed, Cathy?' he answered, "Tommy Smith."[40]

"I don't why Tommy Smith was the first person that occurred to me," Randal says, "It just popped in there. I had no reason other than because of the situation between me and him."

Randal readily agreed to the officers' request for a blood sample and fingerprint analysis, both conducted immediately following the interview. When asked if he would take a polygraph test, Randal readily agreed to that as well. The officers said they would set it up for one day the following week.[41]

After leaving the police station, Randal went to his parent's home to see Heather and Micah. They hugged and cried in one another's arms. Randal's older sister Carolyn was there, as well. That the police wanted Randal to take a lie-detector test and had asked him for blood and fingerprint samples concerned Carolyn. She knew an attorney in Huntsville where she and her husband owned a machine shop. 'You better go talk to this guy,' Carolyn insisted. "I don't need a lawyer," Randal objected, surprised by the suggestion. But Carolyn was adamant, and Randal finally relented.

At the request of the police, Randal met with Stricklend and the other investigators at Cathy's house on the following day. The officers videotaped the encounter, noting Randal's observations. The door chime, which had been mounted on the inside of the front door, was lying on the floor next to the wall, Randal pointed out, and there were several scratches on the front door, which to the best of his recollection had not been there before. When the officers asked him what kind of person he wife was, he described Cathy as "good as gold." When they revisited a question they had posed at the initial interview—*Who might have wanted to kill Cathy?*—Randal gave a different answer. "The only person I can think of would be Judy Bagwell Smith," he admitted hesitantly.[42]

Cathy was buried later that week. Brenda Massingill, who had worked with Randal at Eaton and assisted the Padgetts in their search for a poultry farm, went to the funeral home during visitation to comfort the grieving family. Six-year-old Heather sat curled in her daddy's lap, with her arms wrapped around his neck, clinging to him like a terrified little mouse. Tears streamed down Randal's face. Brenda had to kneel down to be able to hear him. 'I can't let them get my kids, I just can't let them get to my kids,' he whispered, his broad shoulders heaving, choking back the sobs. He feared, as did many in the community, that the killer or killers might strike again.

Law-enforcement officials set up surveillance at the cemetery, monitoring the visitors to Cathy's gravesite.

They had interviewed Judy Bagwell on the morning of the day she and Randal had return from Florida, immediately following their initial interview with him. Judy openly admitted to the affair with Randal and acknowledged that she had had several affairs during her marriage to Tommy Smith. She also admitted to hiding in the backseat of Cathy's car at the church, but she insisted that she had only wanted to talk with Cathy. She said she felt "trapped in the car," when people started coming out of the church, and lay down on the floorboard. She offered no explanation for why she was wearing a wig and gloves. She did, however, offer a somewhat incredible explanation for how she intended to get out of the predicament, saying that she had decided to remain concealed, ride home with Cathy, then walk back to her car—a distance of three miles.[43]

Judy painstakingly described her activities on the Thursday prior to Cathy Padgett's murder, recounting a trip to Huntsville, giving departure and arrival times for each leg of her journey. She was alone all evening, she said, and, made pointed mention of phoning her sister at 10:00 P.M. and going to bed at 10:15 P.M.[44]

Judy Bagwell's ex-husband Tommy Smith was also alone on the night Cathy Padgett was killed. The police had interviewed Smith on the Tuesday following the murder. His statement to police betrayed his jealousy and continued infatuation with his ex-wife. "It tears me up to see her . . . The only reason somebody didn't get shot in my divorce case was because I didn't catch them." In talking about the incident at the church where Judy hid in the back seat of Cathy's car, Tommy Smith admitted to being scared of his ex-wife. "I know the girl. I have lived with her thirteen years." "If she drove up in my yard and wanted to talk to me . . . I would be afraid that she would pull a gun or shoot me or something." He also expressed concerns about being framed for Cathy Padgett's murder, that "somebody . . . could have got in my house with a key and got hair out of the hairbrush [at Cathy's] . . . and planted it back in my house." He acknowledged phoning Judy shortly after their divorce and suggesting they get together for casual sex, but denied having any recent contact with her. Conversely, Judy Bagwell, in her statement to police, said Tommy Smith had phoned her as recently as the previous summer. Law-enforcement officials asked Tommy Smith if they could fingerprint him and take a blood sample, and Tommy Smith agreed.[45]

On August 31, Arab Police investigators seized Randal's pickup truck, his primary mode of transportation, to test the vehicle for blood, hair, and fiber samples.[46]

Randal had not seen or talked to Judy Bagwell since returning from Florida. "In the back of my mind, I kind of suspected Judy," he concedes. "I didn't tell her that, but I knew soon as I let her off, 'I ain't never gonna see you again.' I kept thinking that if I'd been home like I should have been, Cathy might be alive. Judy tried to contact me through mutual acquaintances a couple times, but I didn't want to have anything to do with her."

Randal's sister Carolyn accompanied him on his first visit to see Huntsville attorney Mark McDaniel.

An experienced, highly regarded criminal-defense attorney, McDaniel cut straight to the point. 'Son, I don't care if you did it or not, but if you did do it, I want you to tell me exactly how you did it. Tell me everything you did, where you went, exactly how you did it, and I'll get you off. If you did it, and you don't tell me, something will come up and bite me in the butt at trial, and you'll get hung.'

"Well, you don't need to be asking me this no more," Randal answered in his slow drawl. "I'm telling you now, I ain't done it, and you don't ever have to ask me this again."

Echoing his sister Carolyn's concerns, Mark McDaniel advised him against taking a lie-detector test and said that if he did take one, he needed to have an attorney with him.

Randal retained Mark McDaniel as his legal counsel.

He phoned the police department daily to see if they had any new information. During one such call, the police asked Randal to come down to the station. When he arrived, Investigator Billy Stricklend informed him that they had the polygraph test scheduled. When Randal said he wanted his attorney to accompany him, Stricklend flew into a rage.

'You've been tellin' me all this time you were innocent. Why are you talkin' to a lawyer?' Stricklend demanded, dismissing Randal with a wave of his hand, 'Get out of here!'

Although more than willing to submit to a lie-detector test, Randal was never given one.

Investigator Stricklend already had zeroed in on Randal Padgett as the primary suspect, based on the lab results received from the Alabama Department of Forensic Sciences.

Cathy Padgett had type A blood. Bloodstains from the crime scene matched only Cathy. Randal Padgett and Tommy Smith both had type O blood. The lab results also indicated that the vaginal swabs, as well as stains on Cathy's panties and thigh, contained a mixture of semen and vaginal cells, but an ABO blood type could not be identified from the semen. For 80 percent of the population, ABO blood type can be determined from an examination of other bodily fluids and tissues, including semen, saliva, and skin tissue. For the minority 20 percent of the population, ABO characteristics are not secreted into the fluids and tissues; this group is referred to as nonsecretors. Because no ABO blood factors were identified in the semen, the conclusion followed that Cathy's killer was a nonsecretor.[47]

Randal Padgett was a nonsecretor. Hoping to come up with even more definitive evidence against him, the State investigative team submitted his blood sample to Cellmark Diagnostics in Maryland for DNA comparison to the seminal fluids on the vaginal swabs.[48]

From the outset, law-enforcement officials had refused to tell Randal Padgett anything about his wife's murder, aside from that she was 'cut' and 'it was very brutal.'

"I found out Cathy was raped," Randal says, "when I learned from Mark McDaniel that they were doing a DNA test." As horrible as the news was, Randal was in one sense relieved. "I couldn't wait for the results of that test, so they'd leave me alone and start looking for the right person."

Randal remained close to Cathy's parents, Francis and Hettie Cavanaugh. "They told me, 'We know you didn't do this, Randal. We never even heard you raise your voice to Cathy. If they take you to jail, they may as well take us too.'

"One night, about a month after I found out they were doing a DNA test, the kids and I were over at the Cavanaughs' visiting. Billy Stricklend and Bob Norwood came to the door, and they took me outside and put the handcuffs on me. They wouldn't even let me go back in and say goodbye to my kids. 'I can't believe you're arresting me. You're all messin' up,' I told them. 'No,' they said, 'you're the one that messed up.'"[49]

"They carried me to the Marshall County Jail. I was scared. I'd never been in jail before. I didn't eat the whole time I was in there."

Randal's family rallied forces to make his bail, securing signatures from twenty-one property owners who pledged amounts ranging from $1,400 to $11,400, and after three days he was released on a $100,000 property bond.[50]

He had been arrested on October 5, the same day Cellmark Diagnostics returned its report to the Alabama Department of Forensic Science. The semen DNA extracted from the vaginal swab matched the DNA of the blood sample obtained from Randal Padgett.[51]

Hope and False Hope

"Something's wrong with that test!" Randal insisted when he met with Mark McDaniel.[52]

Charged with "Murder during rape in the first degree," Randal pleaded not guilty at his arraignment on 4 February 1991.[53] The trial date originally was set for March 4, but the court granted McDaniel a continuance to verify the tests conducted by the State.[54]

Fresh samples of Randal's blood and a sample from the vaginal swab were sent to independent laboratories. When the preliminary blood work came back from the serology lab, Mark McDaniel phoned him, ecstatic. "'The lab got a different PGM reading on your blood than the PGM the State reported,' McDaniel tells me, 'This guy will testify that it wasn't your blood the State used for the test!'"

PGM refers to the enzyme phosphoglucomutase. There are multiple forms of PGM. The form of PGM possessed by an individual is an inherited trait, meaning it is distinct and cannot change.[55]

The blood sample labeled Randal Padgett, which the Alabama Department of Forensic Science submitted to Cellmark, was type PGM 2-1. The serology lab used by McDaniel reported Randal's blood was type PGM 1-1. Tommy Smith's blood was also type PGM 1-1, according to the Alabama Department of Forensic Science. Both blood samples were stored in the same lab refrigerator. Had the State inadvertently submitted Tommy Smith's blood, rather than Randal Padgett's? Or had a mix-up occurred at the Cellmark testing facility?[56]

The question as to whose blood Cellmark actually tested seemed to offer a key to solving Cathy's murder and proving Randal's innocence, as well.

Then Lifecodes laboratory returned the results on the DNA test that McDaniel had requested. Like Cellmark, Lifecodes reported that the DNA extracted from the semen on the vaginal swab and DNA from Randal Padgett's blood sample showed a match!

Mark McDaniel confronted Randal. "'What's up with this?' McDaniel asks me. 'I don't know,' I said, 'I don't know what's up with this.' I wondered if when the Department of Forensics sent a swab for the lab to compare for a match, the swab had some of my blood on it. There was no way the DNA could match, because I hadn't been with Cathy in months. And then I got to thinking, there was only one person, besides myself, that had access to my semen—Judy. The only way my semen could have been there was if Judy put it there."

"I'm not proud of talking about this," Randal says. Reluctant to discuss the specifics of his intimate relationship with Judy Bagwell, he refers to sexual intercourse as 'going to bed.' "Starting from about a month before Cathy was killed, after Judy and I went to bed, she got to where she would get up and go to the bathroom. Always, before we would just lie there and fall asleep. It was something I never thought about, until all this stuff came up about the DNA."

In retrospect, two other circumstances also troubled Randal: Judy suggesting he keep his children on the night Cathy was killed and her falling asleep on the trip back from Florida—why was she so exhausted?

But when Randal mentioned his suspicions to Attorney McDaniel, McDaniel dismissed them: "'That's too outlandish,' Mark says to me, 'We can't tell the jury that, we can't point the finger at anybody else. That will make you look bad.' 'Well it needs pointed at somebody,' I said, 'It's pointed at the wrong person now.'"

The local papers' coverage of Cathy Padgett's murder had terrified and traumatized the community with grisly accounts of blood-soaked bed linens and Cathy Padgett's forty-plus stab wounds.

With Randal's arrest, the media coverage changed from horrific to accusing and blatantly false. One story reported that the Padgetts owed $200,000 on the chicken farm, erroneously claiming that Cathy had a $200,000 life insurance policy. The only life insurance Cathy Padgett carried was a modest $20,000 policy provided by her employer. Randall did not even know the amount of coverage provided for in the policy, until after his wife's death.

Cathy's parents turned on Randal. "I don't know what all the police told the Canvenaughs," Randals says. "After I got arrested everything changed. 'How can you believe I done something like this?' I asked Cathy's father. 'Well, they got the hair, and everything keeps piling up,' he says. 'Hair, what hair?' I asked him, 'I ain't heard nothin' about hair.'"

Aside from the suspicious, albeit damning DNA semen match, there was no physical evidence whatsoever linking Randal to his wife's murder—no hair, no fingerprints, no blood.

The Cavanaughs filed for custody of Heather and Micah. Randal had always encouraged and accommodated visits between the children and Cathy's parents. He was shocked. "I got a summons to appear in court. We had a hearing and the court issued an order saying the Cavanaughs got the kids every other weekend and certain holidays. I don't know why they did that. They were getting to see Heather and Micah more before we had the hearing."

In the year and half that elapsed between his arrest and trial, Randal and the children lived with his parents in the nearby Grassy community. Randal's mobile home was small and cramped, and the thought of staying in the house where Cathy had been killed was too horrible to contemplate. He took the children for weekly visits to a psychologist. In the first drawing eleven-year-old Micah made of himself, his lips were turned down in an angry frown. After several months, Micah made a happier drawing of himself, with a smile on his face.

For Randal, though, the days and months dragged on in what seemed like a ghoulish, absurd dream. Mark McDaniel encouraged him to accept a plea deal, with a promise that he'd be out of prison in six years. Randal was appalled. Was this how the criminal justice system worked?

"'Take this plea,' McDaniel tells me, 'and I'll get you a life sentence. You won't have to plead guilty. We'll plead no contest. You won't even have to get up there. You don't have to say a word. They'll send you off to prison, and we'll let you stay down there about a month, then I'll call up Morris Thigpen. He's head of the prison system. Thigpen is one of the best things you've got going for you. I've got another good friend who's a county sheriff, and I'll have Thigpen send you over to this county sheriff's jail. He'll make you a trustee, so you can get out and drive around. Just don't be seen in Arab. Don't be seen in Marshall County. After a while you can go and live in a motel if you want to, just go to the jail and work for them during the day. I'll have you out for good in six years, have you home in six years, and meantime, you won't be in prison.'"

"I can't see spending six minutes in prison for something I didn't do," Randal fired back, "and I ain't gonna do no plea."

When Randal learned that Judy Bagwell had hired an attorney, his initial conversation with Mark McDaniel echoed loud in his mind . . . Son, I don't care if you did it or not, but if you did do it, I want you to tell me everything, where you went, exactly how you did it, and I'll get you off.

Randal confronted McDaniel, asking him what he would do if Judy Bagwell had hired him, "and she fessed up" and admitted to killing Cathy. "What would you do," Randal asked, "knowing that I was going to trial for my life? What would you do about it?"

He was stunned by Mark McDaniel's answer: The basic tenets of his profession enshrined in the doctrine 'lawyer-client privilege' would prohibit him from doing or saying anything.

The results of the fingerprint and palm-print comparison were not turned over to Mark McDaniel until 1 April 1992, a week before the trial began, although Arab Police Lieutenant Billy Stricklend, who headed up the investigation, had received the report on 28 September 1990. All ten palm prints were listed as "unidentified." Of thirteen fingerprints of value, twelve were unidentified. One belonged to Cathy Padgett. None belonged to Randal Padgett or Tommy Smith. The tip of one of Cathy's index fingers had been cut off, leaving way for speculation that two of the unidentified prints may have belonged to Cathy. The other ten were unexplained.[57]

On 29 August 1990, twelve days after Cathy Padgett's murder, the Alabama Bureau of Investigation gave Judy Bagwell a polygraph test. The results indicated that she showed "deception concerning knowledge of who killed Cathy Padgett."[58]

Judy Bagwell was never fingerprinted or asked to submit to forensic sampling of any kind.[59]

The coroner had determined that Cathy Padgett was killed between 1:00 and 2:00 A.M. Truck driver Jimmy Gullion had mentioned to his wife that he had seen a white Ford station wagon with a missing hubcap traveling at a high rate of speed on Bridge Road just before 2:00 A.M. on the night of the murder. A few days later, his wife saw Judy Bagwell's sister in a car that matched Jimmy's description exactly, even the missing hubcap, in the parking lot at the grocery store. The chance of it being a coincidence began to seem even more unlikely when she saw the car again later that week, in the same parking lot at the same grocery store. Judy Bagwell was in the store shopping.[60]

In small towns where community and family ties run deep, people are often reluctant to come forward with information. Jimmy Guillon could not sleep. He did not know what to do.[61] Eventually, though, rumors began to circulate about the white station wagon that Jimmy Gullion saw speeding down Bridge Road on the night of the murder, and at Randal's urging, Mark McDaniel contacted Jimmy Gullion for a full account. McDaniel, however, decided against calling Jimmy Gullion and his wife as witnesses. In explaining his decision to Randal, McDaniel again gave the reason, 'We can't be pointing a finger at someone else.'

The Trial: 8 April 1992

Prior to the onset of the trial, Mark McDaniel discussed his strategy of defense with Randal. "He told me that in most cases the State has this piece of evidence and this piece and this piece, and then they've got their big centerpiece," Randal recalls, recounting McDaniel's explanation. "'All they've got in your case is the centerpiece—the DNA,' McDaniel said. 'We've got to crack holes in that centerpiece.'"

The selection of the twelve-member jury consumed the first two days. Mark McDaniel had requested and been denied a change of venue based on prejudicial pre-trial publicity. Twenty of the thirty-nine prospective jurors had read about the case in the local papers. To sully matters further, during the course of the jury-selection process the judge, Honorable William Jetton, remarked, "I know how I feel about rape, and I know that people that are charged and convicted of rape are in a bad situation in the court that I preside over."[62]

By law, the State and the defense were each allowed to strike fourteen prospective jurors without cause. District Attorney Ronald Thompson used thirteen of his allotted strikes to eliminate men from the jury panel. After elimination of potential jurors who expressed belief that Randal Padgett was guilty, a panel of ten women and two men remained—for the prosecution, a highly favorable gender ratio.[63]

The prosecution planned to argue that Randal Padgett killed his wife because he was having an affair and she would not agree to a divorce. No evidence supported the theory. No evidence whatsoever linked Randal Padgett to Cathy Padgett's murder except for the DNA match reported by Cellmark Diagnostics.

For DNA evidence to be admitted, the State must present proof of the reliability of that evidence. Most of day three and a portion of day four of the trial, conducted out of the presence of the jury, consisted of expert testimony addressing the reliability issue. In keeping with Mark McDaniel's strategy of discrediting the DNA evidence, the defense had hired DNA expert Dr. Michael T. Murray to challenge Cellmark's conclusions. Murray had not arrived when testimony on the reliability question began, and McDaniel asked for a continuance, but Judge Jetton denied the request.[64]

Testifying on behalf of Cellmark, Dr. Charlotte Word admitted that twice the lab had reported erroneous DNA results when the lab had somehow mixed up the samples; however, Dr. Word maintained, these "human errors" had since been corrected. In the absence of the defense's expert witness Dr. Murray, Cellmark's procedures went unchallenged.[65]

When Dr. Murray arrived, he called attention to the general lack of acceptance of Cellmark's techniques within the scientific community and to the unreliability of Cellmark's probability statistics.[66] Interesting in that regard, the State's witnesses could not agree on the probability that Randal Padgett's DNA matched the semen sample, giving statistics ranging from 1-in-940,000 to 1-in-8,600 that the match occurred by chance.[67]

After hearing two days of testimony, Judge Jetton ruled, "I am going to allow the DNA results to go to the jury . . . The matter of product and populations results will be held in abeyance." No testimony on probability statistics would be allowed.[68]

With the jury seated, the State proceeded to present its case against Randal Padgett.

Expert witnesses for the State testified at length about the chemical structure of DNA and DNA-fingerprinting procedures, tedious and highly technical explanations that went on for hours. One man on the jury kept drifting off to sleep, according to Randal.

The jurors may have failed to grasp the complexities underlying the DNA-identification process, but the State expert witnesses drove home the key point in plainspoken, simple language. There was a "match between Randal Padgett and the fraction from the vaginal swab," Dr. Charlotte Word testified, "[the] DNA banding from those two samples are identical . . . It is unlikely that any other person could have donated that sperm sample . . . other than Randal Padgett."[69]

The expressions "match" and "matched" recurred again and again, in testimony by State witnesses, with Defense Attorney McDaniel objecting and, in all instances, overruled.[70]

Worse still, McDaniel's expert, Dr. Michael Murray, gave testimony supporting the Cellmark's findings. In cross-examination, Assistant District Attorney Tim Jolley asked Dr. Murray if, in his expert opinion, Randal Padgett's DNA matched the semen sample from the vaginal swab. Murray replied that he had not had an opportunity to compare the samples. Jolley presented Murray with Cellmark's reports and asked him to formulate a conclusion on the spot. Murray could only reply, that, yes, based on the data he had just been shown, the DNA from the two samples indicated a "match."[71]

Playing to the jurors' emotions, the State introduced into evidence fifteen photographs taken at the crime scene: Cathy Padgett's maimed and mutilated body, positioned crossways on the bed, legs spread, right foot on the nightstand and left foot resting on the floor; close-ups of gaping wounds and bed linens saturated with blood; close-ups of her pubic area; even the tampon her attacker had removed and placed on the pillow.[72]

"I wouldn't look at any of the photographs," Randal says, "I couldn't handle it."

The jurors were so disturbed by the presentation that Judge Jetton called a short recess after only six of the photographs had been shown.[73]

Testimony by Department of Forensic's serologist Rodger Morrison and State pathologist Dr. E. Hunt Sheuerman established that Cathy Padgett was already dead at the time of the sexual assault, and that the act of penetration by the penis or some "other object" may have occurred as much as a quarter hour following her death. Dr. Sheuerman noted that she would have died within seconds of the wound to her heart and that positioning her body and cutting off her panties would have taken several minutes; the evidence indicated that she never moved during the sexual assault and her blood had stopped flowing by then.[74]

McDaniel attempted to question investigators about threatening statements made by Tommy Smith when he was interviewed, but the prosecution objected and the question was not allowed.[75]

Nor would Judge Jetton allow McDaniel to question the investigators about why other possible suspects, namely Judy Bagwell, were not fingerprinted for comparison. The issue of unidentified prints went unexplained, even though none matched Randal Padgett.[76]

Mark McDaniel's strategy of cracking holes in the prosecution's DNA centerpiece had failed miserably, and his haphazard, random efforts to suggest that someone else may have killed Cathy Padgett were blocked.

Randal took the witness stand, but to little avail. "All I could do was sit there and say, 'I didn't do it.'"

Numerous friends of both Randal and Cathy testified that they had never seen the first sign of animosity between the couple. Of the sixteen character witnesses—business owners, clergy, and other trusted members of the community who had known Randal Padgett all his life—several talked about attending Cathy's funeral, and how Randal, a man not given to outward displays of emotion, had wept throughout the service and burial.[77]

At the conclusion of the fifth day of the trial, Monday, April 13, with closing remarks scheduled to begin on the following day, prosecutor Ronald Thompson mentioned to Mark McDaniel that the State had performed additional serological tests on Randal Padgett's blood. The State had decided to repeat the tests, because McDaniel had informed the prosecution of the contradictory PGM reading reported by the lab he employed. The State's second round of tests showed the same PGM reading that McDaniel's lab had reported, a reading different from the State's first test. As noted before, PGM characteristics are inherited; a person's PGM reading does not change. The State's second test showed a PGM 1-1 reading. The State's first test on the blood sample used by Cellmark to generate a DNA match had a PGM 2-1 reading.[78]

Whose blood had Cellmark tested for DNA? There was still the troubling business of the DNA match reported by Lifecodes' lab—a circumstance unknown to the State—but if the blood sample the State forensic lab submitted to Cellmark was contaminated, it was equally plausible that the vaginal swab sample submitted for DNA testing was tainted.

Prosecutor Ronald Thompson had been in possession of the contradictory serological results since April 9, the second day of the trial; but Thompson waited until all of the expert witnesses had left town, before informing Mark McDaniel of the results.[79]

When the trial resumed on the morning April 14, Mark McDaniel asked Judge Jetton to declare a mistrial, on the grounds that the prosecution had withheld exculpatory information, proving Randal Padgett's innocence.[80]

McDaniel called State serologist Rodger Morrison as a witness.[81]

MCDANIEL: Rodger, would a person with a PGM type 1-1, would that be the same blood as a person with the blood type PGM 2-1?
MORRISON: Not generally.
MCDANIEL: They would be different people wouldn't they?
MORRISON: Well—
MCDANIEL: Different blood?
MORRISON: Yes, sir.

Morrison went on to acknowledge that in twenty years of conducting serological tests, he had never seen the same person's blood register two different PGM readings.[82]

Morrison, however, was unqualified to offer an opinion on the significance of the contradictory PGM readings with respect to the reliability of the DNA test; and the DNA experts were no longer available for questioning.[83]

Randal, nonetheless, was hopeful. He sat quietly, listening to Rodger Morrison's testimony. 'I'm going to go free!' he thought, 'I'm going to go free.'

At Judge Jetton's request, Thompson and McDaniel approached the bench. Judge Jetton acknowledged that he was "very confused" by Rodger Morrison's testimony, and that he "had no idea what was going on . . . I hope the jury understands it, because I sure don't." He agreed that the conflicting PGM results constituted "exculpatory" evidence, but he saw no violation in the rules of court. The State had not withheld the information, but had, on the contrary, disclosed the results to the defense.[84]

McDaniel's request for a mistrial was denied.[85]

Once actual testimony had begun, the jury was sequestered. Prior to the evening recess on April 14, Judge Jetton took the added precaution of advising the jurors to avoid newspaper articles and broadcasts about the case, noting "there was an article last night in the paper that would have been devastating if you had read the news."[86]

The inappropriate comment clearly suggested that the press condemned Randal Padgett, as well as alluding to Judge Jetton's personal feelings about the case. McDaniel again moved for a mistrial, and while Judge Jetton conceded that, "I knew when I said it, I should not have," he denied the request.[87]

In his closing remarks, Prosecutor Ronald Thompson told the jurors that they would "never witness a more horrible crime than the crime committed in August of 1990 here in Marshall County." "I can hardly think of anything more despicable than a man to go out and deprive two young children of their mother, brutally murder their mother . . ." Thompson proceeded to shore up his case with fabricated scenarios. He described how Randal had rolled his truck down the hill before cranking the engine so as not to wake his children. "He tried [to rape her] before he killed her, had to try," Ronald Thompson insisted, and then went on to rape her corpse. Thompson also claimed that Cathy refused to agree to the divorce, an entirely unfounded statement, creating a motive where none existed. Acknowledging that the DNA "match" was central to the State's argument, Thompson stressed the infallibility of DNA evidence: "one-third of the people who are DNA tested, the innocent people are exonerated. But, the guilty people are found out."[88]

In the defense's closing, McDaniel countered that an unknown error may have occurred at the Cellmark lab.[89]

The jury reached a decision in less than two hours: guilty.

A Confession Letter Signed "Phil"

On the morning of April 16, the day after the guilty verdict was handed down, the jurors returned to the Marshall County Courthouse to decide on Randal Padgett's punishment. Twenty-five witnesses took the stand, asking the jurors to spare his life. In spite of objections by the prosecution, witness after witness affirmed belief in Randal Padgett's innocence.[90]

"Randal didn't kill his wife" . . . "I don't believe he's guilty at all" . . . "I have a problem believing Randal did this" . . . "I don't believe Randal did it" . . . "There is no way you will ever convince me that he did it."[91]

The witnesses had read the newspaper accounts of the DNA evidence condemning him, but they insisted that the Randal Padgett they knew would never have killed his wife or anyone else.

"He is a deacon at our church" . . . "I work[ed] with him, and I never once heard him raise his voice" . . . "Our house burned in 1986. This man took money out of his savings account and gave it to me to help us get by" . . . "I have never ever heard anything negative ever come out of Randal's mouth."[92]

Randal's mother, sister, and brothers begged for his life. His sister Carolyn told the jurors, "If I could take his place, I would." His brothers Thomas and Ken broke down on the witness stand and wept.[93]

In cross-examining the witnesses, the prosecution repeatedly reminded the jurors of the gory details, how Cathy was "stabbed forty-some-odd times" . . . "she fights back, she grabs the knife, hands and fingers, finger and thumb are almost cut off" . . . she was "raped as she [was] dying."[94]

The jurors had already found Randal Padgett guilty, but something in the testimony of his friends and family evidently moved them. Only three of the jurors wanted to see Randal Padgett executed. Nine out twelve recommended life without parole.[95]

By Alabama law, the final decision rested with the judge. The judicial sentencing hearing was scheduled for May 22.[96]

A few days after the jury trial ended, Mark McDaniel received a letter postmarked Baton Rouge, Louisiana. The first sentence read, "I am the man that killed Cathy Padgett." The correspondence was typewritten, signed "Phil." According to the letter's author, Cathy Padgett had called out, "May the hands of Jesus bind you," during the attack. "Phil" went on to talk about the draperies being pulled back and how the moonlight illuminated her body.[97]

Only the investigators and attorneys knew the draperies were open, a circumstance verified by crime-scene photographs not shown at the trial. Equally suspicious, the attacker reported Cathy's dying words were, "May the hands of Jesus bind you," echoing the expression she used earlier that evening in a conversation with other churchwomen: 'If anyone was in my house, I would just bind them up in the name of the Lord.' The comment appeared in the investigators' notes from interviews with church members—information, likewise, available only to the investigators and attorneys.[98]

Whoever wrote the letter was there, Mark McDaniel was certain. He also had a hunch that the writer was a woman. The author professed that the thrill of the experience "had this man climaxing some eight or nine times over a two-hour period." Was that humanly possible? And why would a man begin a letter, "I am the man who . . . ", by this awkward phrasing specifying his gender? Why not the far more simple and straightforward, 'I killed Cathy Padgett'?[99]

McDaniel showed the letter to Randal, and Randal zeroed in on still other irregularities—single-syllable words misspelled, suggesting that the author was illiterate, an impression contradicted by the many three-and four-syllable words spelled correctly.

Randal believed that Judy Bagwell had written the letter. "I don't think

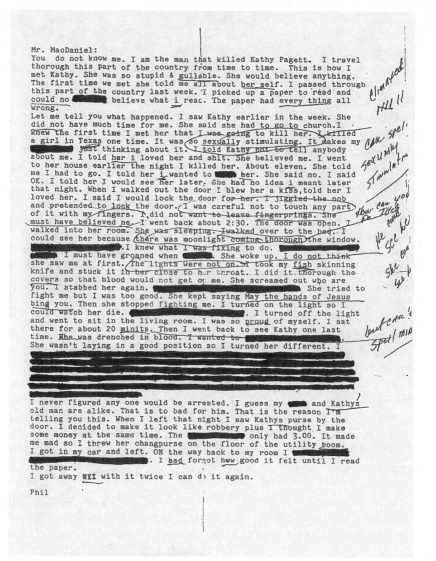

Confession letter from the alleged killer. [COURTESY OF RANDAL PADGETT]

she ever meant for me to be convicted of Cathy's murder," he says. "Her suggesting I keep the kids that night, she meant for that to be my alibi. She didn't think they'd ever test me for comparison to the semen they found, because she didn't think I'd even be a suspect."

But if Mark McDaniel was finally beginning to give credence to Randal's suspicions, it was too late.

McDaniel submitted the correspondence to the State investigative team, requesting that the letter and envelope be tested for fingerprints and saliva DNA and that Judy Bagwell be fingerprinted and DNA-tested for comparison. He also filed a motion asking Judge Jetton to vacate the judgment against Randal Padgett—meaning to declare the judgment void—or variously, to postpone sentencing him, until the tests were completed.[100]

At the May 22 judicial sentencing hearing, Judge Jetton denied both requests, stating "there will be plenty of time to have an investigation regardless of what the sentence may be."[101]

Judge Jetton proceeded to deliver that sentence. "I can see this woman lying in her bed asleep, and I can see Mr. Padgett going down the hall toward that bedroom with a knife in his hand and . . . see Mr. Padgett going into that bedroom and beginning to stab and stab and stab . . . the sentence of this Court for Larry Randal Padgett is death by electrocution."[102]

Brenda Massingill was in the courtroom that day. Her job at Eaton made it impossible for her to attend the trial, but due to a recent illness, she was now on medical leave. Brenda had believed from the outset and continued to believe that Randal Padgett was innocent, regardless of what the papers were saying.[103]

Her conversation with Cathy Padgett, when she phoned about Tommy Smith's offer to buy the farm, haunted her . . . 'Oh, Brenda, if there's anything you can do to help Randal, I'd appreciate it so very much.'

Brenda walked across the street to the jail and asked if she could see Randal before they took him to prison. "Lacy Galloway, one of the chief deputies, took me downstairs and put me in the holding area with Randal. He was in shock. I could tell that. We stood, and I held his hands. I prayed for him and his family—his kids—for Randal's strength and courage, and for the Lord to send us the truth."

In an interview broadcast on local television, D.A. Ronald Thompson called the confession letter "a last ditch effort by the defense. . . a piece of trash, a fabrication."[104] The letter and envelope were never tested. The only people asked to give blood samples for comparison were members of Randal's family, who refused, afraid that they too might be framed.

Death Row: 'No One Ever Gets Out Of Here Alive'

Sentenced to death on his birthday, by midnight of that same day Randal Padgett was on death row at Holman Prison.

"They locked me in this little cell, five feet by eight feet. There was no light in the cell, no lights anywhere, total blackness. I was lying there in the dark like a scared rabbit, and after an hour or so it got a little quieter, and I heard some guy on the tier above me saying prayers. This goes on for a long time. I remember thinking, gee, maybe this place isn't so bad. Then someone yelled 'shut up, can we have a moment of silence,' and the fellow praying let loose with a stream of obscenities, ranting about how he was going to kill the guy's family, how he knew people on the outside, and how he was going to have them kill his mother and kill his sister."

The whispered thought that took shape in Randal's mind was childlike in its simplicity. *This is a bad place. I want out of this place.*

"I spent ninety days when I didn't have any contact with anybody. Ninety days in my cell. Every once in a while they'd let me out into a little dog pen, eight feet by ten feet, for exercise.

"After those ninety days, I got to go to the yard once a day for an hour, with the rest of the people on my tier. There was a volleyball net and a basketball goal. When I first got there, there were weights, too, but somebody ended up getting his head cracked open by one of the weights, and they took the weights away.

"Prison life is like you're on another planet. Everything you know is so distant.

"The guy in the cell next to me was always carryin' on about what he was gonna do to the little high-school girls when he got out. And there was another inmate, an older gentleman—I don't know what his mind was like before he came to that place—but every day about three- thirty he'd start talking about how his brother was gonna come by to get him and what they were gonna do that day, go fishing or whatever.

"There were some real sickos. Varnell Weeks—he was on medication. So long as he took it, he was pretty, well, I don't want to say normal, but he made sense. When he didn't take it, though, he was crazy. One day out in the yard he had a bed sheet wrapped around him and his blanket folded up in a triangle, and he fit the blanket into a corner next to the fence, and went out to the middle of the yard, and dropped the bed sheet, and he was naked as a jaybird. He got down on his knees and started chanting. The fire ants crawled all over him, stinging him, and he just kept on chanting and chanting.

"Sometimes in the middle of the night, along about midnight when it was real quiet, I'd get woken up by Varnell screaming out a word, like maybe '*exercise*,' and then a couple minutes would go by, and he'd scream out a totally different word that didn't have anything to do with *exercise*. All night long, he'd carry on like that, just screaming out words at random.

"I met some pretty decent people in there, too, though. Guys who helped me out when other inmates jumped me. The only time you had trouble was when you were out of your cell—usually.

"There are some evil, evil people down there at Holman.

"The guards would pick certain inmates to be what they called hall runners. It was kind of like being a trustee. If you were a runner, the guards would let you out of your cell. A runner's job was to keep the floors mopped and hand out the food trays. This one runner squirted lighter fluid on a guy in his cage and threw a match in there and set him on fire.

"The guy lived. But another guy who I'd gotten to be friends with, he died of a heart attack. He was complaining one morning of chest pains. They told him it was probably just indigestion, gave him an aspirin, and sent him back to his cell. He died later that day."

'No one gets out of here alive,' one of the other inmates told him.[105]

"They executed three when I was there.

"I remember the first one—about fifteen minutes before execution time, all the inmates started rattling their cell bars or if they had a metal cup or something, beating on the bars, and screaming—it was so loud. I thought to myself, I'm not gonna do this. I don't like it. I don't want any part of it.

"Even before any of this happened to me, I didn't believe in the death penalty. I didn't think it was right. The next time there was an execution, I got up on the bars and screamed and hollered, too.

"On Varnell's execution day, one of the runners came by with a big bag, collecting stuff for Varnell—'Hey, we're giving Varnell a going-away party,' the runner says. There was a commissary, a store at the prison, and if you had money, you could order chips and cookies and Cokes. 'Give him a party?' I said, 'Varnell ain't gonna feel like no party. He's not gonna feel like eatin' anything. He's gonna get killed tonight.'

"The executions really messed with your mind. Trying not to think about it, wondering when your time would be. The day after an execution, it was always real somber. Nobody would play volleyball or basketball. There was a cloud over the whole place.

"Every three or four months I'd have a visitor. Visitors had to be approved, and you could only have eight people on your visitors list. Holman Prison is near Mobile, the corner of the panhandle, right along the Florida line. It was a six-hour drive. My brother or sister would bring my kids to see me every now and then. And a couple people who weren't related to me came—a friend of mine from high school and a neighbor who I'd known most all my life."

In Randal's visits with his children, they made plans for the future, the things they would do when he got out. Randal missed Heather and Micah desperately. Christmas was especially hard, "wondering what they were doing and wishing I could be there with them."[106]

For the men on death row, the aura of gloom and despair intensified during the holidays. "The guys I was close to there . . . we tried to make it festive among ourselves. That was almost impossible."[107]

Randal recalls one Christmas eve when a particularly cruel guard strolled down the tier chortling, 'Well, Christmas eve, I'm going home and open my presents and stand around the tree, and have a fire, and make love to my wife—don't guess you all will be gettin' to do that, will you?'

A Lifeline to the World Outside

"At first all the other inmates were envious of me, because I'd get fifteen to twenty letters a week. But then after a few months that dwindled down to four letters, five letters, and after a year or so, it was just maybe one letter every now and then," Randal pauses, "except for Brenda"—meaning Brenda Massingill.[108]

"Brenda wrote to me at least once a week. At first she'd wait until I'd answer, before writing back. She mentioned something about visits, but I didn't want her to visit. I didn't know why this woman was being so kind to me.

"I learned at the trial that the court system in the United States of America was completely different from what I thought. I used to believe the truth was the foremost thing in the court's mind, but I learned how naïve I was. If a piece of truth comes up that doesn't look good for their side—and I'm not just saying for the prosecution, the defense, too—that piece of truth get whisked through the vent or hid under the rug. In his closing remarks, the district attorney told the jury things that were total lies, saying I rolled my truck down the hill before cranking the engine, so as not to wake my kids, and then snuck off and murdered their mother.

"Mark McDaniel was working on drafting an appeal with attorneys from the Equal Justice Initiative, a group from Montgomery that gives pro bono legal assistance to the wrongfully convicted. 'We'll probably be hearing this one again,' Judge Jetton had said at the trial, when he turned down McDaniel's request for a mistrial. I scarcely knew Brenda, and when she wanted to come visit me, I thought, this is just another one of the prosecution's underhanded tactics—they're afraid I might get a new trial, and they've got a spy. They're sending this woman who's trying to be my friend, and if she gets to come and visit me, no matter if I don't even open my mouth, she's gonna go back and say, 'He told me he did it. He told me he did it.'"

Brenda Massingill was anything but a spy. Freeing Randal Padgett from death row and proving his innocence had become her personal mission in life. She wrote letters to the local papers, key public officials, and attorneys; started a local support group, Citizens' Alliance for Truth; hosted a yard sale to raise money for Randal's legal defense; and together with his brother Ken set up a reward hotline for information leading to the arrest and conviction of Cathy Padgett's murderer.[109]

"I knew Brenda had written to the papers saying that they'd arrested the wrong guy," Randal acknowledges, "and that she'd organized this group that had raised some money for my legal defense. It was a long time, though, before I'd let her come to visit me.

"Finally, through her letters, I came to believe she was sincere and not a spy."

After corresponding with Brenda Massingill for two and a half years, Randal asked to have her name added to his visitors list.

"Brenda came to see me more that last year I was on death row, than anybody else did put together for the entire three and a half years I was in there." The hint of desperate gratitude in Randal Padgett's voice speaks volumes.

Brenda Massingill saw the hand of God at work in her crusade to save Randal Padgett's life. A series of complications from a Teflon implant to treat joint dysfunction in her jaw resulted in her being declared medically disabled. Medical disaster had trailed upon medical disaster, first degeneration of the bone tissue in her skull from the implant, then hepatitis from a blood transfusion.[110] "I knew from the beginning that Randal didn't kill Cathy. But if I'd been working two jobs like I was before, I wouldn't have been able to pursue it," Brenda concedes. "I was homebound for a long time. I didn't even have a car. My energy level and mental concentration weren't what they used to be, but the Lord worked it out for us. After Randal decided to let me come see him, I got involved with a prisoners' support group and met a woman who lived near me who was driving down to Holman to visit another inmate. I rode with her. It was six hours each way, but I went as often as I could, every four to six weeks.

"I didn't have the luxury of offering Randal pity. My role in his life at that time was to build him up and keep him up. 'The word of God says no weapon formed against you is going to prosper,' I'd tell him, 'You've got to get back to The Word. Get back on the program, buddy.' I know it sounded cold and indifferent, but it was the only thing I could offer him. He'd get mad at me, but I was his lifeline, and he knew it. Even his closest friends believed he would die down there in the electric chair."

When Brenda was visiting on an afternoon in mid-January of 1995, a guard interrupted their conversation to give Randal a message to phone his attorney. Not wanting to waste what little time they had together on the phone, he waited until Brenda left to call.

Their prayers had been answered. The Alabama Court of Criminal Appeals had reversed the judgment against Randal and granted him a new trial.

"The State's failure to timely disclose the exculpatory evidence [the conflicting PGM results of the second blood test] denied the appellant the opportunity to prepare what would have been a key portion of his defense," the court concluded, "that is, that the blood sample used to get the DNA match might not have been his."[111]

Brenda got the news six hours later, when she arrived back in Marshall County. The north Alabama television stations were already broadcasting D.A. Ronald Thompson's decision to challenge the appeal ruling. Randal Padgett had been found guilty once, Thompson proclaimed, and if retried he would be found guilty again.

Back to the Marshall County Jail

In most states, indigent defendants automatically qualified for court-appointed legal counsel at all stages of the judicial process. Alabama, however, held that the State was not obligated to supply convicted defendants with legal counsel. The best hope for indigent defendants appealing their conviction was that an attorney would represent them pro bono.*

To pay for the first trial, Randal had depleted his savings and borrowed $50,000, taking out second mortgages on the home-place and chicken-farm properties.[112] Attorney fees and expert-witness fees for the trial had totaled $90,000. While he was on death row, Randal's brother Thomas had managed the chicken farm and, from the proceeds, made interest payments on the $50,000 loan and outstanding $200,000 debt. Mark McDaniel's fee for the appeal added $35,000 to the total moneys owed. McDaniel wanted an additional $90,000 to represent Randal at retrial. He refused to take the case pro bono.

When Randal was granted a new trial, he was transported back to the Marshall County Jail, and at a hearing held soon afterward, the court declared him indigent.

Because his conviction had been reversed, the State was obligated to

---

*In the event the court did appoint legal counsel, the attorney received a maximum of $1,000. Dan Filler, "Death in Alabama: The Problem of Indigent Defense," Concurring Opinions, 13 June 2006, http://www.concurringopinions.com/archives/2006/06/death_in_alabam.html, retrieved 31 May 2007.

supply him with representation and assigned Attorneys Steve Marshall and Dee Walker to his case. They had a maximum budget of $2,000, from which would come their attorney fees, investigative costs, and any other expenses they incurred.*

Dee Walker visited Randal at the jail.

Randal vividly recalls the encounter. "'I don't want this case,' Walker told me, 'This case is a burden to me, but I'm stuck with it. I'm not gonna make any money. I've got a family to feed, and I'm gonna spend my time and money on paying jobs.'

"That scared me. It scared my family, too. They mortgaged Mother's house and borrowed another $50,000 to hire an attorney to represent me."

Family acquaintances advised them to talk with Birmingham attorney Richard Jaffe. Jaffe specialized in death-penalty cases. Familiar with Jaffe's work on behalf of condemned men, Brenda had traveled to Birmingham to hear Jaffe speak a few years before, and following the presentation, she introduced herself and asked Jaffe if he would consider representing Randal. Jaffe explained that he did not take cases away from reputable attorneys; and from what he knew of Mark McDaniel, Randal was in good hands.[113]

Now, though, the circumstances had changed. On a Sunday morning, Randal's three siblings, Carolyn, Thomas, and Ken, sat across from Richard Jaffe at his Birmingham office. They insisted that their brother was innocent. Moved by their sincerity and conviction, Jaffe agreed to take the case.[114]

Randal had spent almost three and half years on death row. He spent the next two years in the Marshall County Jail waiting for a second chance to prove his innocence.

"The inmates were a different kind," Randal says of the other prisoners, "no sickos like at Holman. Most of them were young kids. They all called me Mr. P. I was older, and they'd see me reading the Bible. They'd come to me for advice. I tried to help them along.

"In some ways, though, it was worse than death row. Marshall County had just elected a new sheriff, Mac Holcomb. Holcomb had been in the military. Early morning, they'd play reveille on the speakers and have us come out of our cells and stand at attention for roll call. You had to answer, 'Here, sir.' The rest of the day you'd spend wiping down the jail walls with a little rag or scrubbing the floor with a toothbrush—the jailer came by one morning and threw a handful of toothbrushes under the door and said,

---

*In 1999, Alabama increased attorneys' compensation to $40/hour for out-of-court time and $60/hour for in-court-time. Filler, "Death in Alabama."

'Holcomb wants you to scrub the floor with these.' No sitting, you had to be on your knees scrubbing the floor or moving all the time with your little rag, doing the walls. There was a small exercise yard with a basketball goal, but for the whole two years I was in the Marshall County Jail, Holcomb never once let us go outside.

"He threw me in lockdown for asking for an aspirin. You couldn't question anything Holcomb said or did. For dinner we got a slice of ham so thin you could near see through it and two pieces of white bread—no condiments or salt, ever, with any meal.

"Just before my trial, Holcomb decide to shave everybody's head. When the guards came for me, I said, 'Listen, I'm fixin' to go to court. I don't want to have my head shaved for the trial.' And they said, 'If you don't let us shave your head, we're gonna lock you down and take everything you have away.' 'All right,' I said, 'lock me down.'

"The next day we had a pre-trial hearing, and I told Richard Jaffe about the haircut deal, and Richard brought it up to the judge. The judge told the jailer to take me out of lockdown and not to be shavin' my head.

"That night the deputies came for me and took me down to the sheriff's office. Holcomb had five goons with him. 'Who do you think you are, Padgett?' he says. 'We're gonna strap you down and shave your head whether you like it or not.' And they did. I didn't try to fight them. I would have just gotten smacked around by the five big guys, and they would have shaved my head anyway."

On the outside, Brenda continued with her crusade to prove Randal's innocence. Citizens' Alliance for Truth—the support group founded by Brenda—hired a detective who confirmed that Judy Bagwell was working as a stripper at a Huntsville nightclub.

Richard Jaffe and his associates pored over police reports, forensic data, and Cellmark's test results. His investigator canvassed the city of Arab, checking facts and interviewing local residents.[115] Jaffe requested a change of venue, but was denied.

Richard Jaffe harbored no illusions—he had a tough job ahead of him. Every single member of the jury would know Randal Padgett had been found guilty at his first trial and why.[116]

Equally inauspicious, Randal would again be tried in the court of Judge William Jetton, who overrode the jury's recommendation of life without parole and sentenced Randal to death. In a pre-trial motion, Richard Jaffe asked that Judy Bagwell be fingerprinted. Judge Jetton responded that he did not believe he had the power to order her to submit to the procedure. Jaffe had arranged for Randal to take a polygraph test, and the examiner concluded "Padgett was not being deceptive when he said he did not stab his wife," but Judge Jetton ruled the results of the test could not be presented at the trial.[117]

Randal's family was worried. Randal's sister and brothers talked with Jaffe about the possibility of arranging for a plea deal, and then they went to Randal. The final decision would rest with him.[118]

His siblings tried to persuade him to plead no contest in exchange for a life sentence. When he refused, they accused him of being selfish. 'Think about your mom and your kids. You'll be alive, and maybe you'll get out one day.'

"They begged me," Randal says, recalling the conversation.

Randal held firm. At bottom, his insisting on a trial by jury had very little to do with reason and logic. For Randal it was a matter of faith. "God wasn't going to let me die for something I didn't do. I'd gotten to where I believed that."

The Second Trial: "Look to the Person With the Most to Gain"

The trial began on 8 September 1997. In querying potential jurors, Richard Jaffe encountered opinions ranging from mildly prejudicial to openly hostile. One woman expressed the belief that if someone committed adultery, they probably would commit murder, pointing out that according to the Bible, adultery was a crime punishable by death. Jury selection took eleven days, with the final panel consisting of ten men and two women, the reverse gender-makeup of the first-trial and from the defense's perspective, far more desirable, since men would be more likely than women to sympathize with a man who had had an affair.[119]

Richard Jaffe was well aware that in the jurors' eyes, an individual who previously had been sentenced to death was presumed guilty, and that the attorney representing that individual was regarded as a "sleaze ball." Randal Padgett's was the third death-penalty case Jaffe had tried that year. Much hinged on his opening statement. At the very least, by the time he sat back down, the jury needed to be neutral and receptive to the evidence they would hear.[120]

During Richard Jaffe's opening remarks, the prosecution objected five times in the first five minutes. But Jaffe pressed forward, rephrasing and restating, to raise six questions. Ultimately, all six revolved around two paramount issues: Who had a motive to kill Cathy Padgett, and was Cathy Padgett raped or was what appeared to be rape actually a staged scene?[121]

The confusing and contradictory PGM readings and DNA evidence needed to be addressed, and Jaffe turned over that portion of the case to a young attorney assisting him, Derek Drennan. When Drennan questioned the State forensic serologist Rodger Morrison about the two different PGM readings the lab had reported on Randal Padgett's blood sample, Morrison explained the difference as a function of whether the sample tested was frozen or dried. Morrison said he had researched the issue after his lab reported the contradictory results in 1992 and that his lab no longer considered PGM typing reliable and now used DNA typing for identification purposes instead.[122]

Drennan took issue with the DNA match reported by Cellmark. One of the DNA fingerprints was incompletely represented on the autorad—the X-ray film image charting the sequences. When questioned by Drennan, the Cellmark representative acknowledged that there was "an extract . . . without results" and that no DNA identification could be made from that sample. However, the other DNA fingerprints introduced into evidence, indeed, showed a match.[123]

Randal's daughter Heather had not testified at the first trial and his son Micah testified only briefly; but Heather was in junior high school now, and Micah was in college. Both children testified on their father's behalf, reiterating what they had said from the very beginning, when they first spoke with investigators. The night their mother was killed, they had stayed with their father at his mobile home. They never woke up during the night, never heard a truck motor, never heard their father showering—which someone who participated in the blood-drenched slaying of Cathy Padgett certainly would have needed to do. The tiny trailer, with paper-thin walls, had only two bedrooms. Heather slept in the same bed with her father that night, and Micah slept in an adjoining room, connected via an open doorway without a door.[124]

Randal's next-door neighbor, who worked second shift, corroborated the children's testimony. She said that, on the night of the murder, she arrived home shortly before 1:00 A.M. and stayed up for several hours, during which time she did not hear any vehicle leave or arrive at the Padgett trailer.[125]

To establish definitively that Randal Padgett had no reason to kill his wife, Jaffe called Huntsville divorce attorney Claude Hundley as a witness. Hundley testified that Cathy Padgett had talked with him at length, describing an amicable property settlement and joint-custody arrangement. The divorce was to be uncontested, Hundley noted, and he had agreed to represent both Cathy and Randal, in the event the couple decided to proceed. Other witnesses confirmed that although separated and contemplating divorce, Cathy and Randal Padgett continued to be on good terms.[126]

In his opening statement, Richard Jaffe had remarked on Judy Bagwell's jealousy and her frustration with Randal's refusal to make a commitment to her, as well as to the incident at the church where Judy had hidden in the back seat of Cathy's car, wearing gloves and disguised in a curly black wig. Underlying Jaffe's theory of defense was the supposition that Judy Bagwell had killed Cathy Padgett, and Jaffe proceeded to present the jurors with an array of witnesses and evidence supporting that theory.[127]

Goldkist truck driver Jimmy Gullion testified to seeing a white Ford station wagon with a missing hubcap traveling Bridge Road at a high rate of speed in the early morning hours of August 17, the night of the murder. The Goldkist log verified that Jimmy had made a feed delivery in the area shortly before 2:00 A.M. There were two people in the car, according to Jimmy Gullion, and he was certain that neither one was Randal Padgett. Randal Padgett was a brawny, broad-shouldered man, and the car's occupants were slim. The passenger had brown hair, and the driver, of whom he had a better view, had bushy, black hair, slender arms, and wore a blouse-like top.[128]

Although Jimmy Gullion acknowledged that he could not identify either of the car's occupants, his wife Judy Gullion was able to make a positive identification linking Judy Bagwell and her sister Peggy Binning to an identical car.[129] Judy Gullion testified that several days after her husband mentioned seeing the white station wagon on Bridge Road, she saw Peggy Binning in a white station wagon with a missing hubcap, in the grocery store parking lot. Not long afterward, she saw the car again, in the same parking lot, when Judy Bagwell was in the store shopping.[130]

Another Arab resident, Robin Mason, also testified to twice seeing Judy Bagwell driving a white station wagon, shortly before Cathy Padgett's death. The first occasion was during a visit with Cathy. She and Cathy were standing in the yard talking, when Judy Bagwell drove past, Mason said, and Cathy had remarked, 'We need to pray for her.' Robin Mason later saw Judy Bagwell driving the same white station wagon when she was sitting in her car waiting for a pizza order.[131]

Wilma DeArmond, a former co-worker of Judy Bagwell's, testified about stopping by Judy Bagwell's house on the morning after Judy and Randal returned from Florida. According to DeArmond, Judy Bagwell had a cut on one of her fingers, complained of her arms being sore, and wore a long-sleeved turtleneck—odd given that it was August—leaving way for speculation that she may have been concealing defensive wounds.[132]

Records from Judy Bagwell's employer verified that she did not work the week following Cathy Padgett's murder.[133]

In searching for leads, Richard Jaffe's investigator had interviewed area business owners and their patrons. At neighborhood beauty parlors, the investigator heard the story about Judy Bagwell saving her husband Tommy's semen from three different individuals. Two of the women who spoke openly about the bizarre, fetishlike behavior were reluctant to appear in court. Janice Tidmore, however, agreed to testify. Tidmore had been an acquaintance of Judy Bagwell's when employed at Eaton. The jurors listened spellbound to Tidmore's account of the perverse intimacy Judy Bagwell had described to the women she worked with—how she would save her husband Tommy's semen and use it for facials or mix it with carrot juice in the blender to make a protein drink.[134]

Jaffe brought Judy Bagwell's propensity for semen-saving into focus by calling the jury's attention to the forensic evidence and crime-scene photographs. The autopsy report indicated that Cathy Padgett died within minutes of the fatal wound to her heart. Then her body had been positioned in the unnatural and awkward position in which it was discovered, face up, perpendicular to the head of the bed, one foot on the nightstand and one foot resting on the floor, legs spread wide. Why? And how could someone have lain on top of Cathy Padgett's mutilated body without smearing any blood in the area of her abdomen or vagina, for there was none? Equally significant, there was no trauma whatsoever to the area of her vagina, which was odd given the brutality the attacker had shown when killing her, stabbing her forty-six times.[135]

In fact, there was no evidence that Cathy Padgett's body had moved at all once it was positioned and her panties were cut down the sides to the leg openings. Surrounding her vagina was a perfect concentric circle of semen, unsmeared, and containing no blood. On the inside of her left thigh, though, there was a single bloody fingerprint, which unfortunately had been smeared and rendered unidentifiable during the investigation.[136]

In spite of the compelling testimony and forensic evidence, Richard Jaffe was worried. The issue of motive was key. It hinged on the jealous, obsessive nature of Judy Bagwell's relationship with Randal Padgett, and to understand that relationship, the jurors needed to hear not just Randal's side, but Judy Bagwell's as well. Jaffe decided to put Judy Bagwell on the witness stand. With suspicion directed toward her, there was a risk that she might attempt to exonerate herself by implicating Randal, but it was a risk he had to take.[137]

Richard Jaffe was cautious and gentle in questioning Judy Bagwell. Her testimony was soft-spoken and slow.[138] She admitted that she had a cut on her thumb on the morning following Cathy Padgett's murder, but insisted she cut herself moving a bicycle she had bought for Randal to ride with his children, explaining that there was a piece of sharp metal under the seat—an explanation that did not entirely make sense, since in the normal way of gripping, her thumb would have been on top. As for her wearing a long-sleeved turtleneck in August, she attributed it to her being 'cold natured.'[139]

Judy Bagwell gave the same reason for wearing gloves in mid-September when she hid in the back seat of Cathy's car. She ultimately conceded, though, that she wore the curly black wig because she knew people at the church and did not want to be recognized.[140] She spoke candidly about her tormented state of mind in the aftermath of the incident, when Randal said they needed to stop seeing one another. "I pray every single night that Cathy will die . . . I don't know why she just didn't leave the way anybody else would. Randal loved me and I told her that. She wouldn't leave . . . I just couldn't help myself." Her behavior had become, in her own words, "obsessive," and she began to phone Cathy repeatedly, trying to persuade her to let Randal go.[141]

Underscoring Judy Bagwell's relentless pursuit of Randal Padgett, Richard Jaffe pointed out that, shortly before Cathy Padgett was killed, Bagwell readied a room in her house for Randal's children, furnished with bunk beds identical to those she had seen in Randal's son Micah's room. Was she convinced that Randal had left Cathy for good when he moved out in May of 1990, Jaffe asked? The couple had separated before and then reunited, he reminded her.[142]

Judy Bagwell answered that she did not know. There had been no commitment from Randal, no promise that he actually would divorce Cathy.[143]

Bagwell acknowledged that that she was never fingerprinted, that her house was never searched, and that the investigators who questioned her had discussed granting her immunity if she cooperated.[144]

Asked how an intruder might have gained entrance to Cathy Padgett's home, she replied, "They kept the key in the g—" breaking off just short of telling the jury that she knew the family kept a key hidden in the garage utility room.[145]

Most stunning, though, was Judy Bagwell's response when Jaffe posed the hypothetical question that if, in fact, the DNA match was accurate, and the semen found in Cathy Padgett did belong to Randal Padgett, "Do you know how it got there?"[146]

"It would have to come out [of] me," she said, in a voice choked with emotion, "He wasn't having relations with her."[147]

In the 1987 thriller *Presumed Innocent* by Scott Turow, a jealous wife murders her husband's lover and plants his semen in her corpse. An earlier witness had testified that Judy Bagwell had read the novel shortly before Cathy Padgett was killed.[148]

Judy Bagwell had remarried by the time of the second trial.* Her new husband, a much younger man, knew nothing about her previous affair with Randal Padgett, until she was subpoenaed to appear in court. At the trial, during her testimony, he hung his head, covered his face with his hands, and wept.[149]

Judy Bagwell broke down on the witness stand and wept as well. Richard Jaffe stopped short of asking her outright if she had killed Cathy Padgett. She had said enough.[150]

She had no alibi for her whereabouts on the evening of Cathy Padgett's murder. Nor could she account for how she had spent the $5,000 she withdrew from her retirement fund just prior to Cathy Padgett's death, opening the way to speculation that she may have used the money to purchase the white station wagon mentioned by Jimmy and Judy Gullion and Robin Mason, although both Judy Bagwell and her sister denied ever owning or driving such a car.[151]

In his closing remarks, Richard Jaffe described for the jurors how Cathy Padgett was surprised in her bed, asleep, and stabbed repeatedly through the sheets and covers, fighting for her life, judging from her nearly severed thumb, multiple wounds to her hands, and an unidentified fiber under one of her fingernails. Law-enforcement officials had interviewed Randal Padgett the day after his wife's murder, and he did not have a mark on him. No fingerprints or physical evidence of any kind linked him to the crime scene, aside from the DNA semen match.[152]

"This is a rage killing," Jaffe suggested to the jury. Cathy Padgett was a small woman—five foot three inches tall and of average weight. A "larger person"—like Randal Padgett—could have overpowered her easily. The person who killed Cathy Padgett became embroiled in "a fierce, fierce fight," someone who had stabbed Cathy Padgett forty-six times, and then went on "to stage a rape."[153]

He reminded the jurors of the smeared bloody fingerprint on the inside of Cathy Padgett's left thigh.

"Could it be," Jaffe asked, that Cathy Padgett's body "was positioned for insertion of an object with semen on it, could it be that's how the bloody fingerprint got there?"

Cathy's purse had been thrown on the floor and the contents strewn about. The purse and its contents contained numerous unidentified fingerprints, none of which matched Cathy or Randal Padgett, Jaffe pointed out, and Judy Bagwell by her own admission was never fingerprinted.

"Except for the adultery," there was "nothing in [Randal Padgett's]

*At trial, she went by her married name Judy Bagwell Atanasoff.

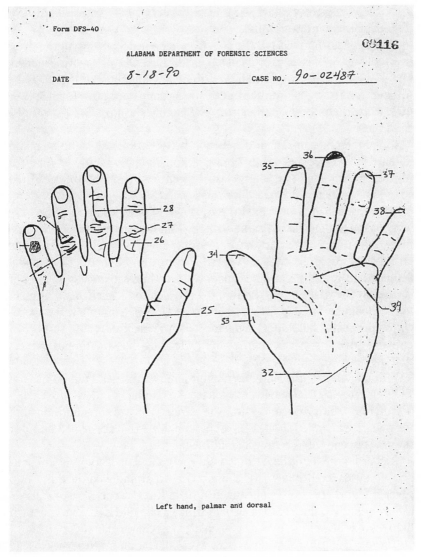

Defensive wounds on Cathy Padgett's left hand. [COURTESY OF RANDAL PADGETT]

background at all to suggest anything but a person of outstanding character," Jaffe stressed. "No violence in his background. No mistreatment of
people. No abuse of women. Or men." Does it make sense that "he kills to
be with Judy Bagwell and then he never sees her again?"

"Look to the person with the most to gain."

At the onset of the trial, convinced they would prevail, the prosecution had ordered a victory cake from a local bakery.[154] Jaffe had succeeded in fracturing that hardy optimism.

Brenda Massingill was in the courtroom every day, sitting in the front row with her briefcase, dressed in business attire. Out-of-town journalists mistook her for an attorney. She was joined by members of the Citizens' Alliance for Truth, who turned out to show their support for Randal. "We prayed for there to be confusion in the enemy's camp," Brenda recalls, "and there was."[155]

In a conference at the judge's bench between Ronald Thompson and Richard Jaffe's associate Derek Drennan, Ronald Thompson had remarked regarding Drennan, 'Judge, if I wasn't a gentleman and an officer of the court, I'd knock the shit out of him right here.'[156]

Thompson had approached the case with the expectation of an easy win, accomplished via the same strategy that had served him well at the first trial—to argue that Cellmark's results showed that DNA found at the crime scene matched Randal Padgett, supporting the theory that Randal Padgett had brutally murdered his wife and then sadistically raped her corpse. By the trial's close, though, the prosecution had changed its tack. In the closing argument delivered by Assistant D.A. Tim Jolley, the prosecution proposed that Randal Padgett raped his wife for the sole purpose of drawing attention away from himself by leading investigators to suspect that the murderer's motive was rape.[157]

In 1990, when Cathy Padgett was murdered, the general public was not widely aware that DNA could be typed to an individual. Underlying the theory of both the prosecution and the defense was the assumption that the person who killed Cathy Padgett was unaware that the semen found at the crime scene could be traced definitively.[158]

Richard Jaffe left the jurors with the following thoughts to ponder, "Judy Bagwell knew two things. One, that she would be the first suspect . . . there was a police record of her in the backseat of Cathy's car . . . And, two, she had to make it look like a man did it . . . [but] her plan didn't work. She didn't plan on Randal getting charged."

The jury had listened to almost two weeks of testimony. Near the close of the second day of deliberation, Richard Jaffe encountered Brenda Massingill outside the courthouse. "Randal will go home when we go," Brenda informed him, calmly confident. "That's what the Lord has told me."[159]

When they were summoned to return to the courtroom, the jury emerged and reported that they were hopelessly deadlocked. Judge Jetton called the attorneys into his chamber. Under the tenets of Alabama law, jury unanimity was required to acquit or convict in capital cases. The jury poll was ten not guilty, two guilty. Judge Jetton announced that he was going to declare a mistrial. The group filed back into the courtroom, Richard Jaffe and Judge Jetton last in line, and in the doorway Jaffe turned to Judge Jetton and said, "Judge, can't you just ask them if there's any way a little more deliberation could be fruitful?" 'No,' Judge Jetton replied, adamantly, 'I've made up my mind. They have been at it for two days.'[160]

The courtroom was packed to capacity, and virtually everyone in the room was praying.

Jetton mounted the bench and addressed the jurors. 'Ladies and gentleman, you've done the best you could, but unfortunately, I'm going to have to declare—,' and then he hesitated, and glanced at Richard Jaffe, and for a moment the two men's eyes locked. 'Ladies and gentleman,' Judge Jetton continued, turning back to the jurors, 'I'm going to ask you one more time, does anyone on this jury think there's any possibility that further deliberations would yield a verdict?'

Several of the jurors answered in the affirmative, and Judge Jetton instructed the panel of twelve to return to the deliberation room. When the debate resumed, the two women jurors, who might have been expected to condemn an adulterer, led the discussion arguing for acquittal. The way in which Cathy Padgett's panties had been cut carefully down the legs with scissors looked like the handiwork of a woman, the two women maintained. Then, one of the women climbed onto the table and posed herself in the way that Cathy's body had been posed, to demonstrate that a woman could not be raped in that position.[161]

Forty minutes later, the jury was back. They informed Judge Jetton that they had reached a unanimous verdict.[162]

In keeping with the dignity and propriety that he demanded in his court, Judge Jetton insisted that there were to be no emotional outbursts when the decision was announced, then nodded to the jury foreman to proceed.[163]

The jury foreman rose to his feet. "We find the defendant Randal Padgett not guilty."

A brief and sudden roar filled the room and then it was quiet except for the hushed weeping of Randal Padgett's children and siblings.

Randal describes the moment in a single word: "Jubilation!"

"They wanted to take me back to the jail to get my stuff, and I said, 'Leave the stuff. I'll come back and get it later.' The jail was right across the street, and when I walked out the front door of the courthouse without my handcuffs and shackles, I could hear the guys in the jail beating on the window bars—just a few at first. The windows were thick bulletproof glass, small windows that you had to stand on your bunk to look out. I flashed them a V for victory, and the whole jail went to throbbing."

"It was total pandemonium," Brenda adds, "stompin' and screaming. I heard later that the sheriff threatened to put the entire cell block in lock-down."

"The Case Is Closed . . . There's Not Enough Evidence to Go After Anybody"

Richard Jaffe has high regard for Judge William Jetton. "He gave us the fairest trial possible," Jaffe insists, "regardless of his personal opinion."[164]

At the first trial, Judge Jetton clearly had believed that Randal Padgett was guilty. But at some point, Judge William Jetton evidently began to sway from that position. Following Randal Padgett's acquittal, Jetton remarked that the verdict did not surprise him, noting that the defense attorneys had done an excellent job of raising reasonable doubt.[165]

More than ten years have passed since the jury ruled that Randal Padgett did not kill his wife, yet, interestingly, the reasonable doubt established at the trial opened up avenues of inquiry that have never been pursued.

Steve Marshall, who briefly represented Randal Padgett as his court-appointed attorney, is now district attorney in Marshall County. He does not anticipate reopening the Cathy Padgett murder case. "There's not enough evidence to go after anybody. As I understand it, the case is closed."[166]

Speculating on why the State has never reopened the investigation, Richard Jaffe cites several obstacles. "They have committed publicly too many times to the position that Randal did it. Also, there are indications that they offered Judy Bagwell immunity. It would be a very difficult case for them. They didn't search her place back when Cathy Padgett was killed, and Judy Bagwell has moved two or three times since then."[167]

During Randal Padgett's appeal, the defense had requested the notes of Alabama Bureau of Investigation agent Tom Taylor, who had assisted with the original investigation. The information was never released to the defense.[168]

Journalists and private investigators requesting access to the Arab Police Department files on the Cathy Padgett murder case are referred to the district attorney's office. The district attorney's office refuses to accommodate requests for information on Cathy Padgett's murder, maintaining that they do not release records to the public, and refers petitioners to the Circuit Court Clerk. The Circuit Court Clerk's office has a record of the opinions granting Randal Padgett a new trial, but the transcripts from the two trials are not on file at the courthouse, which is generally the case in all jurisdictions, nationwide. Trial transcripts are regarded as public records, available upon request for a copying fee, usually a dollar or two per page.

At the Marshall County Circuit Court Clerk's office, petitioners requesting trial transcripts from the two Padgett trials are referred to the court recorder. The court recorder maintains that since Randal Padgett was acquitted, she is not required by law to keep a record of the proceedings.[169] She acknowledges that she has the information, but she refuses to release it, for any price, explaining that she hopes to write a book on the Padgett murder case when she retires. She says she has been offered as much as $1,600 for a transcript of Richard Jaffe's opening and closing remarks, alone—fifty-two pages, at the rate of thirty dollars per page. She declined the offer.*

Randal Padgett's mother took care of his children during his five-year incarceration. His father, who had Alzheimer's disease, died while he was on death row. "I wish he could have waited until I got home," Randal says wistfully. The pain and torment he caused his family weighs heavy with him, guilt over his affair with Judy Bagwell and unfaithfulness to Cathy.

In 2001, the state of Alabama passed a law providing indemnification for unjust convictions, but no one has received compensation under the provisions of the new law. The bill was never funded.[170]

Randal Padgett has gone back to raising chickens and, once again, resides in Marshall County.

When first released, Randal struggled with severe-depth perception impairment. "For two years, the furthest I'd been able to see was maybe thirty feet, since Sheriff Holcomb at the Marshall County Jail never let us go outside. The day they set me free, I was out in the yard at my mother's, and when I looked up from the grass out across the horizon at the tree line, I felt like I was gonna fall, like there was a log rolling out from under me." A few weeks later, he ran into a building abutting a parking space when parking his truck. He had lost the ability to judge distances.

Randal's son Micah lent him gas money during his early days of freedom. He had no income and no job.[171] He sold his house and the 30-acre farm that had once belonged to his grandfather, offsetting some of the debt he had accumulated. When he was arrested, he owed $200,000 on the

*The author was able to reconstruct the story through the generous assistance of Randal and Brenda Padgett, formerly Brenda Massingill, and attorney Richard Jaffe. The Padgetts participated in extensive interviews and supplied the author with the portions of the original trial transcript that they had in their possession, along with appellant briefs and court rulings. Richard Jaffe also agreed to be interviewed and supplied the author with a copy of his opening and closing remarks, which he had purchased from the court recorder in the immediate aftermath of the trial. The author's attempts to gain access to police reports and the trial transcripts in their entirety were thwarted, as has been the experience of everyone known to the author who has sought to acquire information on the Cathy Padgett murder case.

chicken farm, and attorney fees for the two trials and the appeal had amounted to almost $200,000 more. To repay his brother Thomas for managing the chicken farm during his incarceration, Randal gave him half-interest in the business.

He tried to find outside employment to supplement his share of the chicken farm income, only to be turned down time after time. "Most of the places where I put in an application didn't give a reason for not hiring me," Randal says with a shrug, "They just never called me back." He applied for a temporary position with the Census Bureau, and the examiner informed him that he would likely be hired. He had "aced" the proficiency test. Several weeks later, though, Randal received a letter saying the agency rejected his application because he had a prior record with the FBI, stemming from the murder investigation.

Unable to find any other way of making ends meet, Randal borrowed more money, bought out Thomas' interest in the chicken farm, and went back to raising chickens full time. He had taken on responsibility for the $50,000 mortgage on his mother's home, along with his other debt, and in 2005, to fend off bankruptcy, he withdrew every cent from the retirement account he had accumulated during his employment at Eaton Corporation.

But to meet Randal Padgett, unless you pressed him to talk about the dark years, you would never know how tough things were. Along with the chickens, he now raises Boer goats, as well. Standing on the back porch, pointing out across the pasture at a kid goat born just a few weeks before, a boyish grin creases his cheeks. "Will you look at that youngun," he says, delighting in the baby goat's playfulness as it frolics and leaps.

His children Heather and Micah have grown up, graduated from college, and married. Micah and his wife have two children of their own. Randal takes tremendous pleasure in his baby granddaughters. In their presence, as well as in the company of nieces and nephews, Randal and Brenda talk about his incarceration as the time when Randal was away "on vacation."

Brenda calls Randal Padgett "babe" these days.

In 2003, during a short interlude between chicken flocks, Randal and Brenda slipped off to Gatlinburg, Tennessee, to get married. Neither one can pinpoint when they became more than friends, although they both agree that it began during his last few months at Holman Prison. "We didn't know what we were," Brenda says. "It was a very emotional and disturbing time. I'd been single for almost twenty years. I had a deep respect for Randal. The things that he'd gone through, I can't even begin to imagine. The embarrassment, humiliation, and degradation—when I think of

Randal and his goats. [*Leslie Lytle*]

that and how he still held his head up in the county and this community. I don't know when we fell in love. I just wanted to be where the Lord wanted me to be."

Brenda likewise has cashed in her retirement savings to keep the creditors at bay, but as always, Brenda remains confident that things will work out.

For the Padgetts, the long, difficult road they traveled together is a spiritual journey, intrinsically bound up with their faith and trust in God. They frequently are invited to speak about their experience at faith-related venues and educational forums. At Richard Jaffe's request, Randal addressed the annual conference of Alabama Criminal Defense Attorneys and the University of Tennessee School of Law.

Staunch supporters of the death-penalty abolition movement, the couple has attended conferences in Florida and New York and events honoring the death-row exonerated hosted by the Center on Wrongful Convictions at Northwestern University, in Chicago.

Randal and Brenda Padgett. [Leslie Lytle]

For Brenda, a long-time political conservative, campaigning for the abolition of capital punishment is a role she never would have predicted for herself. "I viewed first hand the system of justice in this state, and my views are forever changed. I speak from experience, when I say I know that innocent people are sentenced to die."[172]

Randal takes particular issue with the plea-bargain mechanism. "Ninety percent of criminal cases are plea-bargained before they ever go to trial. I've seen it three or four times, where one guy plea-bargains, and he gets to walk free after a few years and the other guy gets the electric chair—what's fair about that?

"There are innocent people on death row, and after what I went through, I think there might be more than just a few. It's easy to get convicted for something you didn't do."[173]

"When Mark McDaniel told me that he was bound by lawyer-client privilege, if someone he represented confessed to him, I asked him 'Could you sleep at night? Suppose I got convicted and sent to the electric chair, could you sleep at night, knowing you could have saved my life?' 'Well, yeah, I could sleep at night,' he said, 'It's part of my job.'

"I wouldn't have a job like that. I wouldn't." Randal declares, chuckles for a fleeting moment, acknowledging the irony, and then his voice turns somber. "That could really happen. And, boy, that bothers me. After my second trial, they could have launched a new investigation. I know they've got some doubts—but they won't admit they were wrong. How would it look if they were wrong about sending an innocent guy to prison? How would it look—" Randal pauses.

"How would it would it look if they were wrong about sending an innocent guy to his death?"

While in prison in 1995, Randal Padgett wrote a song to be sung to the tune of "That Just About Does It" by Vern Gosdin.

Verse 1
Every night I go to sleep a-cryin'
Looking through these bars with thoughts of dying.
And never having known you like I want to,
And never having held you like I need to.

Sometimes I dream these prison bars are gone.
I dream that I'm not lying here alone.
I dream that I'm far away and free.
I dream I'm holding you so close to me.

Chorus
But I wonder if I'm really gonna make it?
How long can I live on dreams and try to fake it?
What will I ever do,
If I never can have you,
If my dreams don't come true,
Can I take it?

Verse 2
I dream when I see your picture on the wall,
'Til I hear the guard's keys clanging down the hall.
I awaken to my cold and dreary cell
Life, in this place, is pure hell.

Verse 3
You came to me when I really needed a friend.
You said you'd stand by me until the end.
I want to believe that what you say is true.

Conclusion

Guys don't want to be whiners. We don't like to talk about the stuff that happened in there.
—Ron Keine

Girl, I could tell you stuff that would make you cry.
—Michael Ray Graham, Jr.

Michael Graham and the other men whose stories appear in *Execution's Doorstep* did tell me things that made me cry. They asked me not to write about some aspects of their experiences, and I honored those requests. They bared their souls to me, revisiting their torturous ordeals, motivated by a desire to expose the flawed capital justice process—a corrupt, costly, inefficient system they miraculously survived.

A study reviewing death-penalty cases found that from 1900 to 1987 states executed twenty-three individuals who likely were innocent.[1] The actual number of innocent individuals executed may be even higher. Overworked appellate defense attorneys devote their time and energy to saving the living. Nonetheless, since 1987, eight more highly suspect executions have come to light. Investigative journalism by the *Houston Chronicle* brought Ruben Cantu's strong claim to innocence to the public's attention; Larry Griffin's likely innocence was discovered in an investigation launched by the NAACP Legal Defense and Educational Fund. State's attorneys subsequently reviewed the cases of Ruben Cantu and Larry Griffin and concluded that Cantu and Griffin were, indeed, guilty.[2] Judges and prosecutors rarely admit that they have erred. Another executed individual with a strong claim to innocence, Joseph Odell, requested and was denied DNA testing, unavailable at the time of his 1986 trial. In 1997, the state of

Virginia executed Joseph Odell, maintaining it had no obligation to conduct DNA semen tests since, by Virginia law in effect in 1986, a defendant had only twenty-one days from the conclusion of his trial to introduce new evidence. The federal courts affirmed the state's position, citing the 1993 *Herrera v. Collins* ruling, which held that in petitioning for federal habeas corpus review, a defendant must abide by the state's limits for introducing new evidence.[3]

Of the 126 death-row prisoners who have been exonerated since the mid-1970s, only four have received apologies from state officials who played a role in their wrongful convictions and death sentences. Confronted with hard science, the states involved had no choice but to acknowledge their mistakes—all four had DNA evidence backing their claims to innocence. One of the apology recipient's was Ray Krone, an apology tendered after state officials had approached the real killer—identified by a DNA blood match—and tried to persuade him to implicate Krone as an accomplice.[4]

In 75 percent of homicides, no crime-scene DNA evidence exists to test. Only 16 of the 124 exonerated individuals had DNA proof of innocence, the first being Kirk Bloodsworth in 1993. It is unlikely that many more DNA exonerations will occur. For murders occurring twenty or thirty years ago, blood, semen, and tissue samples often have been destroyed or deteriorated. The remaining 110 exonerated men and women scrambled to prove their innocence by disproving the evidence that convicted them.[5]

A number of remedies have been proposed to improve the accuracy and fairness of the capital-punishment process, among them, requiring electronic recording of custodial interrogations; raising the standard for admission of testimony by jailhouse snitches and alleged accomplices; and replacing standard lineups with a sequential, double-blind procedure—fixes that would address some, but far from all of the ills that plague the system.

Research indicates that circumstances specific to capital cases—cases in which the prosecution seeks the death penalty as opposed to a lesser punishment—make capital cases more susceptible to wrongful convictions.[6] Several factors underly the phenomenon.

Capital cases require death-qualified juries—juries excluding those who have a moral objection to imposing the death penalty—and statistics show that death-qualified juries are more likely to reach a guilty verdict.[7] Perhaps individuals who favor the death penalty are more cynical and more easily arrive at a "guilty beyond a reasonable doubt" conclusion. Conversely, it is fair to assume that jurors opposed to capital punishment would be disinclined to reach a guilty verdict if the potential sentence were death. A possible but costly solution might be to appoint two jury panels, one to rule on guilt or innocence and a separate death-qualified panel to rule on the punishment. Significant increases in expense could be expected from the additional court and attorney time needed to select a second jury and to re-present relevant evidence.

Another cause of the high rate of error in capital cases relates to the under-funding of court-appointed defense attorneys and public defenders who, lacking resources to conduct an investigation and prepare a defense, assume that their clients will be found guilty and concentrate their efforts on preparing for the penalty phase of the trial, in the hope of avoiding a death sentence.[8] The situation could be meliorated, but, again, at great financial expense, by leveling the playing field and making the defense's budget equal to that of the prosecution. Law-enforcement officials and state attorneys have virtually no limits on their expense accounts, while court appointed attorneys for indigent defendants typically have abysmally low budgets, often in the $2,000-$5,000 range. Court-appointed attorneys who launch an effective investigation and take the time to prepare an adequate defense (estimated at 500 to 1,000 hours) usually end up working for less than minimum wage.[9]

The most fundamental and insidious cause of excessive error stems from the highly emotional and highly politicized nature of capital cases. With the community traumatized by a heinous and cruel murder, law-enforcement officials are under tremendous pressure to find the killer quickly. The task then falls to state district attorneys to follow through and see to it that the individual is convicted. Police chiefs sometimes are elected, but more often are appointed by elected officials, whose favor they naturally court. County sheriffs usually are elected, as are district attorneys. Speedy apprehension of the alleged perpetrator and seeking and winning a death-penalty sentence against the accused conveys a tough-on-crime philosophy, an important calling-card when election time comes. A prosecutor seeking the death penalty must get a first-degree murder conviction, which requires a unanimous verdict. Prosecutors go to great lengths and great expense to convince the jury of the defendant's guilt and suitability for execution. For some prosecutors, anything less than a death sentence signifies failure. The premium attached to winning a capital conviction—political acclaim and votes—accounts for the exorbitantly high cost of death-penalty trials, expense incurred primarily by the prosecution, much in the form of forensic testing, investigative procedures, and expert-witness fees.[10]

Remember Madison Hobley's sorrowful comment: "They execute nameless people." The dead have no voice, and as noted above, rarely does anyone speak up for them. For judges, prosecutors, and law-enforcement officials who engage in unjust and unethical practices—under the auspices of protecting society from the criminal element—the potential for reward is high, and the risk minimal. A defendant's execution virtually ensures that their wrongdoing will go undiscovered.

In nearly 20 percent of the death sentences overturned on appeal between 1973 and 1995, the higher courts found that law-enforcement officials or prosecutors suppressed evidence of a defendant's innocence. A study completed in 2007 found that, among the 126 individuals wholly exonerated of blame since the death penalty was reinstated in 1976, intentional malice by criminal-justice officials played a role in nearly two-thirds of the cases.[11] Some of the individuals named in the study have civil suits pending. Whether jury awards will be forthcoming remains to be seen. Intentional malice is difficult to prove; and the precedent set in *Imbler v. Pachtman* is difficult to overcome. In that 1976 decision, the U.S. Supreme Court in effect argued that to hold law-enforcement officials and prosecutors accountable for their role in wrongful convictions would "prevent" officials from "the vigorous and fearless performance" of their "duty." In such a political climate, nothing deters officers of the law and court who hope to earn political favors and votes by winning death-sentence convictions. The only remedy for wrongful capital convictions that occur by virtue of officials' unethical actions is to remove the incentive that motivates them.

So long as winning a death sentence functions as a prize by serving as a vehicle to expedite political aspirations, the investigation and prosecution of first-degree murder cases will continue to be plagued by deception and fraud.

I have been asked what I learned in writing *Execution's Doorstep*. The learning curve involved a two-stage process. Early on, I realized that, far more often than I had supposed, a criminal element existed within the criminal-justice system established to serve and protect the citizenry from crime. My research bore out the conlusion of those who have found that political aspirations born of a lust for power and acclaim underscored much of the criminal behavior. In cases where evidence was withheld, suppressed, or manufactured, the crime was obvious. In a more subtle manifestation of subverting justice, officers and officials capitalized on the high-exposure and high-sensationalism quotient of capital murder cases to win public favor, severely impinging on the likelihood that the accused would receive a fair, impartial trial. Then there was the less-overt subversion of justice that followed from indolence and lack of diligence, where officials took the quick and easy route to success and public praise—zeroing in on the first likely suspect, ignoring and failing to pursue alternate leads, instead of conducting a thorough investigation. Certainly, these three circumstances overlap and are interrelated, often with more than one, if not all three, operative when injustice masquerades as justice.

That observation brought me to the second tier of learning. In the capital-justice process, systemic learned behavior governs practice. Underlings emulate their superiors and are rewarded for emulating their superiors. For a young, aspiring assistant district attorney charged with prosecuting a capital murder case to operate counter to the entrenched system requires exceptional courage and selflessness. While it is up to the prosecutor to decide whether to ask for the death penalty, all the individuals associated with the case—the sheriff, deputies, police officers, investigators—stand to get a glory boost that might translate into political reward when the proffered penalty is death. Use of the death penalty to garner laurels for political crowns will continue so long as we have a death penalty. The practice is epidemic within the capital criminal-justice system, and too often the officers and officials who school the up-and-coming generation pass on the disease by example. 'This is how the system works, this how we do things.' To suppose that all of the individuals who use the capital judicial process for political gain eventually could be removed from office is wholly unrealistic; the system is self-sustaining. The death-penalty-reward mechanism that propelled unscrupulous officials to a position of power will propel their successors to a position of power, individuals waiting in the wings to follow in the footsteps of their role models. Tier two of the learning curve in writing Execution's Doorstep led me to the dismal conclusion that, however thorough and far-reaching the reforms designed to ensure that justice is served, guaranteeing that the practice of capital punishment is carried out in a fair and just manner is impossible.

Professor James Liebman, who spearheaded the landmark study on error rates in capital cases, calls the death penalty a "broken system." I would counter Professor Liebman on only one point: the death penalty did not "break." From the outset, the death penalty was an ill-conceived attempt to modify human behavior for the better—an attempt that failed and suffices only to soil and debase everything it touches. As pointed out in the introduction, the death penalty does nothing to deter crime in the culture at large, and among those in the inner circle of the criminal-justice process, there is every indication that the death penalty invites and may even encourage malice and fraud. Except for the United States of America, all of the developed nations have recognized the failure of the death penalty to produce the hoped-for results and abolished capital punishment.

Playwright and political activist George Bernard Shaw summed it up quite succinctly: "Murder and capital punishment are not opposites that cancel one another, but similars that breed their kind."

Appendix
States Paying Restitution for Wrongful Convictions in Capital Cases

Of the thirty-six states that have the death penalty, fourteen pay restitution for wrongful convictions.[1]

State	Requirements	Compensation
Alabama	Conviction vacated or reversed and charges dismissed	Minimum of $50,000 for each year of incarceration; possibility of more if recommended by committee
California	Pardon for innocence or being innocent	$100 per day of incarceration
Illinois	Pardon for innocence	$15,000 maximum for 5 years; $30,000 maximum for 14 years; $35,000 maximum for 15 years or more, plus cost-of-living increase
Louisiana	Conviction reversed or vacated and proof of innocence	$15,000 for each year of incarceration, $150,000 maximum; court may award cost of job-skill training (1 year), medical and counseling service (3 years), tuition at a community college or state university
Maryland	Pardon on grounds that conviction was in error	Actual damages
Missouri	Proof of innocence by DNA evidence	$50 per day of post-conviction confinement
Montana	Exoneration by DNA evidence	Educational aid to persons exonerated by DNA testing

State	Requirements	Compensation
New Hampshire	"Found innocent"	$20,000 maximum
North Carolina	Pardon for innocence	$10,000 for each year of incarceration, $150,000 maximum
Ohio	Conviction vacated or reversed and charges dismissed	$25,000 for each year of incarceration, plus lost wages, costs, and attorney fees
Oklahoma	Conviction vacated and charges dismissed or pardoned, based on a finding the claimant did not commit the crime	$175,000
Tennessee	Exoneration or pardon for innocence	$1,000,000
Texas	Pardon or relief granted on the basis of innocence	$25,000 for each year of incarceration, $500,000 maximum
Virginia	Conviction vacated; accepting award precludes claimant from filing additional claims against the state	90% of the Virginia per capita income for each year of incarceration, up to 20 years; $10,000 tuition in the Virginia Community College system

Acknowledgments

Although it is somewhat atypical for "acknowledgments" to appear at the end of a book, the large number of people who deserve recognition lent itself to such a placement, since the significance of their contribution to *Execution's Doorstep* would be better understood.

Early guidance and assistance in making contact with death-row exonerated individuals came from Edwin Colfax, Larry Marshall, and Rob Warden at the Center on Wrongful Convictions, a project initiated by the Northwestern University School of Law. Rob Warden provided me with dozens of newspaper articles copied from Ron Keine's personal archive, a data source that proved invaluable in pinning down the timeline in his story and verifying data.

Others to whom I am indebted for bringing Ron Keine's story to fruition include Ron's trial attorney Hank Farrah, journalist and author Georgelle Harleman Duncan, and author Dan Johnson, all of whom participated in interviews, contributing contextual background and insight on the many players in the drama, particularly the confessed murderer Kerry Lee. Attorney Farrah also served as a reader, checking for both legal and narrative accuracy. Gratitude, as well, is owed to Pat Seligman, archivist at the Albuquerque Publishing Company Library, who patiently guided me through the permission process for a thirty-year-old photograph. Finally, thanks to Ron's fiancée, Pat Ameel, for sharing her insider's perspective on the difficulties exonerated people face.

Judi Caruso tops my thank-you list for Juan Melendez's story. As Juan's legal advocate, Judi responded to my initial query letter to Juan and set up my first interview with him. Judi ultimately acted as my mentor and advisor, reading early drafts, clarifying legal issues, and putting me in touch with Juan's appellate attorney Martin McClain. Juan's investigator Rosa Greenbaum, likewise, proved to be a rich resource and skilled guide, schooling me on how to navigate the red tape to gain access to the source material I needed. Thanks, too, to Gainesville appellate attorney Susan Cary for information on death-row inmate Melvin Nelson (who died in Juan's arms and not long afterward was granted a new trial) and to Abe Bonowitz, co-founder of Citizens United for Alternatives to the Death Penalty, who helped me locate Rosa Greenbaum and took the stunning photograph of Juan that appears at the opening to his chapter.

My mentor for Michael Graham's story was Michael's appellate attorney John Holdridge. Deep gratitude goes to John, who participated in interviews, fact-checked the manuscript draft, and would have sent me Michael's trial transcript, had his hard-copy files on Michael's case not been destroyed in Hurricane Katrina. John graciously forwarded my request to Nick Brustin with Cochran Neufeld & Scheck, LLP, the law firm handling Michael's civil suit for damages. Nick Brustin saw to it that I received all the documents I needed. Cochran Neufeld & Scheck attorney Jen Laurin also read and fact-checked Michael's story, and Jen went out of her way to search the archives for information I requested. My heartfelt appreciation, likewise, for the insight and perspective offered by Michael's trial attorney, Robert Earle; his fiancée, Cheryl Milton; his mother, Elizabeth Lam; and his stepfather, Doug Lam. Thanks, too, to Doug and his wife Marg for letting Michael and me meet at their home and for granting me access to newspaper articles and letters from their personal archive.

Randal Padgett's story could not have been written without the help of his wife Brenda Padgett. I owe Brenda thanks on multiple fronts, not the least of which is the support she offered me as a strong bond of friendship formed between us in our shared quest to see Randal's story told. Brenda participated in several lengthy interviews and spent days searching her archival newspapers and documents to verify facts and ferret out the answers to my questions. As noted earlier, she and Randal provided me with the portions of the trial transcript in their possession and the appellate brief, which enabled me to reconstruct the trial proceedings. Special thanks also to Richard Jaffe, Randal's attorney at re-trial, who graciously advised me and counseled me throughout, mailed me a copy of his closing remarks and several crime-scene photographs, and reviewed a final draft of the manuscript.

Finding the operative go-between often proved a challenge in its own right, and I thank attorneys Jon Stromsta and Kurt Feuer for directing me to speak with attorney Andrea Lyon, who facilitated my making contact with Madison Hobley. My awe-struck gratitude to Andrea, who was to become my mentor and advisor, patiently explaining the complexities in

Madison's case, providing copies of court opinions, and fact-checking the manuscript draft.

I also want to thank author and editor Laura Barlament, who served as a reader on the Graham and Padgett chapters, and Richard Pult, my editor at UPNE, who deftly zeroed in on problem areas and gently guided me to solutions, subjecting the manuscript to a talk-therapy-type approach, which proved amazingly fruitful.

I can scarcely give thanks enough to my agent Sorche Fairbank for teaching me how to write a well-crafted proposal, for acting as my editor on sample chapters, and, most importantly, for believing in me, coaching me, and encouraging me to pursue my passion in writing this book.

Thanks as well to Sister Helen Prejean, who offered advance praise of the project and championed my efforts in the incipient stages and to Sister Helen's assistant, Sister Margaret Maggio, for her kindness in initiating my contact with the busy Sister Helen.

I also want to mention my dear friend Pat Wiser and my sister Priscilla Lytle, who acted in the guise of my personal cheerleaders, reassuring me and nudging me on through the many hurdles and difficulties writing *Execution's Doorstep* posed.

Above all, my thanks to the five men whose stories are told here: Ron Keine, Juan Melendez, Michael Graham, Madison Hobley, and Randal Padgett. To say that *Execution's Doorstep* could not have been written without them is an understatement of the highest order. Having glimpsed the horror they endured at the close-range of their personal accounting, I remain in awe of their willingness to trust and bare their souls to a woman who appeared out of nowhere and requested permission to tell their stories. Their courage and generosity of spirit borders on the godlike. Before them I am humble. I hope I have honored their legacy.

Notes

Introduction (pages ix–xv)

1. James S. Liebman, Jeffrey Fagan, and Valerie West, "A Broken System: Error Rates in Capital Cases, 1973–1995," Columbia Law School, Public Law Research Paper no. 15, June 2000, http://www2.law.columbia.edu/instructionalservices/liebman/.

2. Unless otherwise noted, the source for the discussion of the appeals process was Liebman, Fagan, and West, "A Broken System."

3. "Lectric Law Library," www.lectlaw.com, retrieved 26 July 2007.

4. Richard Jaffe, telephone interview by author, 10 February 2006.

5. "Innocence: List of Those Freed from Death Row," Death Penalty Information Center, www.deathpenaltyinfo.org retrieved 27 July 2007.

6. Rob Warden, "Set a Fair Price for Wrongful Convictions," *Chicago Sun-Times*, 27 November 2005.

Ron Keine (pages 1–46)

1. Ron Keine, interview by author, tape recording, Winchester, Tennessee, 18–20 February 2005. Unless otherwise noted, the information in this chapter was compiled from the interview sessions with Keine.

2. Douglas Glazier, "New Biker Hearing Asked," *Detroit News*, 23 September 1975; Douglas Glazier, "Break Cited in Biker Case," *Detroit News*, 1 October 1975; Douglas Glazier, "Gun Identified in NM Murder," *Detroit News*, 4 December 1975; Florida Department of Corrections; Douglas Glazier, "Confessed Biker Case Slayer Identified as Drug Informer," *Detroit News*, 30 November 1975; Daniel Stuart Johnson, expert witness, telephone interview by author, 13 November 2005.

3. Glazier, "New Biker Hearing Asked"; Denise Tessier, "Velten Knife Wounds Inflicted after Death, Doctor Testifies," *Albuquerque Journal*, 3 December 1975.

4. Tessier, "Velten Knife Wounds," Glazier, "Gun Identified in NM Murder";

Glazier, "New Biker Hearing Asked"; George Henry Farrah, telephone interview by author, Albuquerque, New Mexico, and Winchester, Tennessee, 14 April 2005 and 8 September 2005; Steve Terrell, "Telling a Story of Horrid Crime, Consequences," *The Santa Fe New Mexican*, 4 June 1995.

5. Tessier, "Velten Knife Wounds"; James Brandenburg, "Don't Vilify Vagos Case Jury," *Albuquerque Journal*, 27 February 2005; Glazier, "New Biker Hearing Asked"; Glazier, "Break Cited in Biker Case"; Farrah interview; Terrell, "Telling a Story."

6. Douglas Glazier, "Ruling Put Off for Bid on New Biker Trial," *Detroit News*, 2 October 1975; Charles W. Daniels, "Prosecutor Misses Point of Death Row Exoneration," *Albuquerque Journal*, 4 March 2005; Johnson interview.

7. *Exonerations and the Death Penalty: An In-depth Look*, video recording of panel discussion, University of New Mexico, 14 February 2005.

8. Tessier, "Velten Knife Wounds."

9. Terrell, "Telling a Story," Johnson interview; Glazier, "Gun Identified," *Exonerations and the Death Penalty*; Daniels, "Prosecutor Misses Point."

10. Johnson interview; Denise Tessier, "Hate, Prejudice Nearly Sent Four to Gas Chamber," *Albuquerque Journal*, 9 July 1978; Daniels, "Prosecutor Misses Point"; Glazier, "New Biker Hearing Asked."

11. *Exonerations and the Death Penalty*.

12. Farrah interview.

13. Douglas Glazier, "Resolution," *Detroit News*, 1 January 1976.

14. Tessier, "Hate, Prejudice."

15. Tessier, "Velten Knife Wounds."

16. Tessier, "Hate, Prejudice."

17. Ibid.

18. Ibid.

19. *Albuquerque Tribune*, 16 February 1974; Ron Keine.

20. Stephen Cain, "Justice Must Serve All—Even Those We Do Not Like," *Detroit News*, 29 December 1974; Ron Keine.

21. Tessier, "Hate, Prejudice."

22. Ibid.; Douglas Glazier, "N.M. Court Orders Transcript in Bikers' Case," *Detroit News*, 6 February 1975.

23. Tessier, "Hate, Prejudice."

24. Sandy McCraw, "'Eyewitness' Says Made Up Testimony," *Albuquerque Journal*, 1 April 1975.

25. Tessier, "Hate, Prejudice."

26. Douglas Glazier, "Cyclists Win Hearing for a New Trial," *Detroit News*, 20 February 1975.

27. Tessier, "Hate, Prejudice."

28. McCraw, "'Eyewitness.'"

29. Tessier, "Hate, Prejudice."

30. McCraw, "'Eyewitness.'"

31. Tessier, "Hate, Prejudice."

32. McCraw, "'Eyewitness'"; Tessier, "Hate, Prejudice."

33. McCraw, "'Eyewitness.'"

34. Ibid.

35. Tessier, "Hate, Prejudice."

36. "Secret Witness Links Cycle Gang to Slaying," *Albuquerque Tribune*, 12 March 1974.

37. Tessier, "Hate, Prejudice."

38. "Secret Witness"; live footage from television broadcasts on the Velten case, courtesy George Henry Farrah.

39. *Albuquerque Tribune*, 13 March 1974.

40. Tessier, "Hate, Prejudice."

41. Stephen Cain, "Biker Witness Tells of Police Threats," *Detroit News*, 10 December 1974.

42. Jim Dawson, "New Trial Considered Milestone," *Albuquerque Journal*, 5 December 1975.

43. Ibid.

44. Tessier, "Velten Knife Wounds."

45. Farrah interview.

46. McCraw, "'Eyewitness.'"

47. Tessier, "Hate, Prejudice."

48. McCraw, "'Eyewitness.'"

49. Glazier, "Cyclists Win Hearing"; Tessier, "Hate, Prejudice."

50. Cain, "Biker Witness."

51. Ibid.

52. Ibid.; Tessier, "Hate, Prejudice."

53. Cain, "Biker Witness"; Cain, "Justice Must Serve All."

54. Cain, "Biker Witness."

55. McCraw, "'Eyewitness'"; Cain, "Biker Witness"; McCraw, "Confession to Killing Is Alleged," *Albuquerque Journal*, 3 April 1975.

56. Cain, "Biker Witness"; McCraw, "'Eyewitness.'"

57. Cain, "Justice Must Serve All."

58. Cain, "Biker Witness."

59. Glazier, "Cyclists Win Hearing"; Glazier, "Parolee Testifies in Biker Case," *Detroit News*, 3 April 1975.

60. Glazier, "Cyclists Win Hearing"; Ron Keine.

61. Cain, "Biker Witness"; Ron Keine.

62. Tessier, "Hate, Prejudice."

63. Glazier, "Cyclists Win Hearing."

64. Ron Keine; "Four Members of Cycle Club Sentenced to Gas Chamber," *Associated Press*, 6 June, 1974.

65. Tessier, "Hate, Prejudice."

66. Tessier, "Hate, Prejudice."

67. John E. Peterson, "Woman Accuses M.M. police," *Detroit News*, 28 December 1974.

68. Dawson, "New Trial."

69. Tessier, "Hate, Prejudice."

70. McCraw, "'Eyewitness'"; Sandy McCraw, "Confession to Killing Is Alleged."

71. McCraw, "Confession to Killing Is Alleged."

72. Tessier, "Hate, Prejudice."

73. Ibid.

74. Ibid.

75. Cain, "Justice Must Serve All."

76. Ibid.

77. Ibid.

78. Tessier, "Hate, Prejudice."

79. Ibid.

80. Ibid.

81. Douglas Glazier, "Figures in Bikers' Case Drop Out Of Sight," Detroit News, 20 July 1975; Tessier, "Hate, Prejudice."

82. Tessier, "Hate, Prejudice."

83. "Four Members of Cycle Club Sentenced to Gas Chamber."

84. Exonerations and the Death Penalty; Keine interviews.

85. Cain, "Biker Witness."

86. "Four Members of Cycle Club Sentenced to Gas Chamber."

87. James S. Liebman, Jeffrey Fagan, and Valerie West, "A Broken System: Error Rates in Capital Cases, 1973–1995," V. The Capital Review Process, First Inspection: State Direct Appeal, Columbia Law School, Public Law Research Paper no. 15, June 2000, http://www2.law.columbia.edu/instructionalservices/liebman/.

88. "Executions in the U.S. 1608–1987, State by State Information," Death Penalty Information Center.

89. Furman v. Georgia, 408 U.S. 153 (1972).

90. "Hate Factory," The Santa Fe New Mexican, 15 October 2005.

91. McCraw, "Confession to Killing Is Alleged."

92. Glazier, "N.M. Court Orders Transcript."

93. Steve Terrell, "Life after death row," Free New Mexican, 16 February 2005.

94. Douglas Glazier, "Why Death Row Bikers Left Detroit," Detroit News, 9 December 1974.

95. Cain, "Biker Witness."

96. Sandy McCraw, "'Eyewitness.'"

97. Douglas Glazier, "Prosecutor Will Check 'Tight Pants' Theory," Detroit News, 13 December 1974.

98. Ibid.

99. McCraw, "'Eyewitness.'"

100. Cain, "Biker Witness."

101. Ibid.

102. Douglas Glazier, "N.M. Court Orders Transcript."

103. Douglas Glazier, "Bikers' Lawyers seek new trial," Detroit News, 28 January 1975.

104. Douglas Glazier, "'You Are Saving Our Lives,'" *Detroit News*, 5 January 1975.

105. McCraw, "Confession to Killing Is Alleged."

106. Stephen Cain, "New Biker Case Suspect Bragged of Other Killings," *Detroit News*, 24 March 1975.

107. McCraw, "'Eyewitness.'"

108. Douglas Glazier, "Bikers Denied a New Trial," *Detroit News*, 10 April 1975.

109. McCraw, "'Eyewitness.'"

110. McCraw, "Confession to Killing Is Alleged."

111. Douglas Glazier, "Bikers Appeal Verdict," *Detroit News*, 21 May 1975.

112. McCraw, "Confession to Killing Is Alleged."

113. Sandy McCraw, "Keine Says Never Saw Killed Man," *Albuquerque Journal*, 4 April 1975.

114. McCraw, "Confession to Killing Is Alleged."

115. McCraw, "Keine Says Never Saw Killed Man."

116. Tessier, "Hate, Prejudice."

117. Glazier, "Bikers Denied a New Trial."

118. Ibid.

119. Glazier, "Bikers Appeal Verdict."

120. Douglas Glazier, "Biker Judge Drops Case in New Trial Bid," *Detroit News*, 24 June 1975.

121. Douglas Glazier, "Confessed Biker Case Slayer Identified as Drug Informer."

122. Glazier, "Biker Judge Drops Case in New Trial Bid."

123. Glazier, "Figures in Bikers' Case Drop Out of Sight."

124. Douglas Glazier, "New Bikers' Case Suspect Balks at Extradition," *Detroit News*, 28 September 1975; Tessier, "Hate, Prejudice."

125. Glazier, "Gun Identified in NM Murder."

126. Glazier, "New Biker Hearing Asked."

127. Glazier, "Break Cited in Biker Case."

128. Glazier, "New Biker Hearing Asked"; Glazier, "Ruling Put Off"; Farrah interview; Glazier, "Break Cited in Biker Case"; Glazier, "Gun Identified in NM Murder."

129. Douglas Glazier, "New Biker Hearing Asked."

130. Farrah interview.

131. Glazier, "Ruling Put Off."

132. Daniels interview.

133. Glazier, "Break Cited in Biker Case."

134. Daniels interview.

135. *Exonerations and the Death Penalty.*

136. Glazier, "Confessed Biker Case Slayer"; Glazier, "New Biker Hearing Asked."

137. Glazier, "Break Cited in Biker Case."

138. Glazier, "Confessed Biker Case Slayer."

139. Glazier, "New Bikers' Case Suspect Balks at Extradition."

140. Glazier, "Break Cited in Biker Case."

141. Glazier, "Confessed Biker Case Slayer."

142. Ibid.

143. Tessier, "Velten Knife Wounds"; Glazier, "Figures in Bikers' Case Drop Out of Sight."

144. Glazier, "Gun Identified in NM Murder."

145. Tessier, "Velten Knife Wounds."

146. Glazier, "Gun Identified in NM Murder."

147. Tessier, "Hate, Prejudice."

148. Tessier, "Velten Knife Wounds."

149. Ibid.

150. Ibid.; Glazier, "Gun Identified in NM Murder."

151. Tessier, "Velten Knife Wounds"; Denise Tessier, "New Velten Trial Ordered," *Albuquerque Journal*, 5 December 1975.

152. Douglas Glazier, "Prosecutor of Bikers Facing Ouster Move," *Detroit News*, 14 December 1975; "Appeal of Freed Bikers Dismissed," *Associated Press*, 25 December 1975.

153. "Bikers' Case Confessor Convicted in Slaying," *Associated Press*, 27 May 1978; Tessier, "Hate, Prejudice."

154. Douglas Glazier, "A Yule Gift for Biker," *Detroit News*, 21 December 1975.

155. Glazier, "Resolution."

156. Douglas Glazier, "Three of four bikers in trouble with law," *Detroit News*, 14 January 1976.

157. Douglas Glazier, "Ex-Death Row Cyclist on Bail in Gun Charge," *Detroit News*, 16 January 1976.

158. Tessier, "Hate, Prejudice."

159. Pat Ameel, interview by author, tape recording, Winchester, Tennessee, 18–20 February 2005.

160. Ron Keine; Tessier, "Hate, Prejudice."

161. Katy Knapp, "Freed Man Blasts Death Row," *Daily Lobo*, 15 February 2005.

162. Ibid.

163. Florida Department of Corrections; Federal Bureau of Prisons; Beaumont Federal Correctional Institution; Ron Keine; Terrell, "Telling a Story"; Steve Terrell, "New Mexico Wrongly Sentenced Bikers to Death," *The Santa Fe New Mexican*, 28 October 2001.

164. Maurice Possley and Steve Mills, "Crimes Go Unsolved as DNA Tool Ignored," *Chicago Tribune*, 26 October 2003. The article recounts numerous cases in which DNA evidence cleared the defendants, but law-enforcement officials refused to consider them innocent or to pursue new suspects through DNA database matching.

165. Liebman, Fagan, and West, "A Broken System," II. Summary of Central Findings.

166. *Imbler v. Pachtman*, No. 74-5435 (1976).

Juan Roberto Melendez (pages 47–91)

1. Unless otherwise indicated, information in this chapter was compiled from a series of interviews with Juan Melendez on 20 December 2004, 5 February 2005, 23 August 2005, 7 October 2005, 9 March 2006, 8 November 2006, and 10 November 2006.

2. The information contained in this section was compiled from the following sources: Gail E. Anderson, Initial Brief of Appellant, *Juan Roberto Melendez v. State of Florida*, Case No. 88961, 29 May 1997, 2, 11, 22, 56, 79; "Summary of Juan Melendez' Case," Floridians for Alternatives to the Death Penalty (FADP); Bill Berkowitz, "A Dead Man Walking toward Freedom?" (P.a.t.r.i.c.k Crusade); *Juan Roberto Melendez v. State of Florida*, No. 66,244, 11 December 1986; Juan Melendez, interviews by author; Rosa Greenbaum, telephone interview by author, tape recording, 26 August, 2005; *Juan Roberto Melendez v. State of Florida*, No. CF-84-1016A2-XX, 5 December 2001; Harold Landrum, Jr., arrest record, 19 October 2005, Polk County Sheriff's Office; Harold Landrum, Florida Department of Law Enforcement, 31 October 2005; Vernon James, arrest record, 19 October 2005, Polk County Sheriff's Office; Vernon James Inmate Record, Florida Department of Corrections, 31 October 2005; Auburndale Police Department, File No. 83-16695, 13 September 1983 and 15 September 1983; Florida Department of Law Enforcement (FDLE) Case #532-1A-0043; *State of Florida v. Juan Roberto Melendez*, Case No. CF 84-1016, 17 September 1984.

3. Lesley Clark, "Freed Inmate Doesn't Hold Grudge," *The Miami Herald*, 5 January 2002.

4. Juan Melendez, summary prepared for Canadian Coalition Against the Death Penalty (CCADP) and interviews with the author.

5. Anderson, Initial Brief, 8; Melendez, interviews.

6. "Summary of Juan Melendez' Case," FADP; Juan Melendez, summary, CCADP; "Summary of Juan Melendez's Case," www.oranous.com.innocence/Juan Melendez, retrieved 27 March 2005; Melendez interviews; Anderson, Initial Brief, 8; Greenbaum interview; Lola Vollen and Dave Eggers, eds., *Surviving Justice: America's Wrongly Convicted and Exonerated* (San Francisco: McSweeney's, 2005), 51.

7. "Summary of Juan Melendez' Case," FADP; Juan Melendez, summary for CCADP; "Summary of Juan Melendez's Case," www.oranous.com.innocence /JuanMelendez; Melendez interviews; Anderson, Initial Brief, 8; Greenbaum, interview.

8. Anderson, Initial Brief, 4, 9, 17; *Juan Roberto Melendez v. State of Florida*, No. CF-84-1016A2-XX; Melendez interviews; FDLE Case #532-1A-0043.

9. *Juan Roberto Melendez v. State of Florida*, No. 88961 (11 June 1998); FDLE Case #532-1A-0043.

10. Anderson, Initial Brief, 60, 62; FDLE Case #532-1A-0043.

11. Melendez interviews; *State of Florida v. Juan Roberto Melendez*, Case No. CF 84-1016; Anderson, Initial Brief, 62.

12. *Juan Roberto Melendez v. State of Florida*, No. 88961.

13. Anderson, Initial Brief, 62.

14. Ibid., 14, 30-31, 63; FDLE Case #532-1A-0043.

15. Anderson, Initial Brief, 4.

16. Ibid., 27–28; Melendez interviews; *State of Florida v. Juan Roberto Melendez*, Case No. CF 84-1016.

17. Anderson, Initial Brief, 6–7, 28, 77–78; Melendez interviews.

18. Melendez interviews; FDLE Case #532-1A-0043.

19. FDLE Case #532-1A-0043.

20. Melendez interviews; "Circuit Judges," http://jud10.org/CircuitCourt/Circuit Judges/alcott.html, retrieved 9 October 2005.

21. Anderson, Initial Brief, 5, 16; *Juan Roberto Melendez v. State of Florida*, No. CF-84-1016A2-XX; *State of Florida v. Juan Roberto Melendez*, Case No. CF 84-1016.

22. *Juan Roberto Melendez v. State of Florida*, No. CF-84-1016A2-XX; Juan Melendez, summary for CCADP.

23. Anderson, Initial Brief, 6, 32.

24. *Juan Roberto Melendez v. State of Florida*, No. CF-84-1016A2-XX; James arrest record; James Inmate Record.

25. Anderson, Initial Brief, 22; James Inmate Record.

26. Anderson, Initial Brief, 22, 32, 67.

27. James Inmate Record.

28. *Juan Roberto Melendez v. State of Florida*, No. CF-84-1016A2-XX; Melendez interviews.

29. Melendez, summary for CCADP.

30. Anderson, Initial Brief, 3–8, 41, 77; *Juan Roberto Melendez v. State of Florida*, No. CF-84-1016A2-XX; *State of Florida v. Juan Roberto Melendez*, Case No. CF 84-1016.

31. Melendez, summary for CCADP.

32. Anderson, Initial Brief, 6–7.

33. *Juan Roberto Melendez v. State of Florida*, No. CF-84-1016A2-XX.

34. Anderson, Initial Brief, 7; FDLE Case #532-1A-0043.

35. Anderson, Initial Brief, 8; Melendez interviews.

36. *Juan Roberto Melendez v. State of Florida*, No. 75081, 12 November 1992.

37. Anderson, Initial Brief, 8–9, 16–17.

38. Ibid., 8–11, 13, 16–17, 42; *Juan Roberto Melendez v. State of Florida*, No. CF-84-1016A2-XX; Melendez summary for CCADP; Melendez interviews; James Inmate Record.

39. *Juan Roberto Melendez v. State of Florida*, No. CF-84-1016A2-XX.

40. Melendez interviews; *State of Florida v. Juan Roberto Melendez*, Case No. CF 84-1016.

41. Melendez summary for CCADP.

42. Berkowitz, "Dead Man Walking."

43. Melendez interviews.

44. Juan Melendez, interview by Judi E. Caruso, video recording, Santa Fe, New Mexico, 8 May 2004.

45. Melendez interviews; *State of Florida v. Juan Roberto Melendez*, Case No. CF 84-1016.

46. Anderson, Initial Brief, 7–8, 53.

47. Ibid., 112, 66–67.

48. *Juan Roberto Melendez v. State of Florida*, No. CF-84-1016A2-XX.

49. Ibid.

50. Judicial Conference of the United States, Committee on Defender Services, Subcommittee on Federal Death Penalty Cases, *Federal Death Penalty Cases: Recommendations Concerning the Cost and Quality of Defense Representation*, prepared by James R. Spencer, Robin J. Cauthron, Nancy G. Edmunds, 1998, Introduction, note 14.

51. Melendez summary for CCADP.

52. Anderson, Initial Brief, 8, 11, 16–18, 41; Sheri Silberstein and Caleb Eber, "Juan Melendez and Bud Welch," Hill Connections, http://hillconnections.org/ri/juanbud3ja.htm.

53. Gary Fineout and Julia Ferrante, "Freed Man Yearns for Simple Pleasures," *Lakeland Ledger*, 5 January 2002.

54. Ibid.; Melendez interviews.

55. Florida Commission on Capital Cases, Locke Burt chairman, *Case Histories*, "A Review of 24 Individuals Released from Death Row," revised 10 September 2002, 77.

56. Fineout and Ferrante, "Freed Man Yearns."

57. The information contained in this section was compiled from interviews by author Juan Melendez, with/and from a presentation by Melendez at the University of the South, Sewanee, Tennessee, 8 March 2006.

58. "Florida's capital post conviction review process," Florida Death Row Advocacy Group, www.fdrag.org/archive.html, retrieved 17 January 2008.

59. *Juan Roberto Melendez v. State of Florida*, No. 66,244.

60. Berkowitz, "Dead Man Walking."

61. *Juan Roberto Melendez v. State of Florida*, No. 75081.

62. *Juan Roberto Melendez v. State of Florida*, No. CF-84-1016A2-XX.

63. Anderson, Initial Brief, 15–18.

64. Melendez summary for CCADP.

65. Anderson, Initial Brief, 36–38.

66. Melendez summary for CCADP.

67. Anderson, Initial Brief, 38.

68. The information in this section was compiled from interviews by the author and by Judi E. Caruso with Juan Melendez.

69. "Lectric Law Library," www.lectlaw.com retrieved 9 March 2005; James S. Liebman, Jeffrey Fagan, and Valerie West, "A Broken System: Error Rates in Capital Cases, 1973–1995," V. The Capital Review Process, Columbia Law School, Public Law Research Paper no. 15, June 2000, http://www2.law.columbia.edu/instructional services/liebman.

70. *Juan Roberto Melendez v. Harry K. Singletary, etc.*, No. 82570, 8 September 1994; Melendez summary for CCADP.

71. "A Review of 24 Individuals Released from Death Row," 74. During this

same period, a habeas petition was filed with the U.S. District Court, but Juan Melendez was freed before the court ever acted on the request.

72. Anderson, Initial Brief, 18–22, 26–33, 36–37, 45.

73. *Juan Roberto Melendez v. State of Florida*, No. CF-84-1016A2-XX; Judi E. Caruso, e-mail correspondence, 10 January 2005.

74. Anderson, Initial Brief, 18–34, 61–63.

75. *Juan Roberto Melendez v. State of Florida*, No. CF-84-1016A2-XX.

76. *Juan Roberto Melendez v. State of Florida*, No. 88961.

77. Anderson, Initial Brief, 43, 53, 57, 66.

78. *Juan Roberto Melendez v. State of Florida*, No. 88961.

79. Melendez summary for CCADP; Rosa Greenbaum, e-mail correspondence, 1 November 2005.

80. Interviews by Caruso and the author with Melendez.

81. *Juan Roberto Melendez v. State of Florida*, No. CF-84-1016A2-XX, Greenbaum, interview by author; Marty Lake Inmate Record, Florida Department of Corrections.

82. *Juan Roberto Melendez v. State of Florida*, No. CF-84-1016A2-XX.

83. Melendez interviews; Melendez presentation, University of the South.

84. Melendez interviews; Silberstein and Eber, "Juan Melendez."

85. Vickie Chachere, "Florida Death Row Inmate to be Released, 99th Freed Nationwide," *Associated Press*, 3 January 2002.

86. Adele Bernhard, "When Justice Fails: Indemnification for Unjust Convictions," table summarizing state statues on indemnification for unjust convictions (6 University of Chicago Law School, Roundtable 73, September 9, 2004); "State by State Information," Death Penalty Information Center.

87. *Imbler v. Pachtman*, No. 74-5435 (1976).

Michael Ray Graham, Jr. (pages 92–135)

1. Michael Ray Graham, Jr., interviews by author, tape recording, 4–5 March, 23 March, 6 April, and 26 May 2006; Christopher Baughman and Tom Guarisco, "Justice for None," *Advocate*, 19 March 2001; Steven M. Pincus, "It's Good To Be Free," www.wmitchell.edu/lawreview/Volume28/Issue1/03_pincus.pdf, retrieved 9 February 2006. Unless otherwise noted, the information in this chapter was compiled from the Graham interviews by the author.

2. Unless otherwise noted, the information in this section was compiled from the Graham interviews; Pincus, "It's Good"; Christopher Baughman and Tom Guarisco, "Justice for None," *Advocate*, 18–20 March 2001 (three-part series); *State of Louisiana v. Michael Graham*, No. 28,734-B, trial transcript, Third Judicial District Court 1987.

3. "Dead Wrong: An Examination of Capital Prosecutions," Administration of Justice Program Accuracy Project, George Mason University, 2001, http://72.14.203 .104/search?q=cache:E8krmoRTcZoJ:pia.gmu.edu/adj/honors/reporttotal.html+ Downsville+Couple+Found+Murdered&hl=en&gl=us&ct=clnk&cd=27, accessed 6 April 2006.

4. Kenneth Larry Averitt, deposition, *Albert Ronnie Burrell and Michael Ray Graham, Jr. v. Tommy Adkins, Dan J. Grady, III, Kenneth Larry Averitt, Donald Holdman, Monty Forbess, Elmer Hearron, Jim Hood, Robert Levy, Bob Buckley, and John and Jane Does 1–40,* Civil Action No. 3:01CV2679, United States District Court, Western District of Louisiana, Monroe Division, 24 May 2004.

5. "Dead Wrong."

6. *State of Louisiana v. Michael Graham,* No. 28,734-B, ruling of Judge Cynthia T. Woodard, Third Judicial District Court, 3 March 2000.

7. Ibid.

8. Elizabeth Lam, interviews by author, tape recording, 24 March and 30 April 2006.

9. Downsville, Louisiana, "Detailed Profile," http://www.city-data.com/city /Downsville-Louisiana.html, retrieved 16 April 2006.

10. Baughman and Guarisco, "Justice for None," 18 March 2001.

11. Farmerville, Louisiana, "Detailed Profile," http://www.city-data.com/city /Farmerville-Louisiana.html, retrieved 16 April 2006.

12. Robert Earle, interviews by author, tape recording, 4 May and 31 May 2006; *State of Louisiana v. Michael Graham,* No. 28,734-B, 3 March 2000.

13. Unless otherwise noted, the information in this section was compiled from Pincus, "It's Good"; *State of Louisiana v. Michael Graham,* No. 28,734-B, 1987; Baughman and Guarisco, "Justice for None," 18–20 March 2001.

14. *State of Louisiana v. Michael Graham,* No. 28,734-B, 3 March 2000.

15. Earle, interviews.

16. Averitt deposition; *State of Louisiana v. Michael Graham,* No. 28,734-B, 3 March 2000.

17. The information in this section was compiled from Graham interviews; Pincus, "It's Good"; *State of Louisiana v. Michael Graham,* No. 28,734-B, 3 March 2000; *State of Louisiana v. Michael Graham,* No. 28,734-B, 1987; Baughman and Guarisco, "Justice for None," 18–20 March 2001; Averitt deposition.

18. *State of Louisiana v. Michael Graham,* No. 28,734-B, 3 March 2000. Unless otherwise noted, the information in this section was compiled from the trial transcript *State of Louisiana v. Michael Graham,* No. 28,734-B, 1987.

19. Graham interviews; *State of Louisiana v. Michael Graham,* No. 28,734-B, 3 March 2000.

20. Graham interviews; Earle interviews.

21. *State of Louisiana v. Michael Graham,* No. 28,734-B, 3 March 2000.

22. Ibid.

23. Pincus, "Its Good"; *State of Louisiana v. Michael Graham,* No. 28,734-B, 3 March 2000.

24. *State of Louisiana v. Michael Graham,* No. 28,734-B, 3 March 2000.

25. The information in the remainder of this section was compiled from the following sources: Earle and Graham interviews; Baughman and Guarisco, "Justice for None," 18 March 2001; U.S. Senate Committee on the Judiciary, testimony of Michael Graham in support of the Innocence Protection Act, 27 June 2001; Lau-

rence Hammack, "Man Finds that Release from Death Row Leads to New Tests," *Roanoke Times*, 21 January 2001.

26. Unless otherwise noted, the information in this section was compiled from the following sources: Pincus, "It's Good"; Baughman and Guarisco, "Justice for None," 18–19 March 2001.

27. Graham interviews; *State of Louisiana v. Michael Graham*, No. 28,734-B, 3 March 2000; Earle interviews.

28. "Innocence, Cases of Innocence 1973–Present," Death Penalty Information Center, http://www.deathpenaltyinfo.org/article.php?scid=6&did=109, retrieved 30 May 2006.

29. The information in this section was compiled from the interviews with Elizabeth Lam and Robert Earle.

30. Baughman and Guarisco, "Justice for None," 20 March 2001.

31. Unless otherwise noted, the information in this section was compiled from the following sources: Graham and Earle interviews; Baughman and Guarisco, "Justice for None," 19 March 2001.

32. Graham interviews; *State of Louisiana v. Michael Graham*, No. 28,734-B, 3 March 2000.

33. The information in this section was compiled from interviews with Elizabeth Lam.

34. The information in this section was compiled from Pincus, "It's Good"; Graham interviews.

35. Unless otherwise noted, the information in this section was compiled from an interview with John Holdridge, tape recording, 12 May 2006.

36. Carol Line, "Death Penalty News—Louisiana, Florida," 2 October 1999, http://venus.soci.niu.edu/~archives/ABOLISH/rick-halperin/oct99/0392.html, accessed 31 May 2006.

37. Pincus, "It's Good."

38. "Execution Database," Death Penalty Information Center, http://www.death penaltyinfo.org/getexecdata.php, retrieved 7 May 2006.

39. Pincus, "It's Good."

40. Ibid.; Baughman and Guarisco, "Justice for None," 19 March 2001.

41. Pincus, "It's Good"; Graham interviews; Michael Ray Graham, Jr., letter to Doug Lam, 12 June 1995.

42. Michael Ray Graham, Jr., letters to Doug Lam, 6 June 1995, 2 January 1996, and 28 March 1996.

43. Elizabeth Lam interview.

44. Elizabeth Lam interview; Doug Lam, interview by author, tape recording, 7 May 2006.

45. Graham interviews; Michael Ray Graham, Jr., letters to Doug Lam, 11 April 1996 and 26 April 1996.

46. Graham letter, 28 March 1996.

47. Graham letter, 2 January 1996; Baughman and Guarisco, "Justice for None," 19 March 2001.

48. Graham letters, 2 January 1996 and 26 April 1996.

49. Graham letter, 26 April 1996; Pincus, "It's Good."

50. Pincus, "It's Good."

51. Michael Ray Graham, Jr., letter to Doug Lam, 29 August 1996; Pincus, "It's Good"; John Holdridge, e-mail correspondence, 12 February 2007.

52. Holdridge interview.

53. Michael Ray Graham, Jr., letter to Doug Lam, 17 September 1996; "Alford Plea Law and Legal Definition," http://www.uslegalforms.com/legaldefinitions /alford-plea/, retrieved 7 May 2006.

54. Graham interviews; Pincus, "It's Good."

55. Graham interviews; Elizabeth Lam interview; Pincus, "It's Good."

56. Graham interviews; report issued by the Mississippi River Commission, New Orleans District, 3 April 2001, www.usace.army.mil/civilworks/cecwb/just _states/just_2002/mvd3.pdf, retrieved 26 March 2006.

57. Graham interviews; Graham letter, 12 June 1995; Hammack, "Man Finds that Release."

58. Holdridge interview; State of Louisiana v. Michael Graham, No. 28,734-B, 3 March 2000; Averitt deposition.

59. Pincus, "It's Good"; Earle interviews.

60. The information in this section was compiled from the ruling of Judge Cynthia T. Woodard, State of Louisiana v. Michael Graham, No. 28,734-B, 3 March 2000.

61. The information in this section was compiled from the following sources: Graham interviews; Pincus, "It's Good"; Baughman and Guarisco, "Justice for None," 20 March 2001.

62. Unless otherwise noted the information in this section was compiled from the following sources: Graham interviews; Pincus, "It's Good."

63. Holdridge, e-mail correspondence.

64. Elizabeth Lam interview.

65. Ibid.

66. Hammack, "Man Finds that Release"; Graham testimony before the U.S. Senate Committee on the Judiciary.

67. Pincus, "It's Good."

68. Ibid., Baughman and Guarisco, "Justice for None," 20 March 2001; Tom Guarisco, "Compensation Sought for Ex-Inmate," Advocate, 23 May 2001.

69. Virginians for Alternatives to the Death Penalty, Spring 2001 Newsletter, http://www.vadp.org/nlspring01.html, retrieved 15 May 2006.

70. Graham testimony before the U.S. Senate Committee on the Judiciary.

71. Doug Lam interview.

72. Elizabeth Lam interview.

73. Cheryl Milton, interview by author, 5 March 2006.

74. Elizabeth Lam interview.

75. Tenney et al v. Brandhove, No. 338, 1951.

76. Averitt deposition; Pincus, "It's Good"; State of Louisiana v. Michael Graham, No. 28,734-B, 3 March 2000.

Madison Hobley (pages 136–182)

1. Madison Hobley, interviews by author, tape recording, Chicago, Illinois, 19–20 February 2007, 6 April 2007, 24 August 2007; Governor George Ryan, speech delivered at DePaul University College of Law, 10 January 2003, http://www.injusticebusters.com/2003/Gov_George_Ryan.htm, retrieved 29 May 2007. The information in this chapter, unless otherwise noted, was compiled from interviews with Hobley.

2. The information appearing in this section was compiled from the Hobley interviews, and from Wallace Best, "Avalon Park," *Encyclopedia of Chicago*, www.encyclopedia.chicagohistory.org/pages/97.html, retrieved 29 June 2007; John Conroy, "The Magic Can," Chicago Reader, 26 May 2000; *The People of the State of Illinois v. Madison Hobley*, No. 81609, 29 May 1998; Steve Mills, "Retrial Denied in Fire Deaths," Chicago Tribune, 9 July 2002.

3. Conroy, "The Magic Can."

4. Edward J. Egan and Robert Boyle, "Madison Hobley Exhibit No. 1," *Report of the Special State's Attorney*, Circuit Court of Cook County, 2006.

5. Ibid.

6. Ibid.

7. Ibid.

8. *The People of the State of Illinois v. Madison Hobley*, No. 81609, 29 May 1998.

9. Egan and Boyle, "Madison Hobley Exhibit No. 1."

10. *The People of the State of Illinois v. Madison Hobley*, No. 81609, 29 May 1998; Edward J. Egan and Robert Boyle, "Madison Hobley," *Report of the Special State's Attorney*, Circuit Court of Cook County, 2006.

11. *The People of the State of Illinois v. Madison Hobley*, No. 81609, 29 May 1998; Egan and Boyle, "Madison Hobley."

12. *The People of the State of Illinois v. Madison Hobley*, No. 81609, 29 May 1998; "Madison Hobley."

13. Conroy, "The Magic Can"; Egan and Boyle, "Madison Hobley" and "Madison Hobley Exhibit No. 1"; *The People of the State of Illinois v. Madison Hobley*, No. 71184, 31 March 1994.

14. *The People of the State of Illinois v. Madison Hobley*, No. 81609, 29 May 1998.

15. Ibid.

16. Conroy, "The Magic Can"; Egan and Boyle, "Madison Hobley."

17. "What Is a Polygraph?" The Polygraph Place, http://www.polygraphplace.com/docs/information.shtml#polygraph, retrieved 29 June 2007.

18. Conroy, "The Magic Can"; *The People of the State of Illinois v. Madison Hobley*, No. 81609, 29 May 1998; Egan and Boyle, "Madison Hobley Exhibit No. 1."

19. Egan and Boyle, "Madison Hobley Exhibit No. 1."

20. Egan and Boyle, "Madison Hobley"; *The People of the State of Illinois v. Madison Hobley*, No. 81609, 29 May 1998.

21. Conroy, "The Magic Can"; *The People of the State of Illinois v. Madison Hobley*, No. 81609, 29 May 1998; "The Illinois Exonerated: Madison Hobley," Center on

Wrongful Convictions, http://www.law.northwestern.edu/depts/clinic/wrongful/exonerations/IL_Hobley.htm, retrieved 29 June 2007.

22. *The People of the State of Illinois v. Madison Hobley*, No. 81609, 29 May 1998.

23. Conroy, "The Magic Can"; *The People of the State of Illinois v. Madison Hobley*, No. 81609, 29 May 1998.

24. *The People of the State of Illinois v. Madison Hobley*, No. 81609, 29 May 1998.

25. Conroy, "The Magic Can"; *The People of the State of Illinois v. Madison Hobley*, No. 81609, 29 May 1998.

26. Madison Hobley interviews; Andrea Lyon, telephone interview by author, 26 April 2007.

27. Conroy, "The Magic Can."

28. Ibid.

29. Ibid., Leonora LaPeter, "Torture Allegations Dog Ex-Police Officer," *St. Petersburg Times*, 29 August 2004.

30. *The People of the State of Illinois v. Madison Hobley*, No. 81609, 29 May 1998.

31. Madison Hobley, e-mail correspondence, 22 June 2007.

32. Conroy, "The Magic Can"; Egan and Boyle, "Madison Hobley."

33. Conroy, "The Magic Can."

34. Madison Hobley e-mail correspondence, 3 July 2007.

35. *The People of the State of Illinois v. Madison Hobley*, No. 81609, 29 May 1998; Celeste Stewart Stack and Paul Tsukuno, *The People of the State of Illinois v. Madison Hobley*, "People's Response in Opposition to Petition for Executive Clemency," Prison Review Board, October 2002; Conroy, "The Magic Can."

36. Conroy, "The Magic Can"; *The People of the State of Illinois v. Madison Hobley*, No. 71184, 31 March 1994.

37. Conroy, "The Magic Can"; Hobley interviews.

38. Barbara Brotman, "The Verdict," *Chicago Tribune*, 30 December 1990; Hobley interviews.

39. *The People of the State of Illinois v. Madison Hobley*, No. 81609, 29 May 1998; Conroy, "The Magic Can."

40. *The People of the State of Illinois v. Madison Hobley*, No. 81609, 29 May 1998.

41. *The People of the State of Illinois v. Madison Hobley*, No. 71184, 31 March 1994; Conroy, "The Magic Can."

42. *The People of the State of Illinois v. Madison Hobley*, No. 81609, 29 May 1998; Conroy, "The Magic Can."

43. *The People of the State of Illinois v. Madison Hobley*, No. 81609, 29 May 1998.

44. Ibid., "The Illinois Exonerated: Madison Hobley."

45. *The People of the State of Illinois v. Madison Hobley*, No. 81609, 29 May 1998; Conroy, "The Magic Can"; Hobley interviews.

46. *The People of the State of Illinois v. Madison Hobley*, No. 81609, 29 May 1998; *The People of the State of Illinois v. Madison Hobley*, No. 71184, 31 March 1994; Hobley interviews.

47. *The People of the State of Illinois v. Madison Hobley*, No. 71184, 31 March 1994.

48. *The People of the State of Illinois v. Madison Hobley*, No. 81609, 29 May 1998;

Notes

The People of the State of Illinois v. Madison Hobley, No. 71184, 31 March 1994; Hobley interviews.

49. Conroy, "The Magic Can"; *The People of the State of Illinois v. Madison Hobley*, No. 81609, 29 May 1998.

50. *The People of the State of Illinois v. Madison Hobley*, No. 81609, 29 May 1998; *The People of the State of Illinois v. Madison Hobley*, No. 71184, 31 March 1994; Hobley interviews.

51. *The People of the State of Illinois v. Madison Hobley*, No. 81609, 29 May 1998.

52. Conroy, "The Magic Can"; *The People of the State of Illinois v. Madison Hobley*, No. 81609, 29 May 1998.

53. Hobley interviews; Barbara Brotman, "The Verdict."

54. Conroy, "The Magic Can"; *The People of the State of Illinois v. Madison Hobley*, No. 81609, 29 May 1998; *The People of the State of Illinois v. Madison Hobley*, No. 71184, 31 March 1994.

55. "Justice for Madison Hobley," International Socialist Organization, http://www.iit.edu/~curtchr1/madison.htm, retrieved 2 July 2007; Conroy, "The Magic Can"; *The People of the State of Illinois v. Madison Hobley*, No. 81609, 29 May 1998; Lyon interview.

56. *The People of the State of Illinois v. Madison Hobley*, No. 81609, 29 May 1998; Brotman, "The Verdict," Lyon interview.

57. *The People of the State of Illinois v. Madison Hobley*, No. 81609, 29 May 1998; Brotman, "The Verdict"; "Justice for Madison Hobley."

58. *The People of the State of Illinois v. Madison Hobley*, No. 81609, 29 May 1998; Brotman "The Verdict."

59. Brotman, "The Verdict."

60. Ibid.; *The People of the State of Illinois v. Madison Hobley*, No. 81609, 29 May 1998.

61. Brotman, "The Verdict"; Hobley interviews.

62. Brotman, "The Verdict"; Hobley interviews.

63. Conroy, "The Magic Can."

64. *The People of the State of Illinois v. Madison Hobley*, "People's Response in Opposition to Petition for Executive Clemency"; Egan and Boyle, "Madison Hobley Exhibit No. 1"; Conroy, "The Magic Can."

65. Conroy, "The Magic Can."

66. Egan and Boyle, "Madison Hobley Exhibit No. 1."

67. John Conroy, "House of Screams," *Chicago Reader*, 26 January 1990; Conroy, "The Magic Can"; LaPeter, "Torture Allegations."

68. Steve Mills, "Man Freed from Death Row Sues City," *Chicago Tribune*, 30 May 2003, http://www.truthinjustice.org/hobley-sues.htm, retrieved 7 March 2007.

69. *The People of the State of Illinois v. Madison Hobley*, No. 71184, 31 March 1994.

70. *The People of the State of Illinois v. Madison Hobley*, No. 71184, 31 March 1994.

71. *The People of the State of Illinois v. Madison Hobley*, No. 71184, 31 March 1994.

72. Lyon interview.

73. Ibid.

74. *The People of the State of Illinois v. Madison Hobley*, No. 81609, 29 May 1998.

75. Conroy, "The Magic Can"; *The People of the State of Illinois v. Madison Hobley*, No. 81609, 29 May 1998.

76. Conroy, "The Magic Can"; *The People of the State of Illinois v. Madison Hobley*, No. 81609, 29 May 1998; Egan and Boyle, "Madison Hobley."

77. Conroy, "The Magic Can"; *The People of the State of Illinois v. Madison Hobley*, No. 81609, 29 May 1998.

78. *The People of the State of Illinois v. Madison Hobley*, No. 81609, 29 May 1998.

79. Ibid.

80. Hobley interviews; *The People of the State of Illinois v. Madison Hobley*, No. 81609, 29 May 1998.

81. Lyon interviews; *The People of the State of Illinois v. Madison Hobley*, No. 81609, 29 May 1998.

82. Lyon interview; *The People of the State of Illinois v. Madison Hobley*, No. 81609, 29 May 1998.

83. Lyon interview; *The People of the State of Illinois v. Madison Hobley*, No. 81609, 29 May 1998.

84. *The People of the State of Illinois v. Madison Hobley*, No. 81609, 29 May 1998; Conroy, "The Magic Can."

85. Conroy, "The Magic Can."

86. *The People of the State of Illinois v. Madison Hobley*, No. 81609, 29 May 1998.

87. "Execution Database," Death Penalty Information Center, http://www
.deathpenaltyinfo.org/executions.php, retrieved 3 July 2007.

88. Eric Zorn, "Gas-Can Mystery May Fuel Retrial In Arson Conviction," *Chicago Tribune*, 12 March 1998.

89. *The People of the State of Illinois v. Madison Hobley*, No. 81609, 29 May 1998.

90. Ibid.

91. Ibid.

92. Susan Dwyer, "Illinois Abolitionists in High Gear," *The New Abolitionist* 28 (May 2003), http://www.nodeathpenalty.org/newabo28/10_ChapterReports.html, retrieved 3 July 2003.

93. Hobley and Lyon interviews.

94. Hobley and Lyon interviews.

95. Hobley interviews; Conroy, "The Magic Can"; Bob Witanek, "Madison Hobley: Torture Victim on Row," Abolish Archives, 20 August 1996, http://venus
.soci.niu.edu/~archives/ABOLISH/summer96/0179.html, retrieved 3 July 2007.

96. Zorn, "Gas-Can Mystery"; Conroy, "The Magic Can"; Lyon interview.

97. Zorn, "Gas-Can Mystery"; Conroy, "The Magic Can"; Lyon interview.

98. Conroy, "The Magic Can."

99. Ibid.; Hobley interviews.

100. Julien Ball, "Justice Denied for Madison Hobley," *The New Abolitionist*, 25 (August 2002), www.nodeathpenalty.org, retrieved 18 March 2007.

101. Lyon interview; Maurice Possley, "Prosecutors Accused of Withholding Evidence in '87 Murders Report on Fingerprints at Issue in Hearing," *Chicago Tri-*

bune, 14 July 2000; *The People of the State of Illinois v. Madison Hobley*, No. 81609, 29 May 1998; Mills, "Retrial Denied."

102. Hobley interviews; *The People of the State of Illinois v. Madison Hobley*, "People's Response in Opposition to Petition for Executive Clemency."

103. Lyon interview.

104. Ibid., *The People of the State of Illinois v. Madison Hobley*, "People's Response in Opposition to Petition for Executive Clemency."

105. Lyon interview; Steve Mills, "Expert Disputes Cops' Testimony on Gas Can in '87 Fire Fatal to 7," *Chicago Tribune*, 21 June 2001.

106. Hobley interviews; Mills, "Expert Disputes Cops' Testimony"; Ball, "Justice Denied."

107. Mills, "Retrial Denied."

108. Ibid., Hobley interviews.

109. Ball, "Justice Denied"; Hobley interviews.

110. Mills, "Retrial Denied."

111. Ibid.; Ball, "Justice Denied."

112. Lyon interviews; Mills, "Retrial Denied."

113. Lyon interview.

114. Jeff Flock, "'Blanket Commutation' Empties Illinois Death Row," CNN, 13 January 2003, http://www.cnn.com/2003/LAW/01/11/illinois.death.row/, retrieved 7 February 2007; "Innocence Cases: 1994–2003," Death Penalty Information Center, http://www.deathpenaltyinfo.org/article.php?did=2340, retrieved 5 July 2007; "Timeline of Governor Ryan's Time in Office," http://deadlinethemovie.com/get_involved/timeline_of_governor_ryans_time_in_office.php, retrieved 8 March 2007; "Report of the Former Governor Ryan's Commission on Capital Punishment," Death Penalty Information Center, http://www.idoc.state.il.us/ccp/ccp/reports/index.html, retrieved 5 July 2007.

115. Hobley and Lyon interviews; Mills, "Retrial Denied."

116. Timeline of Governor Ryan's Time in Office.

117. Ball, "Justice Denied"; Hobley interviews.

118. Lyon interview; Douglas Lee, "Interview with Madison Hobley," *The New Abolitionist* 28 (May 2003), www.nodeathpenalty.org, retrieved 5 July 2007.

119. Jeff Flock, "'A Manifest Injustice Has Occurred,'" CNN, http://ccadp.org/aaronpatterson-released2003.htm, retrieved 18 March 2007.

120. Governor Ryan, speech at DePaul University.

121. Lyon interview.

122. Rosalind Rossi, "Lawyers Demand City Pay Up in Burge Torture Case," *Chicago Sun-Times*, 20 February 2007, www.suntimes.com/news/metro/264489,CST-NWS-burge20.article, retrieved 14 March 2007.

Randal Padgett (pages 183–234)

1. Randal Padgett, interviews by author, tape recording, Guntersville, Alabama, 19 December 2005, 22 September 2006, 22 March 2007, and 26 August

2007. Unless otherwise noted, information in this chapter is compiled from these interviews.

2. *Larry Randal Padgett v. State of Alabama*, CC-91-38, trial record, Marshall Circuit Court 1992, exhibits 139, 199, 141–42.

3. Ibid., exhibits 9–10, 202, 124; Padgett interviews.

4. Padgett interview; *Larry Randal Padgett v. State of Alabama*, CC-91-38, 1992, exhibits 252, 10–11; Brenda Padgett, interviews by author, tape recording, Guntersville, Alabama, 19 December 2005, 5 January 2006, 22 September 2006, and 26 August 2007.

5. Brenda Padgett, interviews; Stephanie Reed and Jake Watson, "DNA: 1:76 Million Chance; Station Wagon Sightings," *The Arab Tribune*, 1 October, 1997.

6. Padgett interviews; *Larry Randal Padgett v. State of Alabama*, CC-91-38, 1992, exhibits 158–60, 163–64.

7. Padgett interviews; *Larry Randal Padgett v. State of Alabama*, CC-91-38, 1992, exhibits 158–60, 163–64.

8. Padgett interviews; *Larry Randal Padgett v. State of Alabama*, CC-91-38, 1992, exhibit 158–60.

9. Padgett interviews; *Larry Randal Padgett v. State of Alabama*, CC-91-38, 1992, exhibits 158–60, 130.

10. Padgett interviews; *Larry Randal Padgett v. State of Alabama*, CC-91-38, 1992, exhibits 158–60; *State of Alabama v. Larry Randal Padgett*, CC96-191, trial transcript, Marshall Circuit Court, 18 September 1997.

11. Padgett interviews; *Larry Randal Padgett v. State of Alabama*, CC-91-38, 1992, exhibits 160–61.

12. Padgett interviews; *Larry Randal Padgett v. State of Alabama*, CC-91-38, 1992, exhibits 160–61.

13. Padgett interviews; *Larry Randal Padgett v. State of Alabama*, CC-91-38, 1992, exhibits 178, 166, 2034–53, 115–16, 106, 98–99; Brenda Padgett interviews.

14. Brenda Padgett interviews.

15. Unless otherwise noted, the information in this section was compiled from interviews with Randal and Brenda Padgett. Information from supplemental sources is referenced in the paragraph or paragraphs in which it appears.

16. *Larry Randal Padgett v. State of Alabama*, CC-91-38, 1992, exhibit 106.

17. Ibid., transcript 2090.

18. Ibid., exhibits 248, 120.

19. Ibid., exhibit 244.

20. References to Tommy Smith are from a police interview with Smith in the trial record for *Larry Randal Padgett v. State of Alabama*, CC-91-38, 1992, exhibits 144–52.

21. *Larry Randal Padgett v. State of Alabama*, CC-91-38, 1992, exhibit 265.

22. Reed and Watson, "DNA"; *Larry Randal Padgett v. State of Alabama*, CC-91-38, 1992, exhibits 247–48, 120, 166, 132.

23. *Larry Randal Padgett v. State of Alabama*, CC-91-38, 1992, exhibit 247–48.

24. *State of Alabama v. Larry Randal Padgett*, CC96-191, 30 September 1997.

25. *Larry Randal Padgett v. State of Alabama*, CC-91-38, 1992, exhibits 140–41.

26. Ibid., exhibit 94.

27. Ibid., exhibit 265.

28. Ibid.

29. Ibid.

30. *State of Alabama v. Larry Randal Padgett*, CC96-191, 18 September 1997; *State of Alabama vs. Larry Randal Padgett*, CC96-191, trial transcript; *Larry Randal Padgett v. State of Alabama*, CC-91-38, 1992, exhibits 265, 202, 9.

31. *State of Alabama v. Larry Randal Padgett*, CC96-191, 18 September 1997 and 30 September 1997.

32. *Larry Randal Padgett v. State of Alabama*, CC-91-38, 1992, exhibits 120, 141.

33. Ibid., exhibit 142.

34. Unless otherwise noted, the information in this section was compiled from interviews with Randal and Brenda Padgett. Information from supplemental sources is referenced in the paragraph or paragraphs in which it appears. *Larry Randal Padgett v. State of Alabama*, CC-91-38, 1992, exhibit 121.

35. Ibid.

36. Ibid.

37. Ibid., exhibit 265.

38. Ibid.

39. Ibid.

40. Ibid.

41. Ibid.

42. *State of Alabama v. Larry Randal Padgett*, CC96-191, 18 September 1997.

43. *Larry Randal Padgett v. State of Alabama*, CC-91-38, 1992, exhibits 247–48; Brenda Padgett e-mail correspondence, 25 March 2007.

44. *Larry Randal Padgett v. State of Alabama*, CC-91-38, 1992, exhibits 249–50.

45. Ibid., exhibits 143–54.

46. Ibid., exhibits 194–95.

47. Ibid., exhibits 196, 257–58; Phillip Jones, "Forensic Analysis of Blood Protein and DNA: A Brief History," *Forensic Focus* (2005), http://www.forensicfocus mag.com/articles/3b1spec1.html, retrieved 9 December 2005.

48. *Larry Randal Padgett v. State of Alabama*, CC-91-38, 1992, exhibits 196, 103.

49. *State of Alabama v. Larry Randal Padgett*, CC96-191, 30 September 1997.

50. *Larry Randal Padgett v. State of Alabama*, CC-91-38, 1992, exhibit 17–23.

51. Ibid., exhibits 103, 203.

52. Unless otherwise noted, the information in this section was compiled from interviews with Randal and Brenda Padgett. Information from supplemental sources is referenced in the paragraph or paragraphs in which it appears.

53. *Larry Randal Padgett v. State of Alabama*, CC-91-38, 1992, exhibits 24–25.

54. Ibid., exhibits 24–25, 29, 46.

55. Jones, "Forensic Analysis."

56. *Larry Randal Padgett v. State of Alabama*, CC-91-38, 1992, exhibit 258; *Larry Randal Padgett v. State*, CR-91-1552, Al. Ct. Crim. App., 13 January 1995.

57. *Larry Randal Padgett v. State of Alabama*, CC-91-38, 1992, exhibits 259–61.

58. Ibid., exhibit 197.

59. *State of Alabama v. Larry Randal Padgett*, CC96-191, 30 September 1997.

60. Reed and Watson, "DNA."

61. Ibid.

62. John Mark McDaniel and William Burgess, Jr., Brief of Appellant, *Larry Randal Padgett v. State of Alabama*, Al. Ct. Criminal App. 1995, 64.

63. Richard Jaffe, telephone interview by author, 3 January 2006; *Larry Randal Padgett v. State of Alabama*, CC-91-38, 1992, transcript 2009; McDaniel and Burgess, Brief of Appellant, 84–85; Padgett interviews.

64. McDaniel and Burgess, Brief of Appellant, 14, 11; *Larry Randal Padgett v. State of Alabama*, CC-91-38, 1992, 4; Brenda Padgett e-mail correspondence, 24 September 2006.

65. McDaniel and Burgess, Brief of Appellant, 8–9.

66. Ibid., 19–20.

67. Ibid., 23.

68. Ibid., 18; *Larry Randal Padgett v. State of Alabama*, CC-91-38, 1992, exhibits 4–6.

69. McDaniel and Burgess, Brief of Appellant, 16–17.

70. Ibid., I–III.

71. Jaffe interview.

72. McDaniel and Burgess, Brief of Appellant, 96–97; *Larry Randal Padgett v. State of Alabama*, CC-91-38, 1992, exhibits 177–81, 183–85, 84–91.

73. McDaniel and Burgess, Brief of Appellant, 96–97.

74. Ibid., 50–51, 53, 56, 60–61; *Larry Randal Padgett v. State of Alabama*, CC-91-38, 1992, exhibit 106.

75. McDaniel and Burgess, Brief of Appellant, IV.

76. Ibid., 28, II.

77. McDaniel and Burgess, Brief of Appellant, xxii.

78. *Larry Randal Padgett v. State*, CR-91-1552, 13 January 1995.

79. Ibid.

80. Ibid., *Larry Randal Padgett v. State of Alabama*, CC-91-38, 1992, exhibit 4.

81. Morrison's testimony is quoted from McDaniel and Burgess, Brief of Appellant, 5.

82. Ibid.

83. *Larry Randal Padgett v. State*, CR-91-1552, 13 January 1995.

84. Padgett interviews; McDaniel and Burgess, Brief of Appellant, 6–7.

85. *Larry Randal Padgett v. State*, CR-91-1552, 13 January 1995.

86. Padgett interviews; McDaniel and Burgess, Brief of Appellant, 32; *Larry Randal Padgett v. State of Alabama*, CC-91-38, 1992, exhibit 4.

87. Padgett interviews; McDaniel and Burgess, Brief of Appellant, 32.

88. Padgett interviews; McDaniel and Burgess, Brief of Appellant, 77–83.

89. Padgett interviews; McDaniel and Burgess, Brief of Appellant, 1.

90. *Larry Randal Padgett v. State of Alabama*, CC-91-38, 1992, exhibit 8, transcript 2117.

91. Ibid., transcript 2019, 2023, 2033–34, 2040–41.

92. Ibid., transcript 2023, 2070–71, 2081–82.

93. Ibid., transcript 2088–92.

94. Ibid., transcript 2034, 2053.

95. Ibid., transcript 2136.

96. Padgett interviews; *Larry Randal Padgett v. State of Alabama*, CC-91-38, 1992, exhibit 8.

97. McDaniel and Burgess, Brief of Appellant, 48, 45; Padgett interviews; *Larry Randal Padgett v. State of Alabama*, CC-91-38, transcript 2141–45; confession letter.

98. McDaniel and Burgess, Brief of Appellant, 45, 47; Padgett interviews; *Larry Randal Padgett v. State of Alabama*, CC-91-38, 1992, transcript 2141–45.

99. *Larry Randal Padgett v. State of Alabama*, CC-91-38, 1992, transcript 2141–45.

100. Ibid., transcript 2141–45; Padgett interviews.

101. *Larry Randal Padgett v. State of Alabama*, CC-91-38, 1992, transcript 2145.

102. Ibid., transcript 2157-2159.

103. Unless otherwise noted, the information from here to the end of this section was compiled from interviews with Brenda Padgett.

104. Brenda Padgett, correspondence, May 1992.

105. "Randal Padgett: Three and a Half Years on Death Row," *The Birmingham News*, 25 July 2004.

106. Peggy Sanford, "Christmas at Home, Not Death Row," *The Birmingham News*, 23 December 1997.

107. Ibid.

108. Unless otherwise noted, the information in this section was compiled from interviews with Randal and Brenda Padgett.

109. Carla Crowder, "Brush with Stars Preceded Poultry Farm," *The Birmingham News*, 25 July 2004.

110. Brenda Padgett, e-mail correspondence, 2 December 2005.

111. *Larry Randal Padgett v. State*, CR-91-1552, Al. Ct. Crim. App., 13 January 1995.

112. Unless otherwise noted, the information in this section was compiled from interviews with Randal and Brenda Padgett.

113. Richard Jaffe, telephone interview by author, tape recording, 10 February 2006.

114. Ibid.

115. Ibid.

116. Ibid.

117. Laranda Nichols, "Polygraph Test Won't Be Allowed in Guntersville Man's Murder Retrial," *The Huntsville Times*, 15 August 1997.

118. Jaffe interview.

119. *State of Alabama v. Larry Randal Padgett*, CC96-191, 18 September 1997; McDaniel and Burgess, Brief of Appellant, 99–100; Jaffe interviews, 3 January 2006 and 10 February 2006; Randal and Brenda Padgett interviews.

120. Jaffe interview.

121. *State of Alabama v. Larry Randal Padgett*, CC96-191, 18 September 1997.

122. Jaffe interview; Stephanie Reed, "Padgett Takes Stand in Murder Defense," *The Arab Tribune*, 1 October 1997.

123. *State of Alabama v. Larry Randal Padgett*, CC96-191, 30 September 1997.

124. *State of Alabama vs. Larry Randal Padgett*, CC96-191, 18 September 1997; Padgett interviews.

125. Reed, "Padgett Takes Stand."

126. *State of Alabama v. Larry Randal Padgett*, CC96-191, 18 September 1997 and 30 September 1997.

127. *State of Alabama v. Larry Randal Padgett*, CC96-191, 18 September 1997; Jaffe interview.

128. Reed and Watson, "DNA"; Jaffe interview.

129. Jaffe interview.

130. Reed and Watson, "DNA."

131. Ibid.

132. *State of Alabama v. Larry Randal Padgett*, CC96-191, 30 September 1997; Jaffe interview; Brenda Padgett interview, 22 September 2006; Reed and Watson, "DNA."

133. *State of Alabama v. Larry Randal Padgett*, CC96-191, 30 September 1997.

134. Jaffe interview; Reed and Watson, "DNA"; Sherry Wilburn, telephone conversation with author, 12 December 2005.

135. *State of Alabama v. Larry Randal Padgett*, CC96-191, 30 September 1997.

136. Ibid.

137. Jaffe interview.

138. Ibid.

139. *State of Alabama v. Larry Randal Padgett*, CC96-191, 30 September 1997; David Moore, "Judge Jetton Dies after Long Bout with Cancer," *Arab Tribune*, 28 April 2004.

140. Moore, "Judge Jetton."

141. *State of Alabama v. Larry Randal Padgett*, CC96-191, 30 September 1997; Moore, "Judge Jetton."

142. *State of Alabama v. Larry Randal Padgett*, CC96-191, 30 September 1997.

143. Ibid.

144. Ibid.

145. Ibid.; Jaffe interview; Randal and Brenda Padgett interviews.

146. *State of Alabama v. Larry Randal Padgett*, CC96-191, 30 September 1997; Moore, "Judge Jetton."

147. *State of Alabama vs. Larry Randal Padgett*, CC96-191, 30 September 1997; Moore "Judge Jetton."

148. Jaffe interview; Brenda Padgett interviews.

149. Randal and Brenda Padgett interviews; Moore "Judge Jetton."

150. Jaffe interview; *State of Alabama v. Larry Randal Padgett*, CC96-191, 30 September 1997.

151. *State of Alabama v. Larry Randal Padgett*, CC96-191, 30 September 1997; *Larry*

Randal Padgett v. State of Alabama, CC-91-38, 1992, 245; Moore, "Judge Jetton"; Reed and Watson, "DNA."

152. All references to Richard Jaffe's closing remarks are taken from the transcript for *State of Alabama v. Larry Randal Padgett*, CC96-191, 30 September 1997.

153. Cathy Padgett's weight and height are from the trial record for *Larry Randal Padgett v. State of Alabama*, CC-91-38, 1992, exhibit 106.

154. Brenda Padgett interviews.

155. Ibid.

156. Jaffe interview; Derek Drennan, e-mail correspondence, 3 August 2006.

157. Jaffe interview.

158. Ibid.

159. Brenda Padgett interviews; Jaffe interview.

160. The account of Judge Jetton's decision to ask the jury for further deliberation is from the interview with Jaffe.

161. Jaffe interview; Padgett interviews.

162. Jaffe interview.

163. Information in the remainder of this section came from interviews with Randal and Brenda Padgett.

164. Jaffe, interview with author, 22 December 2005.

165. Moore, "Judge Jetton."

166. Taylor Bright, "Guilty Until Proven Innocent?" *Birmingham Post-Herald*, December 2005.

167. Jaffe interview.

168. Unless otherwise noted, the information in the remainder of this section was compiled from interviews with Randal and Brenda Padgett.

169. The source for the information contained in this paragraph is the Marshall County court recorder, Sherry Wilburn. The author spoke with her by telephone on 12 and 20 December 2005.

170. Brenda Padgett, e-mail correspondence, 13 November 2005; Adele Bernhard, "When Justice Fails: Indemnification for Unjust Convictions," table summarizing state statues on indemnification for unjust convictions, http://www.innocence project.org/docs/Bernhard_Compensation_Chart.pdf, 6 University of Chicago Law School, Roundtable 73, September 9, 2004, retrieved 23 February 2006.

171. Sanford, "Christmas at Home."

172. Brenda Padgett, "The Innocent Are Sentenced to Die," letter to the editor, *The Birmingham News*, 12 November 2005.

173. Crowder, "Brush with Stars."

Conclusion (pages 235–240)

1. Hugo A. Bedeau and Michael L. Radelet, "Miscarriages of Justice in Potentially Capital Cases," *Stanford Law Review*, 1987.

2. "Executed But Possibly Innocent," Death Penalty Information Center

(DPIC), www.deathpenaltyinfo.org, retrieved 26 July 2007; "Fact Sheet: Inno-cence," National Coalition to Abolish the Death Penalty (NCADP), www.ncadp.org, retrieved 26 July 2007.

3. Sister Helen Prejean, *The Death of Innocents: An Eyewitness Account of Wrongful Executions* (New York: Random House, 2004), 210.

4. "Cases of Innocence," DPIC; Tim Junkin, *Bloodsworth: The True Story of the First Death Row Inmate Exonerated by DNA* (Chapel Hill, N.C.: Shannon Ravenel Books, 2004), 271–75; Ray Krone, interview by author, 13–14 June 2006.

5. Prejean, *Death of Innocents*, 252; "Cases of Innocence," DPIC.

6. Samuel R. Gross, "Lost Lives: Miscarriages of Justice in Capital Cases," 61 *Law and Contemporary Problems* 125 (Autumn 1998).

7. "Fact Sheet: Innocence," NCADP.

8. Ibid.

9. Richard C. Dieter, "With Justice for Few: The Growing Crisis in Death Penalty Representation," DPIC, October 1995.

10. "Fact Sheet: Innocence," NCADP; Margo Hunter, "Improving the Jury System," Public Law Research Institute, http://w3.uchastings.edu/plri/spr96tex/juryuna.html, retrieved 26 July 2007; Prejean, *Death of Innocents*, 100–101.

11. James S. Liebman, Jeffrey Fagan, and Valerie West, "A Broken System: Error Rates in Capital Cases, 1973–1995," Columbia Law School, Public Law Research Paper no. 15, June 2000, http://www2.law.columbia.edu/instructionalservices/liebman/. Richard Moran, "The Presence of Malice," *New York Times*, 2 August 2007.

Appendix: States Paying Restitution for
Wrongful Convictions in Capital Cases (pages 241–242)

1. Adele Bernhard, "When Justice Fails," 6 U Ch L Sch Roundtable 73, 2005.

Index